Unit 10

Drafting financial statements (accounting practice, industry and commerce)

Study Pack

Technician (NVQ Level 4)

Published May 1998 by Financial Training, 10 –14 White Lion Street, London N1 9PE

ISBN 1 85179 726 2

This text has been published by Financial Training, one of the leading providers of training in accountancy and finance. Although it is aimed at students on the Education and Training Scheme of the Association of Accounting Technicians (AAT) it is not published or approved directly by the AAT. Any queries on the Education and Training Scheme and AAT Administration should be addressed to Student Services at AAT, 154 Clerkenwell Road, London EC1R 5AD (0171 837 8600).

We are grateful to the Association of Accounting Technicians for their kind permission to reproduce tasks from the central assessments.

All business entities referred to in this publication are fictitious. Any resemblance to any actual organisation, past or present, is purely coincidental.

Contents

Session 9   Reporting financial performance

Session 10   Fixed assets: tangible assets

Session 11   Fixed assets: intangible assets

Review of Module One

Session 12   Stocks and long-term contracts

Session 13   Accounting for leases and hire purchase contracts

Answers

Practice Central Assessments

Index

Introduction

ASSESSMENT OF UNIT 10

Unit 10 *Drafting financial statements* is assessed by a central assessment. The central assessment lasts for three hours, plus fifteen minutes reading time. During the reading time, you will be allowed to read and write notes on the assessment paper itself but you will not be allowed to write in the answer booklet.

Format of the central assessment

The assessment will be in a number of sections, typically three or four. Marks for each section are not given but candidates are advised how long they should spend on each section.

Overall, the assessor will expect candidates to:

- display basic competence in the preparation of limited company accounts;
- be familiar with basic statutory requirements and the main relevant accounting standards

Sections 1 and 2 of the central assessment will *normally* involve:

- preparation of a profit and loss account and balance sheet from an extended trial balance with some adjustments;

- further questions on, for example,

  - interpretation of accounts;
  - the significance of transactions;
  - journal entries for adjustments;
  - the understanding of key accounting terms/concepts;
  - knowledge of relevant FRSs.

Remaining sections *may* involve, for limited companies or partnerships:

- cash flow statements;
- reconciliation of cash flow statements and operating profit statements;
- partnership appropriation accounts;
- test of candidates' knowledge of law, accounting principles and concepts.

Candidates will be expected to write brief reports or memos to managers or directors explaining, for example, accounting concepts.

Common problems with the central assessment

These are highlighted by the assessor's reports on past assessments. The overall impression given by the assessor's comments is that candidates perform the computational tasks relatively well, but have problems with the written tasks.

The assessor has made the following general criticisms:

- failure to show workings or give sufficient explanation;
- failure to answer the question set;
- failure to demonstrate understanding.

How to tackle the central assessment

- Always read all the instructions carefully before starting.

- Work through the paper in the order set.

- Read the questions. Answer the question that has been set.

- Allocate your time sensibly as instructed between the tasks, although time-pressure should not be a problem if you are well prepared.

- Work methodically through each section. Make sure that you deal with every item of information. Consider ticking each figure in the question as you use it.

- You must aim to get all of the exercise correct if you are to be assessed as competent.

- Plan your approach to the written questions and read all the information carefully. Make sure you understand what you are required to do and what the aim of the communication is. Remember that, in some cases, you may be writing to someone with limited or no knowledge of financial accounting, so you must adapt your approach accordingly.

Notes

(1) Remember that your objective is to prove that you are competent in the unit being assessed. You must therefore aim for 100% accuracy and an extremely high standard of presentation. The actual pass mark is likely to be around 80%, so you cannot afford to ignore any tasks within the assessment.

(2) You must aim to achieve the following:

Good presentation skills: All work should be neat and well presented, as if it were real work. You should use black ink or biro. Pencil is not acceptable, neither is correcting fluid (such as Tipp-Ex). Cross out any errors neatly and clearly. Always use a ruler for underlining. Use the proformas provided. Remember that you are being assessed on your knowledge of disclosure requirements as well as on your knowledge of accounting techniques.

Completeness: All tasks should be complete (for example, columns totalled). You cannot decide to leave out part of an exercise and still hope to be successful.

Good communication skills: Communication skills are fundamentally important in all the assessments for all stages. You are expected to show a good standard of English, including correct spelling and correct use of accounting terms.

Accuracy: All calculations must be completed accurately, such as the calculation of depreciation or minority interest.

Technical knowledge: Any explanations given – for example, the reasons for adopting a particular accounting treatment, etc. – must be accurate. Remember that you are being assessed on your *understanding* of accounting principles.

PERFORMANCE CRITERIA

Each unit is divided into elements which in turn are divided into performance criteria and knowledge and understanding. The performance criteria for Unit 10 *Drafting financial statements* are as follows:

Element 1 Interpret financial statements

- Identify the general purpose of financial statements used in various organisations

- Identify elements in financial statements used in various organisations

- Identify the relationship of elements within financial statements

- Interpret the relationship between elements of limited company financial statements

- Unusual features or significant issues are identified within financial statements

- Valid conclusions are drawn from the information contained within financial statements

- Conclusions and interpretations are clearly presented

Range Statement

1   *Financial Statements*

     Balance sheet, income statements

2   *Elements*

     Assets, liabilities, ownership interest, income, expenditure contribution from owners, distribution to owners, gains and losses

3   *Relationship between elements*

     Profitability, liquidity, efficient use of resources, financial position

Element 2 Draft limited company, sole trader and partnership year end financial statements

- Financial statements are accurately drafted from the appropriate information

- Subsequent adjustments are correctly implemented

- Draft accounts comply with domestic standards and legislation and, where relevant, partnership agreement

- A cash flow statement is correctly prepared and interpreted where required

- Year end financial statements are presented for approval to the appropriate person in a clear form

- Confidentiality procedures are followed at all times

- The organisation's policies, regulations, procedures and timescales relating to financial statements are observed at all times

- Discrepancies, unusual features or queries are identified and either resolved or referred to the appropriate person

Range Statement

1 *Financial Statements*

Profit and loss account, balance sheet, owners capital and current account, cash flow statement, statement of total recognised gains and losses, the supplementary notes required by statute, SSAPs, FRSs or other relevant pronouncements

2 *Domestic Standards*

Relevant SSAPs, relevant FRSs, other relevant pronouncements

3 *Limited company financial statements*

Unitary, consolidated

THE ROLE OF STUDY

Studying for different reasons

Finally, we need to consider the role of study within the scheme. Whatever your previous experience, you will inevitably need to devote a considerable amount of time to studying, even if it is only to familiarise yourself with the coverage and likely content and format of the central assessment. This Study Pack contains study and practice material covering all the performance criteria and knowledge and understanding required for this unit.

The objective of this Study Pack is to provide you with:

- guidance on completing the assessments for this unit

- study material and practice materials to prepare you for the Central Assessment

Using this Study Pack

Whatever your previous experience, you are therefore encouraged to work through the Study Pack, paying attention to the areas which are most relevant to you. Here is a short explanation of the aim of each aspect of this Study Pack and the areas in which they are relevant. This will help you decide.

Sessions 1–22	Study material and examples on particular topics to help you learn the required techniques. The relevant performance criteria are identified at the start of each session. In addition, the knowledge and understanding required for that topic are included within that session.
	The questions at the end of each session are designed to enable you to consolidate your knowledge as you progress through the Study Pack.
Practice central assessments	Two practice central assessments in the style of the real Central Assessment. Try to sit these under exam conditions, giving yourself a sufficient amount of uninterrupted time to complete the task.

Further study material

The Financial Training Company also publishes a *Central Assessment Pack* designed to give you additional practice towards the Central Assessment for this unit. As well as containing new exercises of the sort featured in the real central assessments, it also contains brief revision notes on all major topics and a mock central assessment *in the style of the real central assessment*.

The Central Assessment Packs are available from your usual supplier of Financial Training Company study materials.

PUBLISHER'S NOTE

Financial Training study materials are distributed in the UK and overseas by Stanley Thornes (Publishers) Limited. They are another company within the Wolters Kluwer group. They can be contacted at: Stanley Thornes, Ellenborough House, Wellington Street, Cheltenham GL50 1YD. Telephone: (01242) 228888. Fax: (01242) 221914.

Your chances of success in the AAT assessments will be greatly improved by additional tuition, either at one of Financial Training's centres or by home study. For details of our open learning programmes please contact us at:

The Financial Training Company

1st Floor, Centre City Tower, 7 Hill Street, BIRMINGHAM B5 4UA
Tel: 0121- 625 1296/Fax:0121-625 1297

5th Floor, Market Chambers, 5-7 St Mary Street, CARDIFF CF1 2AT
Tel: 01222-388 067/Fax: 01222-327 408

49 St Pauls Street, LEEDS LS1 2TE
Tel: 0113-245 7455/Fax: 0113-242 8889

3rd Floor, Beckville House, 66 London Road, LEICESTER LE2 0QD
Tel: 0116-285 6767/Fax: 0116-285 6787

3rd Floor, Coopers Building, Church Street, LIVERPOOL L1 3AA
Tel: 0151-708 8839/Fax: 0151-709 4264

10 – 14 White Lion Street, LONDON N1 9PE
Tel: 0171-837 1898/Fax: 0171-278 1693

3rd Floor, Excalibur Building, 77 Whitworth Street, MANCHESTER M1 6EZ
Tel: 0161-236 9646/Fax: 0161-2369047

Provincial House, Northumberland Street, NEWCASTLE-UPON-TYNE NE1 7DQ
Tel: 0191-232 9365/Fax: 0191-232 2115

1st Floor, Victoria House, 76 Milton Street, NOTTINGHAM NG1 3QZ
Tel: 0115-950 8088/Fax: 0115-950 5104

Pegasus House, 463a Glossop Road, SHEFFIELD S10 2QD
Tel: 0114-266 9265/Fax: 0114-268 4084

32 Castle Way, SOUTHAMPTON SO14 2AW
Tel: 01703-220852/Fax: 01703-634379

Swift House, Market Place, WOKINGHAM RG40 1AP
Tel: 0118-9774922/Fax: 0118-9894029

The legal and professional framework

INTRODUCTION

The main purpose of financial statements is to provide information to a wide range of users.

The *balance sheet* provides information on the financial position of a business (its assets and liabilities at a point in time).

The *profit and loss account* provides information on the performance of a business (the profit or loss which results from trading over a period of time).

The *cash flow statement* provides information on the financial adaptability of a business (the movement of cash into and out of the business over a period of time).

Financial statements also show the results of the *stewardship* of a business. Stewardship is the accountability of management for the resources entrusted to it by the owners. This applies to the financial statements of many limited companies.

All users of financial statements need information on financial position, performance and financial adaptability. However, many different groups of people may use financial statements and each group will need particular information. Users of financial statements may include investors, management, employees, customers, suppliers, lenders, the government and the public. Investors need to be able to assess the ability of a business to pay dividends and manage resources. Management need information with which to assess performance, take decisions, plan, and control the business. Lenders, such as banks, are interested in the ability of the business to pay interest and repay loans. The Inland Revenue uses financial statements as the basis for tax assessments.

The law requires limited companies to prepare financial statements annually. These financial statements must be filed with the Registrar of Companies and are then available to all interested parties. Most businesses, whether incorporated or not, are required to produce financial statements for submission to the Inland Revenue.

In the UK, the form and content of limited company accounts is laid down within the Companies Acts. The preparation of limited company accounts is also subject to regulations issued by the Accounting Standards Board.

The form and content of the accounts of other businesses is not prescribed by law. However, the accounts of sole traders and partnerships should be prepared in accordance with current best accounting practice.

COMPANIES ACT 1985

Introduction

The Companies Act 1985 contains the following:

- formats
- fundamental accounting principles
- valuation rules

Formats

Companies must prepare their annual accounts in accordance with certain formats. There are two formats specified for the balance sheet and four formats specified for the profit and loss account. These formats specify the items which must be disclosed in the financial statements and the order in which they must be shown, although they do provide some flexibility in relegating details to the notes to the accounts. We shall study these formats in the sessions on company accounts.

Fundamental accounting principles

The law embodies five accounting principles:

- going concern
- consistency
- prudence
- accruals
- no offset

These accounting principles are well known to accountants and the first four are listed as fundamental accounting concepts in SSAP2 *Disclosure of accounting policies*, which we shall examine later.

When the directors depart from these accounting principles, a note to the accounts must provide particulars of the departure, the reasons for it and its effect.

Valuation rules

The Companies Act 1985 embodies two sets of valuation rules: the **historical cost accounting rules** and the **alternative accounting rules**.

- *Historical cost accounting rules*

    Under these rules, assets are shown on the basis of their purchase price or production cost. Fixed assets with a finite useful economic life must be depreciated on a systematic basis over their useful economic life. Current assets (eg. stocks) must be written down if the net realisable value is lower than the cost.

- *Alternative accounting rules*

    Under these rules, fixed assets other than goodwill, stocks and short-term investments may be shown at their current cost.

COMPANIES ACT 1989

The Companies Act 1989 has to some extent increased the volume of disclosure that companies are required to make in their financial statements. These disclosures are dealt with in later sessions.

One of the most significant requirements is that accounts of public and large private companies must state whether they have been prepared in accordance with applicable accounting standards (ie. SSAPs and FRSs – see below) and give details of, and the reasons for, any material departures.

ACCOUNTING STANDARDS

Accounting standards give guidance in specific areas of accounting. There are two types of accounting standard currently in issue:

- *Statements of Standard Accounting Practice (SSAPs)*

   SSAPs were created by a body known as the Accounting Standards Committee (ASC). The ASC was abolished in July 1990.

- *Financial Reporting Standards (FRSs)*

   The Accounting Standards Board (ASB) took over the role of setting accounting standards from the ASC in August 1990. One of the ASB's first acts was to adopt all 22 existing SSAPs. The SSAPs therefore continue to be applicable to all sets of accounts.

   The new accounting standards created by the ASB are known as *Financial Reporting Standards*. In preparing company accounts, both SSAPs and FRSs should be complied with. Failure to do so can lead to the company being ordered to redraft its accounts (*S12 CA 1989*).

   The board consists of nine qualified accountants and is monitored and funded by a body, the Financial Reporting Council, whose members are drawn from accounts user groups (eg. Stock Exchange, CBI) as well as the accounting profession.

Urgent Issues Task Force (UITF)

This is a committee of the ASB. It deals with urgent and emerging issues, particularly where the normal standard setting process would be too slow to implement changes. It issues consensus pronouncements which are known as *UITF Abstracts*.

Aims of accounting standards

The aim of the ASB is to establish and improve standards of financial accounting and reporting for the benefit of users, preparers and auditors of financial information.

Accounting standards:

- are authoritative statements of how particular types of transaction and other events should be reflected in financial statements

- are applicable to all financial statements that are intended to give *a true and fair view*

- need not be applied to immaterial items.

Compliance with accounting standards will normally be necessary for financial statements to give a true and fair view. Only in exceptional circumstances will departure from the requirements of an accounting standard be necessary in order for financial statements to give a true and fair view.

Members of professional bodies are expected to observe accounting standards, whether they are acting as directors or officers of a company or as auditors or reporting accountants. They should use their best endeavours to ensure that accounting standards are observed by others and that significant departures found to be necessary are adequately disclosed and explained in the financial statements.

Main types of standard

There are four main types of standard, although several contain features of more than one type:

(a)   *Informational:* These require explanation of what has been done. The best example is SSAP2 *Disclosure of accounting policies*, discussed below.

(b)   *Additional disclosure:* Some standards call for the disclosure of information not required by law. Thus FRS1 *Cash flow statements* requires all but small companies to include a cash flow statement in their financial statements.

(c)   *Presentation:* These require a standard presentation of information. An example is FRS3 *Reporting financial performance*, which requires, for example, analysis of results between continuing operations and discontinued operations. In many British standards, guidance on presentation is relegated to non-mandatory appendices.

(d)   *Valuation (or measurement):* These standards contain rules on how items in a balance sheet and profit and loss account should be valued (or measured). An example is SSAP9 *Stocks and long-term contracts*.

While there has been relatively little opposition to standards of the first type, many have spoken out against standards of the other three types, particularly those which specify valuation or measurement rules. It has been argued that these restrict the exercise of professional judgement by the accountant.

MANAGEMENT ACCOUNTS

As well as producing financial statements for external users, businesses may also produce financial statements for internal use. These are often known as *management accounts*.

These accounts provide the information which management needs in order to control the business, to take decisions and to plan for the future. Therefore they are likely to be very much more detailed than the financial statements produced for external users. Whereas published financial statements are based on historical information, management accounts may include forecast information, such as cash flow statements.

Financial statements intended for third parties are normally produced annually. Management accounts may be produced quarterly or monthly.

Management accounts do not have to comply with the requirements of the Companies Acts. They may be drafted in whatever form management wish.

Management accounting as such (for example, recording cost information) is outside the scope of this unit. The emphasis of this unit falls upon financial accounting, that is, drafting financial statements primarily intended for external users. However, you are required to be able to present final accounts to management and proprietors in a clear and intelligible form. In practice, this means that you may be asked to draft accounts in a format other than the Companies Act format, or in greater detail than that required by the Companies Act.

For example, it may be appropriate to produce a manufacturing account as well as a trading and profit and loss account (see Session 6). Alternatively, the business may be organised in several different divisions and therefore it may be important for management to know the gross or operating profit achieved by each of these divisions. The management accounts of a partnership or a sole trader often contain detailed schedules showing the make-up of items such as drawings, which would not normally be included in the accounts presented to third parties. Generally, the more detailed the accounts the more useful they are likely to be, provided that they are not so detailed that a mass of irrelevant data obscures the really important items. In the absence of any specific instructions, you should use your judgement to make the best use of the available information to present management with the form of accounts most likely to be useful to them.

OTHER PROFESSIONAL REQUIREMENTS

Confidentiality

In the course of preparing accounts, you are likely to acquire confidential information. This applies whether you are working in practice and preparing accounts for a client or whether you are preparing accounts for your own employer.

Confidential information should not be disclosed, either to anyone within the organisation or to a third party unless permission has been obtained from the client, employer or other proper source. Under very exceptional circumstances, an accountant may have a legal duty to disclose information to a third party (for example, if a client has committed an illegal act).

An accountant should not make use of confidential information for personal gain, for example, by dealing in the shares of a client company.

Some businesses treat the financial statements themselves as strictly confidential, at least until they are published. This is particularly likely in the case of a public company or a large partnership, but may apply to any business.

There are obvious examples of the type of information which is likely to be confidential (for example, directors' salaries). Other information may be less obviously sensitive but still regarded as confidential in some organisations. In practice, confidentiality procedures vary from organisation to organisation, but they must always be followed strictly.

Policies and procedures

Most organisations are likely to have their own policies, regulations and procedures for preparing financial statements. These govern the method of preparing the financial statements, the accounting policies and systems used, and the way in which financial information is presented. Accounting procedures will vary according to the size and structure of the organisation and the nature of the business.

Timescales are likely to be important in most organisations. Limited company final accounts must be filed with the Registrar of Companies within ten months of the end of the financial year (or seven months if the company is a public company). Deadlines are likely to be particularly tight if the company has to report its results to the public and the financial press, or where it is owned by another company, particularly if that company is overseas.

Many businesses are required to produce accounts within a timescale in order to raise finance or as a condition of continued support from banks.

The professional accountant must observe the policies, regulations, procedures and timescales of the organisation for which financial statements are prepared.

Dealing with discrepancies and unusual items

In drawing up financial statements you are likely to have to resolve matters such as discrepancies and the treatment of unusual items.

Earlier in your studies you will have learned the importance of procedures such as reconciling control accounts and ensuring that the trial balance balances. Extending the trial balance may give rise to differences, especially where the nominal ledger contains a large number of individual accounts. When producing the first draft of a set of accounts, it is not uncommon to find that the balance sheet does not balance or that the figure for retained profit in the profit and loss account does not agree to the figure in the balance sheet! A methodical approach is necessary in order to resolve all discrepancies (unless they are immaterial enough to be safely ignored).

Drafting final accounts, particularly statutory accounts for limited companies, can be a complex operation. Accurate information about items contained in the accounts is essential so that the correct accounting treatment can be determined and the correct disclosures made. You may not necessarily have access to all the information which you need. For example, if a business acquires a type of fixed asset which it has not previously held, it will be necessary to determine its useful economic life in order to decide how it should be depreciated. If you cannot resolve items yourself, you should refer them to the appropriate person.

There is another reason why it is important to identify discrepancies and unusual items. An accounting system which is not properly controlled increases the scope for errors in the financial statements and may be an invitation to fraud.

SUMMARY

The legal and professional framework for preparing financial statements consists of:

- the Companies Acts (which apply to limited company financial statements)

- Accounting Standards (which apply to all financial statements giving a true and fair view)

The professional accountant must observe the requirements of the Companies Acts and Accounting Standards and must also:

- follow confidentiality procedures;

- observe the policies, regulations, procedures and timescales of the organisation for which financial statements are prepared.

The conceptual framework

ACCOUNTING CONCEPTS

Introduction

- The Companies Act 1985 and SSAP2 *Disclosure of accounting policies* outline the four most fundamental accounting concepts recognised by the accountancy profession.

- The Companies Act 1985 outlines a further principle of non-aggregation (no offset).

- Current accounting practice recognises other important concepts of materiality and commercial substance over legal form.

- The Companies Act 1985 identifies the *true and fair* principle.

SSAP2: Disclosure of accounting policies

Introduction

SSAP2 states that 'it is fundamental to the understanding and interpretation of financial accounts that those who use them should be aware of the main assumptions on which they are based'.

To achieve this, the statement defines accounting concepts and bases (on which accounting policies depend) and recommends disclosure in accounts of significant accounting policies.

Definition of concepts, bases and policies

- **Fundamental accounting concepts**

  - These are the *broad basic assumptions* which underlie the periodic financial accounts of business enterprises.

  - SSAP2 recognises four fundamental concepts.

  - The relative importance of each will vary according to the circumstances of the particular case.

The going concern concept

It is assumed that the enterprise will continue in operational existence for the foreseeable future.

The accruals concept

Revenues and costs are 'matched' with one another in the period to which they relate. If this conflicts with prudence, prudence must prevail.

The consistency concept

Like items are treated in a similar manner within each accounting period and from one period to the next.

The prudence concept

Revenues and profits are not included in the accounts until they are realised but provision is made for losses and liabilities immediately, even if the loss will not occur until the future.

- **Accounting bases**

    – These are the *methods* developed for applying fundamental accounting concepts to financial transactions and items, for the purpose of financial accounts.

    – In order to decide in which periods revenue and expenditure will be brought into the profit and loss account and the amounts at which material items should be shown in the balance sheet, business enterprises will select specific accounting bases most appropriate to their circumstances and adopt them.

- **Accounting policies**

    These are the specific accounting bases judged by the business enterprises to be most appropriate to their circumstances and adopted by them for the purpose of preparing their financial accounts.

Illustration

Consider fixed assets and depreciation.

The company's accounting *policy* would be to depreciate plant and machinery.

The accounting *base* would be to depreciate plant and machinery over an expected useful life of ten years. Thus a change in the average expected useful life would be a change in accounting base but *not* a change in accounting policy.

Since depreciation should be allocated so as to charge a fair proportion of the cost or valuation of the asset to each accounting period expected to benefit from its use, it is invoking the *accruals concept*.

SSAP2 – Text

The text of the standard is as follows:

- *Disclosure of adoption of concepts which differ from those generally accepted*

    If accounts are prepared on the basis of assumptions which differ in material respects from any of the generally accepted fundamental concepts, the facts should be explained.

    In the absence of a clear statement to the contrary, there is a presumption that the four fundamental concepts have been observed.

- *Disclosure of accounting policies*

  The accounting policies followed for dealing with items which are judged material or critical in determining profit and loss for the year and in stating the financial position should be disclosed by way of notes to the accounts. The explanation should be clear, fair and as brief as possible.

Non-aggregation principle (CA 1985)

In determining items in the accounts, assets and liabilities should not be offset against one another.

Illustrations

- Compensating inaccuracies in individual accounts should not be lost in one large total.

- If a company borrows money to buy a building, the building should be shown in fixed assets and the loan in creditors.

The concept of 'true and fair'

The Companies Act 1985 section 226 requires the directors of a company to prepare for each financial year of the company a balance sheet as at the last day of the year and a profit and loss account.

It continues, insisting that the balance sheet shall give a *true and fair* view of the state of the affairs of the company as at the end of the financial year and the profit and loss account shall give a *true and fair* view of the profit or loss of the company for the financial year.

So, where accounts are drawn up to comply with the Companies Acts, the concept of *true and fair* is a legal one.

Truth implies that the figures are mathematically accurate and factually correct.

Fairness implies that the information is presented in a manner which is free from bias.

The question as to whether or not a particular company's financial statements are true and fair can ultimately be decided by the courts.

The concept of true and fair may also apply to the financial statements of sole traders and partnerships.

Other important accounting concepts

- *Substance over form*

  Under this concept, transactions and other events are accounted for and presented in financial statements in accordance with their economic substance and financial reality and not merely with their legal form.

  For example, leasehold buildings are owned by the landlord rather than the occupier, but the occupier is using them for his business in the same way as if they were freehold. Thus it is appropriate to treat them as a fixed asset, provided that it is made clear that the premises are leasehold.

- *Materiality*

    - The omission or mis-statement of an item in a financial statement is material if, in the light of surrounding circumstances, the magnitude of the item is such that it is probable that the judgement of a reasonable person relying upon the report would have been changed or influenced by the inclusion or correction of the item.

        (Statement of Financial Accounting Concept No 2 issued by FASB)

    - There is no rigid or officially recognised definition. It is a practical rule.

    - It allows other rules to be ignored if the consequences of doing so are considered insignificant and cut off all proportion to the time and cost involved in rigidly following those other rules.

    - Accounting standards do not apply to immaterial items.

- *Realisation*

    Transactions are normally recorded when there is a legal requirement to accept liability for them; that is, when the legal title is transferred.

    This means that a transaction may be included in an earlier accounting period than the one in which cash is eventually exchanged.

- *Historical cost*

    Quantitative information recorded in monetary values is normally retained at its historical cost.

    In the case of goods purchased, this will be at the price originally paid for them and, in the case of sales, at the agreed price for which the goods were eventually sold.

- *Relevance*

    The overall message that the accounts are trying to relay may be obscured if too much information is presented.

    Accounting statements should contain only information that complies strictly with the specific requirements of the user.

- *Objectivity*

    The preparation of accounting statements involves a considerable amount of individual discretion.

    They should be prepared with the minimum amount of personal bias and the maximum amount of overall objectivity.

THE STATEMENT OF PRINCIPLES

Introduction

One of the first priorities of the ASB has been to develop a Statement of Principles. At present it exists as an Exposure Draft.

The aim of the Statement of Principles is to develop a conceptual framework for the preparation of financial statements. A conceptual framework is a basic set of rules or principles. From these basic rules, more detailed rules for specific issues can logically be developed.

A conceptual framework provides a clear and authoritative statement and includes the following:

- the primary statements to be presented
- the qualities they should possess
- the meaning of key accounting terms
- the criteria which must be met before items are recognised in the financial statements
- the amounts at which recognised items should be measured

UK accounting practice has been consistently criticised for its lack of coherent and consistent underlying principles. Unlike some other standard setting bodies, such as the International Accounting Standards Committee and the Financial Accounting Standards Board in the United States, the ASC did not develop any kind of conceptual framework.

The remainder of this section summarises key points from the draft Statement of Principles.

Introduction (to the Statement of Principles)

Users	*Need information to assess ability of enterprise to*
Investors	pay dividends, manage resources
Employees	provide employment/remuneration
Customers	continue in operational existence
Suppliers	repay debts, continue in operational existence
Lenders	pay interest, repay loans
Government	pay tax, manage and account for resources
Public	provide goods and services, provide employment
	Need information on
All	financial position, performance and financial adaptability

Chapter 1: The objective of financial statements

Primary objective

To provide information to a wide range of users on:

	Primarily provided by
Financial position	balance sheet
Performance	profit and loss account and statement of movement in reserves
Financial adaptability	cash flow statement and certain notes to the accounts

The information is provided so that they can assess the stewardship of management and make economic decisions.

Chapter 2: Qualitative characteristics of financial statements

Threshold quality

Information is only useful if it is material (ie. if its omission or misstatement could influence economic decisions taken by users on the basis of the financial statements).

Qualitative characteristics relating to content

Characteristics relating to content make (material) information useful.

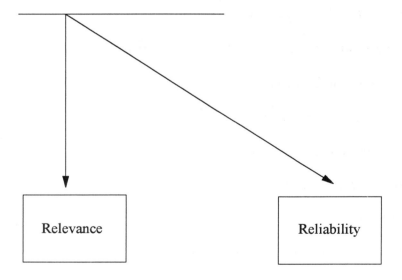

relevant = influences decisions

Information is *relevant* if:

(a) it possesses predictive and/or confirmatory value; and

(b) the aspects to be conveyed have been selectively determined ('choice of aspect').

reliable = free from error or bias

Information is *reliable* if it reflects substance and is:

(a) neutral (free from bias);

(b) prudent;

(c) complete; and

(d) validly described and measured.

Qualitative characteristics relating to presentation

Characteristics relating to presentation, if lacking, limit the usefulness of material information.

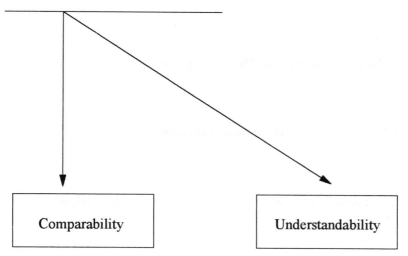

Comparability
Information is *comparable*
if it is consistent

–   for an enterprise over time;
        and

–   between enterprises.

Understandibility
Information is *understandable*
if it is meaningful to a user with:

–   a reasonable knowledge of
        business, economic activities
        and accounting; and

–   a willingness to study the
        information with reasonable
        diligence.

Aspects of comparability:

–   disclosure (eg. accounting
        policies, corresponding
        amounts);

–   compliance with accounting
        standards.

Aspects of understandability:

–   users' abilities;
–   presentation.

Chapter 3: The elements of financial statements

Assets

Rights or other access to future economic benefits controlled by an entity as a result of past transactions or events.

Liabilities

An entity's obligations to transfer economic benefits as a result of past transactions or events.

Ownership interest

The ownership interest is the residual amount found by deducting all liabilities of the entity from all the entity's assets.

Gains

Increases in equity other than those relating to contributions by owners.

Losses

Decreases in equity other than those relating to distributions to owners.

Contributions from owners

Increases in equity resulting from investments made by owners in their capacity as owners.

Distributions to owners

Decreases in equity resulting from transfers made to owners in their capacity as owners.

Chapter 4: Recognition in financial statements

Recognition

An item should be recognised in financial statements if:

- it meets the definition of an element of financial statements – asset, liability, ownership interest, gain, loss, etc;

- there is sufficient evidence that the change in assets or liabilities inherent in the item has occurred (including, where appropriate, evidence that a future inflow or outflow of benefit will occur); and

- it can be measured at a monetary amount with sufficient reliability.

Change in assets or liabilities

There are three classes of past events that may involve a measurable change in assets or liabilities and hence that may trigger recognition:

- transactions;
- contracts for future performance ('contract'); and
- other events.

Reliable measurement

Methods of reliable measurement include:

- transaction price (historic cost);
- market-based measures (eg. replacement cost, net realisable value);
- the expected value of a group of items.

Chapter 5: Measurement in financial statements

Valuing assets

Two methods:

- historical cost; and
- current value.

Historical cost is the actual cost of acquiring the asset.

Current value is the value in use.

- Value in use is given by discounting the estimated future cash flows associated with using the asset in the business, using a suitable discount rate.

Chapter 6: Presentation of financial information

Components of financial statements

These comprise the:

– profit and loss account (P&L a/c);	) statements of financial
– statement of total recognised gains and losses (STRGL);	) performance
– balance sheet; and	
– cash flow statement.	

Statements of financial performance

Statements of financial performance contain all the gains and losses recognised in respect of the period:

- they are included in the STRGL if they relate to assets and liabilities concerned with carrying out the entity's operations (eg. fixed assets);

- all others are included in the P&L a/c.

Balance sheet

The balance sheet and notes provide information on and the interrelationships between its:

- resource structure (major classes and amounts of assets); and
- financial structure (major classes and amounts of liabilities and equity).

It is helpful to users if assets, liabilities and equity are reported in classes.

Presentation of information in the balance sheet can help a user to assess future cash flows. For example, assets held for sale should be reported separately from those held on a continuing basis.

A balance sheet does not purport to show the value of a business enterprise. However, together with other financial statements and other information, balance sheets should provide information that is useful to those who wish to make their own assessment of a company's value.

Cash flow statement

A cash flow statement reflects cash receipts classified by major sources and cash payments classified by major uses. It provides useful information on a company's activities in:

−   generating cash through operations;
−   using cash to repay debt;
−   using cash to distribute dividends; and
−   re-investing to maintain or expand operations.

This helps in the assessment of a company's risk, liquidity, viability, adaptability and the way in which profits are converted to cash. Assessment of prospects for future cash flows is hindered by the effect of timing differences between, for example, cash receipts and sales. Therefore, cash flow statements should be used in conjunction with the other primary statements when assessing future cash flow prospects.

Financial adaptability

This is the ability of an enterprise to take effective action to alter the amounts and timing of cash flows so that it can respond to unexpected needs or opportunities. Examples of financial adaptability are:

−   raising new capital, perhaps by issuing debt securities at short notice;
−   raising cash by selling assets without disrupting operations; and
−   achieving a rapid improvement in net cash inflows from operations.

Financial adaptability helps a company ride through a bad patch, take advantage of profitable investment activities and, as such, often indicates a lower risk company.

The primary statements give information relevant to financial adaptability, for example:

−   the cash flow statement reports cash flow from operations and, in general, a higher cash inflow from operations means that the company is better able to withstand adverse changes in operating conditions;

- statements of financial performance help to assess the ability of the company to reduce expenses if income declines; and

- the balance sheet gives details of available resources and claims on those resources.

Chapter 7: Reporting entity

- The *reporting entity* is the entity that is the subject of a given set of financial statements.

- An entity must be a *cohesive economic unit* (ie have a unified control structure) in order to *supply* meaningful financial statements.

- Consolidated financial statements reflect a parents' *control* of the assets and liabilities of its subsidiaries by aggregating the assets, liabilities and results of a parent and its subsidiaries.

- The boundary of the reporting entity is set by the extent of *control*, whether it is an individual entity or a group.

- Control is the *power to direct*. To have control an entity must have:

  - the *ability to deploy* the economic resources, whether assets or entities; *and*
  - the *ability to benefit* (or to suffer) by their deployment.

QUESTION

Briefly define the four fundamental accounting concepts referred to in SSAP2.

SUMMARY

SSAP2 sets out the four fundamental accounting principles:

- going concern
- accruals
- consistency
- prudence

The Companies Act 1985 sets out the same fundamental principles with one further addition:

- non-aggregation (no offset)

Introduction to final accounts

TYPES OF BUSINESS ORGANISATION

There are three main types of profit making business organisation:

- sole trader (sole proprietor)
- partnership
- limited company

Sole trader

As the name suggests, this is an organisation owned by one person.

Accounting conventions recognise the business as a *separate entity* from its owner. However, legally, the business and personal affairs of a sole trader are not distinguished in any way. The most important consequence of this is that a sole trader has complete personal unlimited liability. Business debts which cannot be paid from business assets must be met from the sale of personal assets, such as a house or car.

Sole trading organisations are normally small because they have to rely on the financial resources of their owner.

The advantages of operating as a sole trader include flexibility and autonomy. A sole trader can manage the business as he or she likes and can introduce or withdraw capital at any time.

Partnership

A partnership is two or more persons associated for the purpose of a business or a profession. Like a sole trader, a partnership is not legally distinguished from its members. Personal assets of the partners may have to be used to pay the debts of the partnership business.

The advantages of trading as a partnership stem mainly from there being many owners rather than one. This means that:

- more resources may be available, including capital, specialist knowledge, skills and ideas;

- administrative expenses may be lower for a partnership than for the equivalent number of sole traders, due to economies of scale; and

- partners can substitute for each other.

Partners can introduce or withdraw capital at any time, provided that all the partners agree.

Limited company

A limited company is a distinct, artificial 'person' created in order to separate legal responsibility for the affairs of a business (or any other activity) from the personal affairs of the individuals who own and/or operate the business.

The owners are known as *shareholders* (or members) and the people who run the business are known as *directors*. In a small corporation, owners and directors are often the same person.

Sometimes the owner of a company is another company; at some stage in the chain, however, there will be human owners! If one company owns another company, the owner is known as the parent company and the other company is known as the subsidiary company; collectively, the two companies are known as a *group*.

The consequences of separate legal personality

Limited liability

The company's debts and liabilities are those of the company and not those of the members.

Each member of a limited company is liable to contribute if called on to do so only the amount he has agreed to pay on his shares.

Perpetual succession

Unless the company is wound up, it continues in existence regardless of the death, bankruptcy, mental disorder or retirement of any of its members (this is in contrast with the position of a partnership which automatically dissolves where one of the partners dies or retires).

Property holding

The property of a registered company belongs to the company. A change in the ownership of shares in the company will have no effect on the ownership of the company's property. (Compare this with partnerships where the firm's property belongs directly to the partners who can take it with them if they leave the partnership.)

Transferable shares

Shares in a registered company can often be transferred without the consent of the other shareholders. (In the absence of agreement to the contrary, a new partner cannot be introduced into a firm without the consent of all existing partners.)

Contracts with members

A registered company can contract with its members and can sue and be sued on such contracts. (A partner cannot enter into contracts with his own firm.)

Suing and being sued

As a separate legal person, a company can sue and be sued in its own name. Judgements relating to companies do not affect the members personally.

Number of members

There is no upper limit on the number of members in a company.

In a partnership, except in certain restricted categories, such as accountants and stockbrokers, the maximum number of partners is 20. This limitation on numbers makes it difficult for a partnership to raise large amounts of capital.

Security for loans

A company has greater scope for raising loans by, for example, borrowing on debentures (long-term borrowings) and may secure them with floating charges.

(A floating charge is a mortgage over the constantly fluctuating assets of a company providing security for the lender of money to a company. It does not prevent the company dealing with the assets in the ordinary course of business. Such a charge is useful when a company has no fixed assets such as land, but does have a large and valuable stock in trade.)

The law does not permit partnerships or individuals to secure loans with a floating charge.

Taxation

Because a company is legally separate from its members, it is taxed separately from its members. Tax payable by companies is known as *corporation tax*. Partners and sole traders are personally liable for tax on the profits made by their businesses.

The rate of corporation tax (currently 33%) is lower than the top rate of income tax (currently 40%).

Disadvantages of incorporation

The disadvantages arise principally from the restrictions imposed by the *Companies Act 1985*.

Formalities, publicity and expenses

When they are being formed, companies have to register and to file a Memorandum and Articles of Association (formal constitution documents) with the Registrar. Registration fees and legal costs have to be paid.

Most limited companies' accounts are subject to an annual audit inspection (although this requirement is being lifted for small companies). The costs associated with this can be high. Partnerships and sole traders are not subject to this requirement unless as members of professional bodies whose own rules apply.

A registered company's accounts and certain other documents are open to public inspection. The accounts of sole traders and partnerships are not open to public inspection.

Capital maintenance

Limited companies are subject to strict rules in connection with the introduction and withdrawal of capital and profits.

Management powers

Members of a company may not take part in its management unless they are directors, whereas all partners are entitled to share in management, unless the partnership agreement provides otherwise.

PREPARING FINAL ACCOUNTS

Final accounts are the end result of a process of summarising, classifying and structuring large quantities of data. The objective of preparing final accounts is to turn individual transactions into useful information.

Whether the accounts are being prepared for a sole trader, a partnership or a limited company, the steps in the process are basically the same.

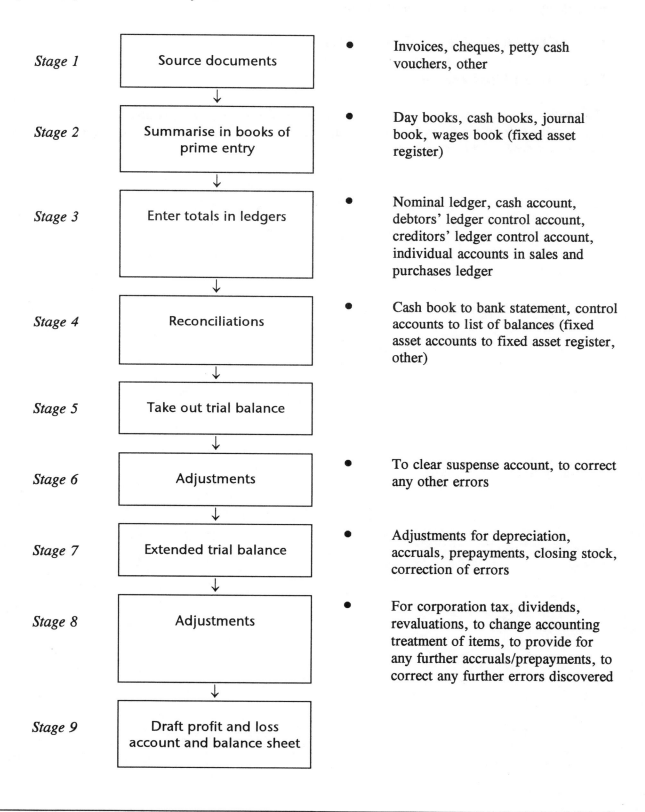

Stage 1 — Source documents
• Invoices, cheques, petty cash vouchers, other

Stage 2 — Summarise in books of prime entry
• Day books, cash books, journal book, wages book (fixed asset register)

Stage 3 — Enter totals in ledgers
• Nominal ledger, cash account, debtors' ledger control account, creditors' ledger control account, individual accounts in sales and purchases ledger

Stage 4 — Reconciliations
• Cash book to bank statement, control accounts to list of balances (fixed asset accounts to fixed asset register, other)

Stage 5 — Take out trial balance

Stage 6 — Adjustments
• To clear suspense account, to correct any other errors

Stage 7 — Extended trial balance
• Adjustments for depreciation, accruals, prepayments, closing stock, correction of errors

Stage 8 — Adjustments
• For corporation tax, dividends, revaluations, to change accounting treatment of items, to provide for any further accruals/prepayments, to correct any further errors discovered

Stage 9 — Draft profit and loss account and balance sheet

The first few stages should be familiar to you as you have covered them in your earlier studies. Your studies for Unit 14 will focus on the later stages:

- making final adjustments
- drafting the final accounts

In practice, there is normally a further set of adjustments, particularly where the accounts to be drafted are those of a limited company. These adjustments arise from the review of the draft accounts by management and from the audit.

THE ACCOUNTS OF A SOLE TRADER

The profit and loss account

The *profit and loss account* is a summary of a business' transactions for a given period. In practice, as you will see from the following pro forma, it is commonly split into two parts and referred to as a *trading and profit and loss account*.

Pro forma trading and profit and loss account for the year ended ...

		£	£
Sales			X
Less:	**Cost of sales**		
	Stock, at cost on 1 January (opening stock)	X	
	Add: Purchases of goods	X	
		X	
Less:	Stock, at cost on 31 December (closing stock)	(X)	
			(X)
Gross profit			X
Sundry income:			
	Discounts received	X	
	Commission received	X	
	Rent received	X	
			X
			X
Less:	Other expenses:		
	Rent	X	
	Rates	X	
	Lighting and heating	X	
	Telephone	X	
	Postage	X	
	Insurance	X	
	Stationery	X	
	Office salaries	X	
	Depreciation	X	
	Accountancy and audit fees	X	
	Bank charges and interest	X	
	Bad and doubtful debts	X	
	Delivery costs	X	
	Van running expenses	X	
	Advertising	X	
	Discounts allowed	X	
			(X)
Net profit			X

① – **Trading account**
② – **Profit and loss account**

Explanations

- The *trading account* discloses the *gross profit* generated by the business by comparing sales with the cost of those sales. A shopkeeper, for example, will purchase for resale items from various suppliers (wholesalers); by adding a profit margin to this cost, the selling price of the goods will be computed and this margin is the *gross profit*.

- *Cost of sales* is calculated by taking the cost of the goods available for sale during the year of period (ie. opening stock plus purchases) and deducting the cost of the goods which were unsold (ie. closing stock). Sales and cost of goods sold relate to the *same* number of units.

- The *profit and loss account* shows other items of income and expenditure earned or incurred by the business, in order to arrive at *net profit*.

- In a manufacturing industry, further analysis is needed of the figure for cost of sales. This is dealt with in Session 6. Similarly, service industries may have different ways of defining goods and net profit.

The balance sheet

The *balance sheet* is a statement of the financial position of a business at a given date, usually the end of the period covered by the *profit and loss account*. It is a snapshot at one given moment.

Pro forma balance sheet at ......

	Cost £	Depreciation £	£
Fixed assets			
Freehold factory	X	X	X
Machinery	X	X	X
Motor vehicles	X	X	X
	X	X	X
Current assets			
Stocks		X	
Debtors	X		
Less: Provision for doubtful debts	(X)	X	
Prepayments		X	
Cash at bank		X	
Cash in hand		X	
		X	
Current liabilities			
Trade creditors	X		
Accrued charges	X		
		(X)	
Net current assets			X
Long-term liabilities			X
12% loan			(X)
Net assets			X

	£
Representing:	
Capital at 1 January	X
Profit for the year	X
	——
	X
Less: Drawings	(X)
	——
Proprietor's funds	X
	——

Explanations

- *Fixed assets:* Assets acquired for use within the business with a view to earning profits, but not for resale. They are normally valued at cost less accumulated depreciation.

- *Current assets:* Assets acquired for conversion into cash in the ordinary course of business; they should not be valued at a figure greater than their realisable value.

- *Current liabilities:* Amounts owed by the business, payable within one year.

- *Net current assets:* Funds of the business available for day-to-day transactions. This can also be called *working capital.*

- *Long-term liabilities:* Funds provided for the business on a medium to long-term basis by an individual or organisation other than the proprietor. Long-term liabilities are repayable in more than one year.

Within these main headings, the following items should be noted:

- *Fixed assets*

  Depreciation is an amount charged in the accounts to write off the cost of an asset over its useful life.

- *Current assets*

  Debtors are people who owe amounts to the business.

  Provision for doubtful debts refers to those amounts owed which the proprietor is unsure of collecting.

  Prepayments are items paid by the company before the balance sheet date but relating to a subsequent period.

- *Current liabilities*

  Trade creditors are those suppliers to whom the business owes money.

  Accrued charges are amounts owed by the business, but not yet paid, for other expenses at the date of the balance sheet.

  Current liabilities are repayable within one year.

MAKING ADJUSTMENTS

Adjustments to the initial trial balance, the extended trial balance and the draft accounts are made by drawing up and posting a *journal entry*.

In practice, journals may be used in several ways:

- to record major or unusual transactions;
- to record period-end adjustments (eg. depreciation, stock, doubtful debts); and
- to facilitate the correction of errors, and to explain the nature of the errors.

Journals are recorded in the journal book. This is a book of prime entry and is not part of the double entry. From the journal book, the journals are posted to the relevant accounts in the nominal ledger.

Example 1

On 31 March 19X5 we purchased a new motor vehicle for £20,000 in cash. If we were going to record this in the books we would:

Debit:	*Motor vehicles*	*£20,000*	
Credit:	*Cash*		*£20,000*

Solution

This statement of the double-entry is sometimes known as a *journal*.

In the journal book itself, the transaction would be recorded as follows:

Date	Narrative	Account No	Dr £	Cr £
31.3.X5	Dr Motor Vehicles	M1	20,000	
	Cr Cash	C41		20,000
	Purchase of new motor vehicle (registration P666 BLR)			

When period-end adjustments are made, the journal is drawn up and the trial balance or draft accounts are adjusted. (These journals are not normally posted to the nominal ledger until the accounts have been finalised. The nominal ledger accounts are then balanced off and the new balances brought down for the start of the next accounting period.)

Example 2

Flagg extracted the following trial balance from his ledgers at 31 March 19X4:

	£	£
Petty cash	48	
Capital		3,830
Drawings	3,360	
Sales		49,457
Purchases	37,166	
Purchases returns		504
Stock (1 April 19X3)	5,057	
Fixtures and fittings	1,704	
Debtors	4,366	
Sundry creditors		4,987
Carriage on purchase	262	
Carriage on sales	442	
Rent and rates	1,104	
Light and heat	180	
Postage and telephone	204	
Sundry expenses	456	
Cash at bank	4,328	
	58,677	58,778

The trial balance did not agree. On investigation, Flagg discovered the following errors:

(1) In extracting the schedule of debtors, the credit side of a debtor's account had been overcast by £24.

(2) An amount of £10 for carriage on sales had been posted in error to the carriage on purchases account.

(3) A credit note for £41 received from a creditor had been entered in the purchase returns book but no entry had been made in the creditor's account.

(4) £84 charged for repairs to Flagg's private residence had been charged, in error, to the sundry expenses account.

(5) A payment of a telephone bill of £51 had been entered correctly in the cash book but had been posted, in error, to the postage and telephone account as £15.

Solution

The adjustments are as follows:

			Dr £	Cr £
1	Debit	Debtors	24	
	Credit	Suspense account		24
	Being correction of undercast in debtor's account			
2	Debit	Carriage on sales	10	
	Credit	Carriage on purchases		10
	Being correction of wrong posting			
3	Debit	Creditors	41	
	Credit	Suspense account		41
	Being correction of omitted entry			
4	Debit	Drawings	84	
	Credit	Sundry expenses		84
	Being payment for private expenses			
5	Debit	Postage and telephone	36	
	Credit	Suspense account		36
	Being correction of transposition error			

Journals 1, 3 and 5 clear the suspense account:

Suspense account

	£		£
Difference per trial balance	101	Debtors	24
		Creditors	41
		Postage	36
	101		101

The trial balance is then corrected:

	Opening £	Adjustments £	Dr £	Cr £
Petty cash	48		48	
Capital	(3,830)			3,830
Drawings	3,360	84	3,444	
Sales	(49,457)			49,457
Purchases	37,166		37,166	
Purchases returns	(504)			504
Stock at 1 April 19X3	5,057		5,057	
Fixtures and fittings	1,704		1,704	
Debtors	4,366	24	4,390	
Creditors	(4,987)	41		4,946
Carriage on purchases	262	(10)	252	
Carriage on sales	442	10	452	
Rent and rates	1,104		1,104	
Light and heat	180		180	
Postage and telephone	204	36	240	
Sundry expenses	456	(84)	372	
Cash at bank	4,328		4,328	
	(101)	101	58,737	58,737

THE EXTENDED TRIAL BALANCE

A trial balance is simply a list of all the balances on the ledger accounts *before* year-end adjustments are made. These adjustments need to be made before the preparation of the profit and loss account and balance sheet and they normally include the following:

- correction of errors
- recognition of accruals and prepayments
- provision of the year's depreciation charge
- review of the charge for bad and doubtful debts
- inclusion of closing stock

The extended trial balance is a worksheet which takes us from the trial balance to the profit and loss account and balance sheet.

Layout of a typical extended trial balance

Account	Trial balance		Adjustments		Profit and loss account		Balance sheet	
	Dr £	Cr £	Dr £	Cr £	Dr £	Cr £	Dr £	Cr £

The names of the ledger accounts and the corresponding amounts per the trial balance are entered into the first three columns.

The adjustments columns are used for all of the year-end adjustments mentioned above.

Example 3

Trial balance at 31 December 19X6

	Dr £	Cr £
Shop fittings at cost	2,000	
Depreciation provision at 1 January 19X6		100
Leasehold premises at cost	12,500	
Depreciation provision at 1 January 19X6		625
Stock in trade at 1 January 19X6	26,000	
Debtors at 31 December 19X6	53,000	
Provision for doubtful debts at 1 January 19X6		960
Cash in hand	50	
Cash at bank	2,250	
Creditors for supplies		65,000
Proprietor's capital at 1 January 19X6		28,115
Drawings to 31 December 19X6	2,000	
Purchases	102,000	
Sales		129,000
Wages	18,200	
Advertising	2,300	
Rates for 15 months to 31 March 19X7	1,500	
Light and heat	1,800	
Bank charges	200	
	223,800	223,800

The following adjustments are to be made:

(1)   Depreciation of shop fittings   £100
*   Depreciation of leasehold premises   £625*

(2)   A debt of £500 is irrecoverable and is to be written off; the doubtful debts provision is to be increased to 2% of the debtors.

(3)   Advertising fees of £200 have been treated incorrectly as wages.

(4)   The proprietor has withdrawn goods costing £1,000 for his personal use; these have not been recorded as drawings.

(5)   The stock in trade at 31 December 19X6 is valued at £30,000.

(6)   The electricity charge for the last three months of 19X6 is outstanding and is estimated to be £400.

Solution: Preparation of the extended trial balance

Stage 1: The balances per the trial balance are recorded in the correct columns and the total of the debit balances is agreed to the total of the credit balances.

Stage 2: We shall now deal with the adjustments (apart from accruals and prepayments).

- **Correction of errors**

Two errors need to be corrected. One of the errors concerns the drawings of the proprietor, ie. the fact that some of the purchases were bought for his own use. To correct this, we should decrease the purchases and increase the drawings, ie:

Debit	Drawings	1,000	
Credit	Purchases		1,000

The other error concerns the mis-classification of advertising fees as wages. To correct this, the following adjustment is necessary:

Debit	Advertising	200	
Credit	Wages		200

- **Provision of the year's depreciation charge**

The charge for the year is £725 and we need to charge this to the *depreciation expense* account and also to increase the *provision for depreciation*, ie. the accumulated depreciation carried forward. The double-entry is:

Debit	Depreciation expense account	725	
Credit	Provision for depreciation: shop fittings		100
Credit	Provision for depreciation: leasehold premises		625

We will need to set up the depreciation expense account as none exists.

- **Provision for doubtful debts**

The debtors amount to £52,500 after the write-off of the bad debt of £500. A provision of £1,050 (£52,500 × 2%) is therefore required at 31.12.X6. The provision brought forward at the beginning of the year was £960; therefore it should be increased by £90 (1,050 – 960). The total charge to the profit and loss account is £590 (the debt written off plus the increase in the provision). The double-entry is:

Debit	Bad and doubtful debts expense	590	
Credit	Provision for doubtful debts		90
Credit	Debtors		500

The bad debt expense account will need to be created.

- **Inclusion of closing stock**

Closing stock appears in both the profit and loss account and the balance sheet.

- In the profit and loss, it is a reduction of cost of goods sold and hence is a *credit.*
- In the balance sheet, it is an asset and hence is a *debit.*

Accordingly we set up two stock accounts: one for the balance sheet and one for the profit and loss account. The adjustment is:

Debit	Stock (balance sheet)	30,000	
Credit	Stock (profit and loss account)		30,000

If you turn to the extended trial balance on page 35, you will see that each of these pairs of double-entry has been recorded in the adjustment columns. As the debit entries should always equal the credit entries, it is a useful check to cast the debit and credit adjustment columns to see that the totals are equal.

Stage 3: We now have to deal with the last adjustments, ie. the accruals and prepayments.

● **Electricity**

The profit and loss account charge for the year needs to be increased by £400 and a creditor for £400 must be established. The double-entry is:

Debit	Light and heat	400	
Credit	Accruals		400

The accruals account will need to be set up.

● **Rates**

The profit and loss account charge for the year should be £1,200 (12/15 × £1,500), and there should be a prepayment of £300. The double-entry is:

Debit	Prepayments	300	
Credit	Light and heat		300

Stage 4: We have now recorded all of the adjustments and we need to prepare the trading and profit and loss account and balance sheet. This is achieved by the following:

● Cross-cast each account and enter the total in the appropriate column of the profit and loss account or balance sheet. Some examples are as follows:

– Fittings (2,000 + 0 = £2,000) are recorded in the *debit* column of the balance sheet.

– Provision for depreciation on fittings (100 + 100 = £200) is recorded in the *credit* column of the *balance sheet.*

– Purchases (102,000 – 1,000 = £101,000) is recorded in the *debit* column of the *profit and loss account.*

Note: Accruals are added to the original trial balance amount whereas prepayments are subtracted.

● Add the debit and credit sides of the profit and loss account. The differences between these two columns is a profit (if the credits exceed the debits) or a loss (if the debits exceed the credits). The difference is recorded in the correct column of the profit and loss account (so that the two sides now balance) and the double-entry is with the balance sheet.

● Add the debit and credit columns of the balance sheet. These should agree unless you have made any errors.

Stage 5: The trading and profit and loss account and balance sheet are then prepared from the relevant columns.

The completed extended trial balance is shown overleaf:

Extended trial balance at 31 December 19X6

Account	Trial balance Dr £	Trial balance Cr £	Adjustments Dr £	Adjustments Cr £	Profit and loss account Dr £	Profit and loss account Cr £	Balance sheet Dr £	Balance sheet Cr £
Shop fittings	2,000						2,000	
Provision for depreciation 1.1.X6		100		100				200
Leasehold premises	12,500						12,500	
Provision for depreciation 1.1.X6		625		625				1,250
Stock 1.1.X6	26,000		30,000	30,000	26,000	30,000	30,000	
Debtors	53,000			500			52,500	
Provision for doubtful debts 1.1.X6		960		90				1,050
Cash in hand	50						50	
Cash at bank	2,250						2,250	
Creditors		65,000						65,000
Capital		28,115						28,115
Drawings	2,000		1,000				3,000	
Purchases	102,000			1,000	101,000			
Sales		129,000				129,000		
Wages	18,200			200	18,000			
Advertising	2,300		200		2,500			
Rates	1,500			300	1,200			
Light and heat	1,800		400		2,200			
Bank charges	200				200			
Depreciation – shop fittings			100		100			
Depreciation – leasehold premises			625		625			
Bad debts expense			590		590			
Prepayments			300				300	
Accruals				400				400
					152,415			
Net profit					6,585			6,585
	223,800	223,800	33,215	33,215	159,000	159,000	102,600	102,600

The trading and profit and loss account and balance sheet are now drafted from the extended trial balance. (For the purpose of this example, we are assuming that there are no further adjustments to the extended trial balance; in practice, this might not be the case. Any further adjustments would be made by drawing up and posting journal entries, exactly as before.)

Trading and profit and loss account for the year ended 31 December 19X6

	£	£
Sales		129,000
Less: Cost of sales		
Opening stock	26,000	
Purchases	101,000	
	127,000	
Closing stock	(30,000)	
		(97,000)
Gross profit		32,000
Less: Expenses		
Wages	18,000	
Advertising	2,500	
Rates	1,200	
Light and heat	2,200	
Charges	200	
Depreciation (100 + 625)	725	
Bad debts	590	
		(25,415)
Net profit		6,585

Balance sheet at 31 December 19X6

	Cost £	Accumulated depreciation £	Net book value £
Fixed assets			
Shop fittings	2,000	200	1,800
Leasehold premises	12,500	1,250	11,250
	14,500	1,450	13,050
Current assets			
Stocks		30,000	
Debtors (52,500 – 1,050)		51,450	
Prepayments		300	
Cash at bank		2,250	
Cash in hand		50	
		84,050	
Current liabilities			
Creditors	65,000		
Accruals	400		
		(65,400)	
Net current assets			18,650
Total assets less current liabilities			31,700

	£
Represented by:	
Capital	28,115
Add: Net profit for the year	6,585
	34,700
Less: Drawings	(3,000)
	31,700

FURTHER POINTS

Users of the accounts and their needs

The form and content of sole trader accounts are not prescribed by law. Therefore the accounts of sole traders may be drawn up in any format that the owner wishes. This is determined by the needs of the users of the accounts.

For a sole trader, the most probable users are:

- the owner of the business (who is almost certainly also the manager of the business)
- the Inland Revenue
- any third parties which may have provided finance (normally the bank)

The owners of a business are interested in its profitability and in the components of that profit. They need detailed information about the cost of sales and expenses. They probably need to compare the performance of the business in the current period with its performance in previous periods. The owners of a business should also be interested in its solvency. Even if the business is making profits, it cannot survive without cash, or the ability to generate cash.

The Inland Revenue uses the accounts to determine the amount of tax payable. This is based on adjusted net profit. Certain expenses are not allowable for tax purposes. Depreciation and losses on sales of fixed assets are not allowable as deductions from profit. However, capital allowances, calculated in a form prescribed by the Inland Revenue, are allowable. For these reasons, accounts should include details of expenses and of additions and disposals of fixed assets.

Loan creditors are primarily interested in the ability of the business to pay interest and to repay loans. They are likely to focus on the balance sheet as well as on the profit and loss account.

The form of accounts

General principles which should be observed in preparing accounts include the following:

- *Aggregation:* information must be detailed enough to be useful but not so detailed as to obscure the general picture. For example, descriptions of each transaction or event taking place during the period would be of little use.

- *Classification:* items should be grouped according to their nature or function and items which have similar characteristics should be grouped together. For example, all fixed assets appear under the same heading and cost of sales is differentiated from other expenses.

- *Structure:* the prominence given to disclosure should be appropriate to the overall significance of the item within the accounts as a whole. For example, if a business were required to supply a breakdown of individual items within a particular account heading, this information would normally be disclosed in a note, rather than on the face of the profit and loss account.

- *Consistency:* because businesses need to compare their current performance and position with those of previous periods, accounts should normally be presented in the same format each year.

Current best practice

Sole traders are not obliged to follow accounting standards when drawing up accounts. However, accounts should normally be drawn up in accordance with current best practice (which may mean compliance with accounting standards). It should be noted that accounts cannot show a true and fair view unless they comply with accounting standards.

In practice, many accounting standards are unlikely to be relevant to the accounts of sole traders. Those which are most likely to apply include the accounting standards which you have already met earlier in your studies:

- SSAP2 *Disclosure of accounting policies*
- SSAP5 *Accounting for value added tax*
- SSAP9 *Stocks and long-term contracts*
- SSAP12 *Accounting for depreciation*

Other accounting standards likely to be relevant to sole traders include the following:

- SSAP17 *Accounting for post balance sheet events*
- SSAP18 *Accounting for contingencies*
- SSAP22 *Accounting for goodwill*
- FRS5 *Reporting the substance of transactions*

These accounting standards are covered later in this Study Pack.

QUESTIONS

1   VB Ltd

VB Ltd, a chemical company, extracted a trial balance from its ledgers on 30 April 19Y0 and found that the sum of the debit balances did not equal the sum of the credit balances. A suspense account was opened and used to record the difference. VB Ltd does not use control accounts for its customer and supplier accounts.

The company carried out an investigation into the cause of the difference and found the following:

(1) Cash sales of £246 had been debited to the sales returns account and the cash book.

(2) An invoice to a customer for £1,249 had been posted to the customer's account as £1,294.

(3) Bank charges of £37 had not been entered in the cash book.

(4) Value added tax of £45 had been included in the sum posted to the purchases account from a supplier's invoice.

(5) A contra entry of £129 had been debited to the customer account and credited to the supplier account.

(6) An invoice for rates for the six-month period ending 30 September 19Y0 amounting to £13,500 had not been entered in the ledgers and remained unpaid on 30 April 19Y0.

(7) A carriage invoice of £52 had been debited to carriage outwards but it related to the purchase of goods from a supplier of the company.

(8) A bad debt of £40 which should have been written off had been forgotten and remained as a balance on the customer's account.

Required

Show the journal entries necessary to correct *each* of the above (including a narrative) and state the effect of each correction on the profit of the company for the year ended 30 April 19Y0.

---

2 Robert Bridges

Robert Bridges extracts his nominal ledger trial balance at 31 December 19X8 as follows:

	£
Capital at 1.1.X8	24,376
Drawings	2,015
Fixed assets	4,900
Provision for depreciation	1,250
Stocks at 1.1.X8	3,180
Debtors	4,723
Provision for bad debts	76
Petty cash	100
Creditors	1,485
Sales	36,823
Purchases	29,467
Discount received	518
Discount allowed	581
Rent	300
Rates	750
Electricity	224
Casual wages	1,069
Telephone	18
Travel expenses	367
Sundries	909

Robert has forgotten to extract the balance on his cash book of which £15,000 represents the balance on a deposit account and the remainder the balance on the current account.

The following year-end adjustments need to be made:

(1)　Closing stock is valued at £4,567.

(2)　Depreciation is to be charged at 25% on written-down value, with a full year's depreciation in the year of purchase and none in the year of sale.

(3)　Rent has been paid to 30 September 19X8 and rates to 31 March 19X9.

(4)　£1,200 interest is due on the deposit account.

(5)　In 19X9 Robert paid £63 for electricity for the three months, December 19X8 and January and February 19X9.

(6)　Robert has promised his assistant a bonus of £25 for 19X8.

(7)　It is decided to merge the telephone and sundry expenses.

(8)　A bad debt of £7 is to be written off, £16 is to be specifically provided against and the general provision is to be increased to 2% of remaining debtors.

(9)　An asset costing £400 with accumulated depreciation of £100 had been sold for £100. The only entries made were to credit the fixed asset account with the sale proceeds and to debit cash.

Required

(a)   Prepare an extended trial balance.

(b)   Prepare a trading and profit and loss account for the year ended 31 December 19X8.

(c)   Prepare a balance sheet at 31 December 19X8.

SUMMARY

The journal is used to record period-end adjustments. It must be accompanied by narrative stating the nature of the transaction.

The extended trial balance is simply a worksheet showing the adjustments made to the figures in the trial balance to lead to the profit and loss account and balance sheet.

Procedure:

- Set out initial trial balance.

- Deal with adjustments.

- Ddeal with accruals and prepayments.

- Add the columns across into P + L and B/S columns.

- Add the columns down.

- Prepare profit and loss account and balance sheet from the relevant columns.

Sole traders are not required to prepare their accounts in a standard format or to observe accounting standards. In practice, applicable accounting standards should normally be followed.

The accounts of partnerships

INTRODUCTION

What is a partnership?

The Partnership Act 1890 defines a partnership as 'the relation which subsists between persons carrying on a business in common with a view of profit'.

The existence of a partnership is usually a matter of fact constituted by agreement (either orally or in writing) between those who wish to carry on business together. The essence of a partnership is that each partner is an agent of all the others for the purposes of the business. Each partner is bound by the acts of all the other partners and each partner can be sued in his own name for the whole of any partnership debts.

Basic rules

Let us look first at the basic rules you must know before starting partnership accounts.

- To record a partner's interests in the business, we will need:

    (i)   a *capital* account, which shows his share of fixed capital of the firm, and
    (ii)   a *current* account recording his share of profits/losses and his drawings.

    There will be one account for *each* partner and these accounts should always be shown in *columnar* form.

    Capital and current accounts normally appear as *credit* balances. The partnership (ie. the business) has a liability to the partners as individuals. A debit balance on a current account means that the partner is a *debtor* of the business. This occurs if a partner draws more money out of the business than his profit share entitles him to draw.

- Whether you need both capital and current accounts depends on the instructions of the particular question you are dealing with. If the option is left open to you, use one account only and call it the *capital account*.

- If you do need both, there is a general rule as to the distinction between the two accounts and the types of item which should be passed through them. It is best to use the capital account to record adjustments to the amount of fixed capital of any partner and the effect of any alteration in the value of goodwill, ie. items of a permanent nature.

Partnership agreement

The basis of a partnership is agreement and trust. It is much better to have a written agreement to which reference may be made by all partners. An agreement may however be created in any of the following ways:

- deed
- writing
- word of mouth
- course of dealing

The agreement will cover rights and duties of partners and is likely to include a number of items of accounting importance including:

- partners' capital and current accounts
- profit and loss sharing ratio
- partners' drawing rights
- interest on capital, current and drawings accounts
- partners' salaries
- valuation of goodwill
- provision relating to death or retirement of partners

RIGHTS OF PARTNERS

The division of profits and losses between partners depends upon the arrangements laid down in the partnership agreement.

The following provisions of the Partnership Act 1890 (S24) give the rights of partners to the following *in the absence of agreement to the contrary*:

- All partners are entitled to share equally in capital and profits and must contribute equally to losses.

- Partners are not entitled to interest on capital.

- Partners are not entitled to salaries.

- A partner is entitled to interest at 5% per annum on advances beyond the amount of his agreed capital (ie. on loans).

Questions normally give all relevant details of the partnership agreement. In the absence of this information you should apply the provisions above.

APPROPRIATION OF PROFIT

The profit and loss account of a partnership is the same as that of any other trading entity but, once the net trading profit has been found, a further account is necessary to show the implementation of the partnership agreement and the resulting division of profits between the partners. This is called an *appropriation account*. Thus the appropriation account does not contain items that are charges against profit; it simply shows how the final profit is divided. Where changes have occurred to the partnership during the accounting period, it may be necessary to allocate or apportion profit between the periods and to construct a separate appropriation account for each period.

Profit and loss appropriation account

This account starts with the net profit divisible between the partners and shows the division between them. It may reflect any or all of the following:

- interest on current accounts;
- interest on capital accounts;
- salaries;
- division of remaining profit in agreed ratio;
- any adjustment to reach guaranteed minimum share for one of the partners.

Interest on capital and current accounts is normally calculated on the balance at the period-end. A partnership agreement may provide for interest on debit balances as well as on credit balances. Interest on debit balances is a deduction from profit share.

It is important to remember that any interest on loans from partners, in excess of agreed capital, is a charge against profit (ie. an expense), and does not appear in the appropriation account.

Example

A, B and C are in partnership. Their first year's trading produces a profit of £27,000 before taking account of the items covered below. The partnership agreement specifies:

Interest on capital at 10% per annum; no interest on drawings.
A is to receive a salary of £6,000 per annum.
Profits are to be shared 1:2:3 between A, B and C respectively.

Partners' capitals are:

A	*£6,000*
B	*£4,000*
C	*£8,000*

In addition to the above capital, C has advanced a further £15,000 and interest on this amount has been agreed at 12% per annum.

Drawings during the year were as follows:

A	*£8,000*
B	*£5,000*
C	*£10,000*

Solution

The first step is to find the net profit divisible between the partners as follows:

	£
Profit in question	27,000
Deduct: Interest on loan – £15,000 × 12%	1,800
Divisible profit	25,200

Next we construct a profit and loss appropriation account giving effect to the agreement between the partners.

Profit and loss appropriation account

			£	£
Net profit (as above)				25,200
Interest on capital				
	A	10% × 6,000	600	
	B	10% × 4,000	400	
	C	10% × 8,000	800	
				(1,800)
				23,400
Salary A				(6,000)
				17,400
Profit in agreed ratios				
	A	1/6 × 17,400	2,900	
	B	2/6 × 17,400	5,800	
	C	3/6 × 17,400	8,700	
				17,400

Finally, we must construct the partners' current accounts to reflect the other side of these entries.

Partners' current accounts

	A £	B £	C £		A £	B £	C £
Cash book				Interest on loan			1,800
– drawings	8,000	5,000	10,000	Interest on capital	600	400	800
				Salary	6,000		
Balances c/f	1,500	1,200	1,300	Profit share	2,900	5,800	8,700
	9,500	6,200	11,300		9,500	6,200	11,300

Although interest on the loan is charged to profit and loss account, it is still credited to the current account of C. Drawings are debited directly to the current accounts and must *never* appear in the profit and loss account or appropriation account.

Changes during a year

Where a change takes place in a partnership during an accounting period, it will be necessary to produce two appropriation accounts dealing with each period separately. In order to do this the profit must be divided between the periods before and after the change. This may involve the following:

(a)   a simple time-apportionment of profit on a month-by-month basis.

(b)   a time-apportionment of gross profit on a month by month basis and a division of other expenses on either a time basis or according to factual information;

(c)   an apportionment of gross profits according to the level of sales in each period and a breakdown of expenses using the following methods:

(i)   *pro rata* to sales;
(ii)   apportioned on a time basis;
(iii) according to the facts given.

The last of these three methods, (c), is the most complicated so we will examine this method using a simple illustration. Remember, methods (a) and (b) use part of the methods we will adopt here, but both are simplifications of this approach.

Example

A and B are in partnership sharing profits and losses equally. The profit and loss account for the year to 31 December 19X1 was as follows.

	£	£
Sales		60,000
Cost of sales		30,000
Gross profit		30,000
Packing and distribution	9,000	
Rent, rates etc.	6,000	
Depreciation – car	800	
		15,800
Net profit		14,200

Owing to the workload taken on by B following A's illness in June, it was agreed that B should receive a salary of £6,000 pa and the remaining profits should be shared A 2/3 and B 1/3. This new agreement was to operate as from 1 July 19X1.

Sales in the period January to June were £20,000.

B was also to have personal use of the firm's motor car which was purchased on 1 July.

Solution

The first step is to work out the net profit for each period. Expenses will be apportioned as follows:

Cost of sales	)	
Packing and distribution	)	in proportion to sales
Rent and rates etc.	–	time basis
Depreciation – car	–	last period only

The rules for appropriation can then be applied.

Profit and loss appropriation account

		1 January to 30 June		1 July to 31 Dec	
		£	£	£	£
Sales			20,000		40,000
Cost of sales			(10,000)		(20,000)
			10,000		20,000
Packing and distribution		3,000		6,000	
Rent, rates etc.		3,000		3,000	
Depreciation		–		800	
			(6,000)		(9,800)
Net profit			4,000		10,200
Appropriations					
Salary – B		–	–	3,000	(3,000)
			4,000		7,200
Share of profit	A	2,000		4,800	
	B	2,000		2,400	
			4,000		7,200

GOODWILL

Definition

There are many ways in which goodwill can be defined – the most generally accepted definition is:

'Goodwill is the difference between the value of a business as a whole and the fair value of its separable net assets'.

So a business may have net assets that have a current market value of, say, £50,000 yet someone may be prepared to pay £80,000 for the business as a whole. Why? What does the extra £30,000 goodwill represent?

Sources of goodwill

Goodwill may arise from a large number of sources, some of which are:

- reputation of owners;
- quality of goods;
- site monopoly or advantage;
- advantageous patents or trade marks;
- growth element.

Unrecorded goodwill

It is normal for a business to show no value for goodwill on its balance sheet because of its volatile nature and the uncertainty as to its true value (you will recall a company can only include purchased goodwill in its balance sheet).

Whenever a change occurs in a partnership, it is necessary to record the goodwill prior to making the change and normally it is then written off once the change has occurred.

This adjustment in respect of unrecorded goodwill is required whenever any of the following takes place:

(a)   admission of a new partner;
(b)   retirement of a partner;
(c)   death of a partner;
(d)   change in profit-sharing ratio;
(e)   any combination of (a) to (d) above.

The adjustment to be made in respect of unrecorded goodwill is always the same:

Credit Old partners' capital accounts with unrecorded goodwill in the old profit-sharing ratio
Debit   Goodwill account

This records the goodwill and the change may now be made.

Credit Goodwill account
Debit   New partners' capital accounts in the new profit-sharing ratio

This now eliminates goodwill from the balance sheet of the firm.

Often, no goodwill account is opened. This does not mean that goodwill can be ignored but that a shortcut is taken. The entries are commonly shortened to:

Credit Old partners in old profit-sharing ratio
Debit   New partners in new profit-sharing ratio

Example

A and B are in partnership sharing profits equally. No goodwill exists in the books of the partnership and the partners wish to continue this policy. They agree that in the future A should receive 60% of the profits and B only 40%.

Goodwill is valued at £60,000.

Solution

		£	£
Credit	A Capital account		30,000
	B Capital account		30,000
Debit	Goodwill	60,000	
Credit	Goodwill		60,000
Debit	A Capital account	36,000	
	B Capital account	24,000	

This would appear in the ledger accounts as follows:

Goodwill	**Capital**

	£		£		A £	B £		A £	B £
Capital	60,000	Capital	60,000	G'w'l c/f	36,000	24,000 6,000	G'w'l c/f	30,000 6,000	30,000
					36,000	30,000		36,000	30,000
				b/f	6,000		b/f		6,000

The entries in the goodwill account may be omitted because the £60,000 is simply entered and then written out.

Why do this? To ensure that B gets full credit for his 50% share of goodwill generated to the date of change of profit share ratio.

Suppose that, one year later, the goodwill had risen to £80,000 and that the partnership was sold, realising this in the form of a profit. Ignoring the other assets of the business, the effects on the partners would be:

Capital

Capital

	£		£		A £	B £		A £	B £
Capital	80,000			b/f c/f	6,000 42,000	38,000	b/f Goodwill – Cash	48,000	6,000 32,000
					48,000	38,000		48,000	38,000
							b/f	42,000	38,000

The capital accounts therefore reflect the proper claims the partners have on the realised goodwill:

	A	B
50% share of original goodwill	30,000	30,000
60%/40% share of goodwill generated in last year (£20,000)	12,000	8,000
	42,000	38,000

Other assets

Before any change can occur in a partnership, all assets and liabilities must be recorded at their correct value just like the goodwill we saw above. Unlike the goodwill, these assets are normally left at their new values in the partnership books. The entries required when an asset is to be increased in value are therefore:

Debit Asset account with the amount of the revaluation
Credit Old partners in old profit-sharing ratio

(The reverse entry is made to reduce an asset in value.)

Where a number of assets are to be revalued, it is normal to open a revaluation account into which all the increases and decreases may be collected, with the net difference being transferred to the partners' capital accounts in their profit-sharing ratio.

Example

A and B are in partnership, sharing capital and profits in the ratio 1:1. They decide to change the profit ratio to 2:1. The book value of the assets and their true value at the date of change are as follows:

	Book value £	Revalued value £
Freehold land and buildings	*100,000*	*200,000*
Motor vehicles	*25,000*	*35,000*
Debtors	*30,000*	*20,000*
Creditors	*10,000*	*10,000*
Total net assets	*165,000*	*265,000*

Ignore goodwill.

Required

Write up the ledger accounts to record the revaluation.

Solution

Steps

(1)   The partners' capital accounts must show a total of £165,000 (the total net assets) divided in the ratio 1:1 (£82,500 : £82,500). They will appear as follows:

Capital account				
	A £	B £		A £	B £
			b/f	82,500	82,500

(2)   The asset accounts will be debited or credited with the increase or decrease in value, and the appropriate amount entered in the revaluation account. These later entries are shown below (the entries in the asset accounts are not shown).

Revaluation account				
	£	£		£	£
Debtors	10,000		Freeholds		100,000
			Vehicles		10,000

(3)   The balance on the revaluation account is written off to the capital account in the ratio 1:1 – the old profit-sharing ratio.

Capital account

	A	B			A	B
	£	£			£	£
				b/f	82,500	82,500
				Revaluation	50,000	50,000

Revaluation account

		£	£			£	£
Debtors			10,000	Freeholds			100,000
Capital accounts			100,000	Vehicles			10,000
			110,000				110,000

Note: The fact that the profit-sharing ratio has changed does not alter the partners' ownership of the assets that exist at the date of change, in exactly the same way that their share of goodwill existing at the date of change did not change.

ADMISSION OF NEW PARTNERS

Cash paid by incoming partners

All cash paid by an incoming partner, however described, must be credited to his account in the partnership.

Transactions of this type are often described in somewhat confusing and misleading terms. The most common descriptions are outlined below.

(a)   C is admitted as a partner and introduces cash of £12,000.

Entries		£	£
Debit	Cash	12,000	
Credit	C's capital account		12,000

(b)   C is admitted as a partner and pays A and B £6,000 each.

		£	£
Debit	A's capital account	6,000	
	B's capital account	6,000	
Credit	C's capital account		12,000

(c)   C is admitted as a partner and pays A and B £6,000 each, purchasing one sixth share of goodwill from each.

The entries are the same as in (b) above but this also tells us C's share of profit:

$1/3$ $(1/6 + 1/6)$

and the valuation of goodwill: $1/6 = £6,000$ ∴ Goodwill = £36,000

Example

A and B are in partnership, sharing profits 1:1. The total net assets (excluding goodwill) amount to £200,000. No goodwill account is maintained in the books. They agree to admit C into partnership on 1 January 19X5, when the new profit-sharing ratio will be 1:1:1. C agrees to pay £20,000 for his share of the goodwill.

Required

Show how the above transaction will be recorded in the books of the partnership.

Solution

Steps

(1)   Calculate the goodwill.

C's share of goodwill is $\frac{1}{3}$ = £20,000
Therefore the goodwill   = £60,000

(2)   Write the goodwill into the books in the old profit ratio (A:B; 1:1).

(3)   Write the goodwill out of the books in the new profit ratio (A:B:C; 1:1:1).

(4)   Record the payment of £20,000 by C.

The partners' capital account will appear as follows (S = Step):

Capital account

	A £	*B* £	*C* £		*A* £	*B* £	*C* £
c/f	130,000	130,000		b/f	100,000	100,000	
				Goodwill			
	130,000	130,000		(S1, 2)	30,000	30,000	
					130,000	130,000	
				b/f	130,000	130,000	
Goodwill (S3)	20,000	20,000	20,000	Cash book			
c/f	110,000	110,000		(S4)			20,000
	130,000	130,000	20,000		130,000	130,000	20,000
				b/f	110,000	110,000	–

Comment on solution

If the goodwill were written back again in the new profit ratio 1:1:1, each partner would be credited with £20,000, giving A and B £130,000 (ie. their original share of the net assets and goodwill) and C £20,000 (the value of the cash paid in).

Example

Merriman, Jolly and Jape were in partnership, sharing profits one-half, one-third, one-sixth respectively.

On 1 January 19X1 they admitted Giggle into partnership on the following terms.

Giggle to have one-sixth share which he purchased entirely from Merriman, paying him £4,000 for that share of goodwill. Of this amount, Merriman retained £3,000 and put the balance into the firm as additional capital. Giggle also brought £2,500 capital into the firm.

It was agreed that the investments should be reduced to their market value of £1,800 and that the plant should be reduced to £2,900 as on 31 December 19X0.

The balance sheet of the old firm at 31 December 19X0 was as follows.

	£	£
Fixed assets		
Plant	3,500	
Furniture	1,000	
Investments	3,000	
		7,500
Current assets		
Stock	5,000	
Debtors	6,000	
Cash at bank	4,000	
	15,000	
Current liabilities		
Creditors	10,500	
		4,500
		12,000
Capital accounts		
Merriman		6,000
Jolly		4,000
Jape		2,000
		12,000

Required

(a)   *Prepare the opening balance sheet of the new firm as at 1 January 19X1.*

(b)   *Prepare the capital accounts of the partners for the year to 31 December 19X1.*

Solution

The steps involved in solving this problem are as follows:

Steps

(1)   Prepare the revaluation account, identify the profit or loss and transfer it to the old partners in their profit-sharing ratio.

(2)   Work out the total value of goodwill.

$1/6 = £4,000$, total goodwill $= £4,000 \times 6 = £24,000$

Credit the old partners in the old ratio and debit the new partners in the new ratio.

(3)   Calculate the new ratio.

Merriman's share $= 1/2 - 1/6 = 1/3$

Therefore, new ratio is $1/3 : 1/3 : 1/6 : 1/6 = 2:2:1:1$

(4)   Record the private settlement between Merriman and Giggle.

(5)   Record the cash introduced by Merriman and Giggle.

(6)   Balance the partners' capital accounts and draft the new balance sheet.

The answer would appear as follows.

(a)   **Balance sheet at 1 January 19X1 (Step 6)**

		£	£
Fixed assets			
	Plant	2,900	
	Furniture	1,000	
	Investments	1,800	
			5,700
Current assets			
	Stock	5,000	
	Debtors	6,000	
	Cash at bank	7,500	
		18,500	
Current liabilities			
	Creditors	10,500	
			8,000
			13,700

		£
Capital accounts		
	Merriman	6,100
	Jolly	3,400
	Jape	1,700
	Giggle	2,500
		13,700

(b)

Partners' capital accounts

	M £	Jo £	Ja £	G £		M £	Jo £	Ja £	G £
Revaluation	900	600	300	–	Bal b/f	6,000	4,000	2,000	–
Bal c/f	6,100	3,400	1,700	2,500	Cash	1,000	–	–	2,500
	7,000	4,000	2,000	2,500		7,000	4,000	2,000	2,500
					Bal b/f	6,100	3,400	1,700	2,500

Note: There is no entry in the partners' capital accounts for goodwill as the settlement between Merriman and Giggle took place outside the partnership, ie. Giggle gave Merriman a cheque for £4,000. Alternatively, the transaction could have gone through the books and appeared as follows:

Partners' capital accounts

	M £	Jo £	Ja £	G £		M £	Jo £	Ja £	G £
Revaluation	900	600	300	–	Bal b/f	6,000	4,000	2,000	–
Goodwill	8,000	8,000	4,000	4,000	Goodwill	12,000	8,000	4,000	–
Cash	3,000	–	–	–	Cash	–	–	–	6,500
Bal c/f	6,100	3,400	1,700	2,500					
	18,000	12,000	6,000	6,500		18,000	12,000	6,000	6,500
					Bal b/f	6,100	3,400	1,700	2,500

Workings

Revaluation account (Step 1)

	£		£
Investments	1,200	Partners' capital accounts	
Plant	600	Merriman	900
		Jolly	600
		Jape	300
	1,800		1,800

Cash at bank

	£		£
Balance b/f	4,000		
Merriman (Step 5)	1,000		
Giggle (Step 5)	2,500	Balance c/f	7,500
	7,500		7,500
Balance b/f	7,500		

RETIREMENT OF PARTNERS

Introduction

If a partner retires, he will be sacrificing his share of future profits and will, therefore, want compensation for this.

He will also want his share of existing assets of the business.

Partnership Act 1890

Section 42 gives the following rights to an outgoing partner:

(a)   Where a partner dies or ceases to be a partner and the surviving partner continues in business without a settlement of accounts, the outgoing partner is entitled (in the absence of any agreement to the contrary) to (i) or (ii) below:

      (i)   such post-dissolution profits as the court may find attributable to the use of his share;

      (ii)   interest at 5% per annum on the amount of his share.

(b)   Where, by agreement, an option is given to surviving partners to purchase the interest of an outgoing or deceased partner and that option is exercised, the outgoing partner (or his estate) is not entitled to any further share in profits.

      If this option is *not* exercised (a) applies.

Section 43 provides that, subject to agreement to the contrary, the amount due to an outgoing partner (or his estate) is a debt accruing from the date of dissolution or death.

Goodwill

On retirement, a partner will want his share of the goodwill that he has helped the business acquire over the years.

Double-entry

Dr   Goodwill account
      Cr   Partners' capital account in the old profit-sharing ratio

To bring goodwill temporarily into the books.

Dr   Partners' capital account in new profit-sharing ratio
      Cr   Goodwill

To remove goodwill from the books.

These are exactly the same entries as on admission.

Revaluation account

The retiring partner will also want his share of the existing assets. Since balance-sheet values are unlikely to reflect the true asset values (especially property), some assets will have to be revalued.

Double-entry

(a)   To revalue an asset upwards:

Dr   Asset account
      Cr   Revaluation account

with increase in value.

(b)   To revalue an asset downwards:

Dr   Revaluation account
      Cr   Asset account

with decrease in value.

(c)   The revaluation account is cleared to the existing partners' capital accounts.

(d)   If the revaluation account is not to remain in the books, then the procedure is reversed and the revaluation account is cleared to the new partners' capital accounts in the new profit-sharing ratio.

Example

M, N and P are in partnership sharing profits and losses equally. P wishes to retire.

The partnership balance sheet shows:

	£
Property (market value £80,000)	60,000
Debtors (recoverable value £9,500)	10,000
Bank	50,000
	120,000

	£
Capital accounts	
M	40,000
N	40,000
P	40,000
	120,000

Required

(a)   *Prepare the revaluation account.*

(b)   *Prepare the partners' capital accounts.*

(c)   *Prepare the revised balance sheet – the partners do not wish the revaluations to remain in the books.*

Solution

(a)

Revaluation account

		£		£
Debtors	(2)	500	Property account (1)	20,000
M	(3)	6,500		
N	(3)	6,500		
P	(3)	6,500		
		20,000		20,000

Narrative

	£	£

(1) Dr   Property account   20,000
     Cr   Revaluation account   20,000

with increase in value of property.

	£	£

(2) Dr   Revaluation account   500
     Cr   Debtors account   500

with decrease in recoverable value of debtors.

(3) Clear balance to the partners in the old profit-sharing ratio.

	£	£

     Dr   Revaluation account   19,500
     Cr   Partners' capital account
                  M   6,500
                  N   6,500
                  P   6,500

The balance sheet would now incorporate revaluations showing:

	£
Property	80,000
Debtors	9,500
Bank	50,000
	139,500

	£
Capital accounts	
M	46,500
N	46,500
P	46,500
	139,500

Capital account

	M £	N £	P £		M £	N £	P £
Bal c/f	46,500	46,500	46,500	Bal b/f	40,000	40,000	40,000
				Revaluation a/c	6,500	6,500	6,500
	46,500	46,500	46,500		46,500	46,500	46,500

(b)   P retires and the business must pay him the amount he is owed, ie. the balance on his capital account.

Dr   P Capital account   £46,500
   Cr   Bank account   £46,500

The balance sheet now shows the following.

	£
Property	80,000
Debtors	9,500
Bank	3,500
	93,000

	£
Capital accounts	
M	46,500
N	46,500
	93,000

Capital accounts

	M £	N £	P £		M £	N £	P £
Bank			46,500	Bal b/f (a)	46,500	46,500	46,500
Bal c/f	46,500	46,500	–				
	46,500	46,500	46,500		46,500	46,500	46,500

(c)   The revaluation account is not to remain in the books. It must be reversed.

					£	£
(1)	Dr	Revaluation account			20,000	
	Cr	Property account				20,000
(2)	Dr	Debtors' account			500	
	Cr	Revaluation account				500

with reversal of revaluation entries.

				£	£
(3)	Dr	Partners' capital account	M	9,750	
			N	9,750	
	Cr	Revaluation account			19,500

Clear revaluation account to partners' capital account in the new profit-sharing ratio.

Showing the accounts in full now:

Revaluation account

	£		£
Debtors	500	Property	20,000
Capital accounts			
M	6,500		
N	6,500		
P	6,500		
	20,000		20,000
Property (1)	20,000	Debtors (2)	500
		Capital accounts	
		M (3)	9,750
		N (3)	9,750
			20,000
	20,000		

Capital accounts

	M £	N £	P £		M £	N £	P £
Bank a/c			46,500	Bal b/f	40,000	40,000	40,000
Revaluation				Revaluation (a)	6,500	6,500	6,500
(c) (3)	9,750	9,750					
Balance c/f	36,750	36,750	–				
	46,500	46,500	46,500		46,500	46,500	46,500

Revised balance sheet for MN at 31 December 19XX

	£
Property	60,000
Debtors	10,000
Bank	3,500
	73,500

	£
Capital accounts	
M	36,750
N	36,750
	73,500

DISSOLUTION

A partnership may be ended for various reasons – the partners' wish to retire, or to pursue other interests, or to take advantages of the status of a limited company.

The approach is similar to the changes in partnership, with the use of a realisation account instead of revaluation account.

On dissolution, the assets of the partnership will have to be sold and the liabilities met. It may happen that the proceeds are not equal to the net book value of the net assets of the partnership and this will give rise to a profit or loss on realisation. This must be credited or debited to the partners in their profit-sharing ratio.

Example

Ted, Tony, Jim and Willie run a business in partnership. At 31 December 19X4 the partners decide to sell their business to one of their competitors. The balance sheet showed the following position, the partners sharing profits equally:

Balance sheet at 31 December 19X4

	Cost £	Dep'n £	£
Fixed assets			
Lease	10,000	3,000	7,000
Fixtures and fittings	1,500	900	600
Motor van	800	250	550
	12,300	4,150	8,150
Current assets			
Stock		8,500	
Debtors		7,600	
Bank		3,200	
		19,300	
Current liabilities			
Creditors		3,900	
			15,400
			23,550
Capital accounts			
Ted			6,000
Tony			4,000
Jim			3,000
Willie			2,000
			15,000
Current accounts			
Ted		2,080	
Tony		2,460	
Jim		2,120	
Willie		1,890	
			8,550
			23,550

The following assets were sold for cash:	£
Lease	9,000
Fixtures and fittings	400
Stock	8,200
Debtors	7,500
Goodwill	12,000
Total proceeds	37,100

The motor van was taken over by Jim at a valuation of £630. The creditors were paid in full and the bank account was closed.

Required

Close off the books of the following partnership as at 31 December 19X4.

Solution

Step 1: Prepare a realisation account.

As the partnership is terminating, all the ledger accounts in the partnership's books have to be closed. The most practical way of doing this is to transfer all the assets that are being sold or taken over to a **realisation account**, the journal entry being:

Dr: Realisation account
Cr: Asset accounts

with the book value of the assets being sold or taken over.

In the case of this business all the assets, except the bank account, are being disposed of, so the realisation account after the above journal entry should look like this:

Realisation account

	£
Lease	7,000
Fixtures and fittings	600
Motor van	550
Stock	8,500
Debtors	7,600
	24,250

Step 2: Deal with the sale proceeds of the assets.

The realisation account must be credited with the sale proceeds of the assets (including goodwill) sold for cash as well as the value at which Jim (who becomes a debtor) is going to take over the motor van, the journal entries being:

Dr: Bank account
Cr: Realisation account

with the assets being sold for cash (see ledger account in step 3 below).

Dr: Partner's current account
Cr: Realisation account

with the asset being taken over by one of the partners at the agreed value (see ledger account in step 3 below).

Financial Training

Step 3: Close off the realisation account.

The realisation account, which is similar to a disposal of fixed assets account, now shows a profit which is divided between the partners in their profit-sharing ratio and transferred to their respective current accounts as shown.

Realisation account					
	£	£			£
Sundry assets		24,250	Bank (assets sold for cash)		37,100
			Jim's current account		630
Profit of £13,480					
Ted (¼)	3,370				
Tony (¼)	3,370				
Jim (¼)	3,370				
Willie(¼)	3,370				
	———				
		13,480			
		———			———
		37,730			37,730
		———			———

Step 4: Close off the remaining accounts.

The only accounts left in the books now are the partners' capital and current accounts, the creditors' accounts, and the cash book. After paying off the creditors there should be just enough money in the bank to pay the amounts due to the partners. The partners' current and capital accounts can be combined at this stage.

Cash book					
	£			£	£
Balance per balance sheet	3,200	Creditors			3,900
Realisation account	37,100	Partners' capital accounts			
		Ted		11,450	
		Tony		9,830	
		Jim		7,860	
		Willie		7,260	
				———	
					36,400
	———				———
	40,300				40,300
	———				———

Partners' capital accounts

	Ted £	Tony £	Jim £	Willie £		Ted £	Tony £	Jim £	Willie £
Realisation account Motor van			630		Balance per Balance sheet	6,000	4,000	3,000	2,000
					Current a/c balances	2,080	2,460	2,120	1,890
Cash book	11,450	9,830	7,860	7,260	Realisation a/c Profit	3,370	3,370	3,370	3,370
	11,450	9,830	8,490	7,260		11,450	9,830	8,490	7,260

As you can now see there was exactly enough money in the bank to pay off the partners so the books have now been closed.

DRAFTING PARTNERSHIP ACCOUNTS

Partnerships are not required to draw up accounts in a prescribed format.

The comments made in Session 3 regarding the users of sole trader accounts, general principles of drafting accounts and applicable accounting standards also apply to partnerships.

QUESTIONS

1   Brick and Stone

The following list of balances as at 30 September 19Y0 has been extracted from the books of Brick and Stone trading in partnership, sharing the balance of profits and loss in the proportions 3 : 2 respectively.

	£
Printing, stationery and postage	3,500
Sales	322,100
Stock in hand at 1 October 19X9	23,000
Purchases	208,200
Rent and rates	10,300
Heat and light	8,700
Staff salaries	36,100
Telephone charges	2,900
Motor vehicle running costs	5,620
Discounts allowable	950
Discounts receivable	370
Sales returns	2,100
Purchases returns	6,100
Carriage inwards	1,700
Carriage outwards	2,400
Fixtures and fittings	
At cost	26,000
Provision for depreciation	11,200
Motor vehicles	
At cost	46,000
Provision for depreciation	25,000
Drawings	
Brick	24,000
Stone	11,000
Current account balances at 1 October 19X9	
Brick	3,600 credit
Stone	2,400 credit
Capital account balances at 1 October 19X9	
Brick	33,000
Stone	17,000
Debtors	9,000
Creditors	8,400
Balance at bank	7,700 debit

Additional information

(1)   £10,000 is to be transferred from Brick's capital account to a newly opened Brick loan account with effect from 1 July 19Y0.

The terms of the loan applied a rate of 10% per annum.

(2)   Stone is to be credited with a salary at the rate of £12,000 per annum from 1 April 19Y0.

(3)   Stock in hand at 30 September 19Y0 has been valued at cost at £32,000.

(4)   Telephone charges accrued due at 30 September 19Y0 amounted to £400 and rent of £600 was prepaid at that date.

(5)   During the year ended 30 September 19Y0, Stone has taken goods costing £1,000 for his own use.

(6)   Depreciation is to be provided at the following annual rates on the straight-line basis:

Fixtures and fittings	10%
Motor vehicles	20%

Required

(a)   Prepare a trading and profit and loss account for the year ended 30 September 19Y0.

(b)   Prepare a statement showing the appropriation of profit for the year ended 30 September 19Y0.

(c)   Prepare a balance sheet as at 30 September 19Y0 which should include summaries of the partners' capital and current accounts for the year ended on that date.

2   Short and Round

The following list of balances as at 30 June 19X6 has been extracted from the books of Short and Round who have traded in partnership for many years.

	£
Fixtures and fittings – cost at 1 July 19X5	25,000
Provision for depreciation at 1 July 19X5	12,200
Motor vehicles – cost at 1 July 19X5	36,000
Provision for depreciation at 1 July 19X5	21,000
Trade debtors	32,500
Trade creditors	24,200
Cash at bank	19,400
Cash in hand	1,200
Loan from Jones	15,000
Provision for doubtful debts	700
Stock at cost at 1 July 19X5	27,500
Sales	569,800
Purchases	469,880
Carriage in	2,200
Rent	27,600
Heat and light	2,300
Telephone	1,900
Postage and stationery	1,750
Wages and salaries	14,500
Capital accounts as at 1 July 19X5	
Short	22,500
Round	17,500
Current accounts as at 1 July 19X5	
Short	3,790 credit
Round	1,040 credit

Additional information

(1) Interest at the rate of 8% per annum is payable annually in arrears on the loan from Jones; the loan was received on 4 July 19X5.

(2) Telephone charges accrued due at 30 June 19X6 amounted to £360 and rent of £2,800 was prepaid at that date.

(3) All sales produce a uniform rate of gross profit.

(4) Provision is to be made for depreciation as follows:

> Fixtures and fittings – 10% per annum on cost
> Motor vehicles – 25% per annum on cost

(5) No interest is payable on the partners' capital accounts, but Round is to be credited with a salary of £10,000 from 1 November 19X5.

On this date, the partners also decided to change their profit-sharing ratio from Short 70%, Round 30% to Short 60%, Round 40%.

(6) A doubtful debt provision of 5% of trade debtors is to be maintained.

(7) One quarter of sales took place in the first third of the year, but all indirect expenses accrued evenly throughout the year.

(8) Short and Round took out drawings for the year of £14,000 and £12,000 respectively.

(9) Stock in hand at 30 June 19X6 was valued at £31,200.

Required

(a) Prepare the trading, profit and loss account for the year ended 30 June 19X6.

(b) Prepare a statement showing the appropriation of profit for the period prior to the change in PSR and for the period after the change.

(c) Prepare the balance sheet as at 30 June 19X6.

3 Metro, Goldwyn and Mayer

Metro and Goldwyn, who make up their accounts to 31 March in each year, carried on a retail business sharing profits and losses: Metro two-thirds and Goldwyn one-third.

On 1 July 19X7, they admitted Mayer as a partner and from that date profits and losses were to be shared: Metro two-fifths, Goldwyn two-fifths and Mayer one-fifth. Mayer introduced £3,000 into the firm on 1 July 19X7, of which it was agreed £2,000 should be his fixed capital, the balance being credited to his current account.

Interest on fixed capital is allowed at the rate of 6% per annum but no interest is charged or allowed on current accounts.

The trial balance of the partnership at 31 March 19X8 was as follows:

	£		£	£
Leasehold premises purchased 1.4.X7	8,000	Capital accounts 1.4.X7		
		Metro	4,000	
Motor vehicles, at cost	2,600	Goldwyn	3,000	
				7,000
Shop fittings, at cost	1,600			
Purchases	21,500	Current accounts 1.4.X7		
Balance at bank	3,060	Metro	1,200	
Employees' salaries, including partners' drawings	7,200	Goldwyn	900	
Stock, 31.3.X7	3,800			2,100
Debtors	1,500	Mayer		3,000
Professional charges	360	Sales (£8,000 for three		
Shop wages	3,320	months to 30.6.X7)		40,000
Rent, rates, lighting and heating	1,400	Provision for depreciation at 31.3.X7		
General expenses (£910 for three months to 30.6.X7)	2,800	Motor vehicles	1,400	
		Shop fittings	600	
				2,000
		Creditors		2,800
		Provision for doubtful debts at 31.3.X7		240
	57,140			57,140

You are given the following further information:

(1) For the purpose of the partnership changes, the value of the goodwill of the firm was agreed to be £15,000. No account for goodwill is to be maintained in the books but adjusting entries for the transactions between the partners are to be made in their current accounts.

(2) The stock at 31 March 19X8 amounted to £4,100.

(3) The following partners' drawings are included above under 'Salaries': Metro £1,200, Goldwyn £720 and Mayer £500.

(4) A motor vehicle which had cost £1,000 and on which depreciation of £700 had been provided had been sold on 1 June 19X7 for £400 and the proceeds credited to the motor vehicles account, no other entry having been made apart from that in the cash book.

(5) Provision is to be made for depreciation for the year on motor vehicles and shop fittings at the rates of 20% and 10% respectively, calculated on cost at the end of the year.

(6) At 31 March 19X8, rent paid in advance amounted to £200 and general expenses accrued amounted to £120.

(7) Mayer is to be credited with a salary at the rate of £300 per annum as from the date of his admission as a partner.

(8)   Professional charges include £160 in respect of the acquisition of the leasehold premises. This amount is to be capitalised as part of the cost of the lease, the total cost of which is to be written off in twenty equal annual instalments.

(9)   Doubtful debts (for which full provision is to be made) amounted to £279 at 30 June 19X7 and to £298 at 31 March 19X8.

Required

(a)   Prepare the trading and profit and loss account for the year ended 31 March 19X8, apportioning:

      (i)   gross profit on the basis of sales;
      (ii)   expenses (unless otherwise indicated) on a time basis.

(b)   Prepare the balance sheet at that date.

(c)   Prepare the partners' current accounts in columnar form.

4   Jack, Hugh and Clive

Jack, Hugh and Clive were in partnership, sharing profits and losses: Jack 50%, Hugh 30% and Clive 20%.

The draft balance sheet of the partnership at 30 June 19X3 was as follows:

	Cost £	*Dep'n* £	£
Fixed assets			
Freehold premises	10,000	2,000	8,000
Plant and equipment	6,000	1,800	4,200
Motor vehicles	4,000	1,900	2,100
	20,000	5,700	14,300
Current assets			
Stock		3,600	
Debtors	5,200		
Less: Provision for doubtful debts	400		
		4,800	
Bank balance		8,300	
		16,700	
Current liabilities			
Provision for repainting of premises	1,400		
Creditors	4,600		
		6,000	
Net current assets			10,700
			25,000
Less: Loan from Jack			3,000
			22,000
Representing			
Capital accounts			
Jack			12,000
Hugh			6,000
Clive			4,000
			22,000

Jack retired on 30 June 19X3 and Hugh and Clive continued in partnership, sharing profits and losses: Hugh 60% and Clive 40%.

Jack's loan was repaid on 1 July 19X3 and it was agreed that 10% of the outstanding balance due to him should be paid as soon as the amount was computed. The balance was to remain on loan to the partnership.

It was agreed that the following adjustments should be made to the balance sheet as at 30 June 19X3:

(1) The freehold premises were to be revalued at £15,000 and the plant and equipment at £3,500.

(2) Jack was to be charged £400 for one of the motor vehicles taken over by him, this vehicle having a book value of £450.

(3) The provision for doubtful debts was to be increased by £200.

(4) The provision for repainting of the premises was to be increased to £2,000.

(5) £400 was to be written off the stock in respect of damaged and obsolete items included therein.

(6) A provision of £250 included in creditors was to be written back.

For the purpose of the retirement the value of the goodwill of the firm was agreed to be £7,000.

No account for goodwill was to be maintained in the books, adjusting entries for the transactions between the partners being made in the capital accounts.

Required

(a) Prepare the revaluation account.
(b) Prepare the partners' capital accounts.
(c) Prepare Jack's account, showing the outstanding balance due to him.
(d) Prepare the balance sheet of Hugh and Clive at 1 July 19X3.

5   Vigor, Twist and Slater

Vigor, Twist and Slater were in partnership sharing profits: Vigor one-half, Twist one-third and Slater one-sixth.

A summary of the balance sheet of the partnership at 31 March 19X0 was as follows.

	£	£		£	£
Fixed capital accounts			Fixed assets		7,000
Vigor	5,000		Stock		3,400
Twist	3,000		Debtors		4,500
Slater	2,000		Cash		6,100
		10,000			
Current accounts					
Vigor	2,400				
Twist	1,800				
Slater	1,300				
		5,500			
Loan account					
Twist		2,000			
Creditors		3,500			
		21,000			21,000

The fixed assets included two motor cars having book values of £700 and £500.

The partners, wishing to retire from the business, sold the stock and fixed assets, other than the motor vehicles, for £15,000 in cash.

The debtors realised £4,200 and the creditors were settled for £3,300.

The partners agreed that the following should be the basis of distribution on dissolution of the partnership:

(1)   Vigor is to take over one car at a valuation of £800 and Twist the other at £460.
(2)   The balances are to be settled in cash.

Required

(a)   Prepare a realisation account.

(b)   Prepare a cash account.

(c)   Prepare the partners' capital and current accounts in columnar form, showing the final settlement between them.

6   Barrow, Mark, Williams and James   (AAT Pilot CA D94)

Data

You have been approached by a partnership, Barrow, Mark, Williams and James, to help finalise their accounts for the year to 30 June 1994.   A bookkeeper working for the partnership has prepared a profit statement for the year. The net profit has been agreed at £40,000 *after* deduction of salaries and loan capital interest. You have been given a memo detailing the following information by the bookkeeper.

(1)   Interest is payable on loans at a rate of 5% per annum; interest on capital is paid at the same rate, based on the year-end capital amounts. No interest is allowed on balance of current accounts.

(2)   Drawings made for the year ending 30 June 1994 were as follows:

	£
Barrow	17,000
Mark	20,000
Williams	5,000
James	13,000

(3)   Mark is entitled to a salary of £7,000 per annum and James is entitled to £6,000 per annum.

(4)   Barrow invested a further £10,000 capital into the partnership on 1 January 1994. James invested a further £5,000 on 1 February 1994.

(5)   Barrow's loan account with the partnership stands at £6,000.

(6)   The profit/losses are shared 3:4:2:1 by Barrow, Mark, Williams and James.

(7)   You have been supplied with the balance sheet of the partnership as at 30 June 1993.

Balance sheet of Barrow, Mark, Williams and James as at 30 June 1993

	£	£
Fixed assets		
Motor cars	19,000	
Fixtures and fittings	9,300	
		28,300
Current assets		
Stock	10,000	
Debtors	7,000	
Bank	13,000	
	30,000	
Current liabilities		
Creditors	9,000	
Net current assets		21,000
Total assets less current liabilities		49,300

Represented by:

	£	£
Capital accounts		
Barrow	15,000	
Mark	15,000	
Williams	3,000	
James	5,000	
		38,000
Current accounts		
Barrow	2,500	
Mark	1,800	
Williams	(1,000)	
James	2,000	
		5,300
Loan account		
Barrow		6,000
Capital employed		49,300

Assessment tasks

Task 1

Based on the above information, draw up an appropriation account for the partnership of Barrow, Mark, Williams and Jones for the year ended 30 June 1994.

Task 2

Prepare the partners' current and capital accounts for the year ended 30 June 1994.

Task 3

Most partnerships make a partnership agreement; what happens if there is no such agreement?

Task 4

Explain the difference between an appropriation and an expense, illustrating your answer with reference to partners' capital and loans.

Task 5

List *three* reasons why you might choose to go into partnership rather than sole tradership if you were to go into business.

SUMMARY

Partnerships and formation

- The amount owed by the business to each partner is reflected in the total of each partner's capital and current account.

- Typically, the capital account is used for recording fixed capital.

- The current account is used for all other items, the most important of which are profit share and drawings.

- Profit is shared by the partners in accordance with their agreement.

- If there is no agreement, the Partnership Act 1890 states how profit is to be shared.

- Double-entry:

| Drawings | Dr | Partners' current account |
| | | Cr Bank account |

| Interest on loan to partnership* | Dr | Profit and loss loan interest account |
| | | Cr Partners' current account |

| Interest on capital | Dr | Appropriation account |
| | | Cr Partners' current account |

| Salaries | Dr | Appropriation account |
| | | Cr Partners' current account |

| Profit share | Dr | Appropriation account |
| | | Cr Partners' current account |

(* Special case)

Admission and retirement

- On admission, the assets and future profits (goodwill) must be valued.

- Goodwill adjustments

    Dr   Goodwill account
         Cr   Partners' capital account in the old profit-sharing ratio (PSR)

with goodwill temporarily created in the books.

    Dr   Partners' capital account in the new PSR
         Cr   Goodwill account

with goodwill removed from the books.

Financial Training

- Revaluation adjustments – upwards (decrease is the opposite)

  Dr   Asset account
      Cr   Partners' capital account in the old PSR

  with the balance on the revaluation account.

- If it is decided not to carry the valuation in the books

  Dr   Partners' capital account in the new PSR
      Cr   Asset account

  with the reversal of the revaluation entries.

- Capital introduced on admission

  Dr   Bank
      Cr   New partner's capital account

Dissolution

- Prepare a realisation account

  Dr   Realisation account
      Cr   Asset accounts

  with the book value of the assets being sold or taken over

- Deal with the sale proceeds of the assets

  Dr   Bank account
      Cr   Realisation account

  with cash received from the sale of assets

  Dr   Partners' current account
      Cr   Realisation account

  with assets taken over by the partners at the agreed value

- Close off the realisation account

  Dr   Realisation account
      Cr   Partners' current accounts

  with the balance on the realisation account (profit) in their profit sharing ratio

- Close off the remaining accounts (partners' capital and current accounts may now be combined)

  Dr   Partners' capital accounts
      Cr   Bank account

  with the balances on the capital accounts.

Introduction to limited company accounts

INTRODUCTION

We have already seen that a limited company is regarded as separate from its owners, the shareholders. The 'limited' part of a company's name refers to the fact that the shareholders are limited in their liability for the company's debts – the most they can lose is the total amount paid/payable on the shares held by them.

This means that companies will often be owned by shareholders who are independent of the management. They may also have other major loan investors. The financial statements therefore are of great importance in communicating between the company and its investors.

The main differences between the accounts of a company and those of a sole trader are:

- the format of the company accounts, which is governed by Schedule 4 of the Companies Act 1985, as modified by the Companies Act 1989;

- the treatment of profit in the profit and loss account;

- the composition of capital in the balance sheet.

PRO FORMA COMPANY PROFIT AND LOSS ACCOUNT

	£
Turnover	X
Cost of sales	(X)
	—
Gross profit	X
Distribution costs	(X)
Administrative expenses	(X)
Other operating income	X
	—
	X
Interest payable and similar charges	(X)
	—
Profit on ordinary activities before taxation	X
Corporation tax	(X)
	—
Profit on ordinary activities after taxation	X
Dividends paid and proposed	(X)
	—
Profit for the financial year	X
Retained profit brought forward	X
	—
Retained profit carried forward	X
	—

ANALYSIS OF EXPENSES

Unlike the profit and loss account of a sole trader, the profit and loss account of a limited company does not show the different types of expenses separately. Instead, expenses are grouped under the headings 'distribution costs' and 'administrative expenses'.

The best approach is:

- cross-reference workings for the main headings (distribution costs and administrative expenses);

- as you come across each expense, put it under the appropriate working heading;

- transfer the total at the end into the profit and loss account.

Do not spend hours deciding which heading for each expense – it won't really matter, as long as you've dealt correctly with the obvious ones and have shown clearly what you've included.

As a rule of thumb, you could use the following guide:

Distribution costs

- Salesmen's salaries and commissions
- Depreciation of showroom, delivery vehicles and salesmen's cars
- Advertising
- Delivery costs

Administrative expenses

Other expenses that are not shown under distribution costs, interest payable, tax or dividends!

This will include rent, light and heat, directors' remuneration, auditors' remuneration, depreciation on offices and staff cars, and other overheads.

Other operating income

The main example you might come across under this heading is rent receivable.

CORPORATION TAX

The company is a separate legal entity and is subject to tax. Tax payable by companies is known as *corporation tax*. This is an appropriation of the company's profits and therefore appears in the profit and loss account.

Generally, tax will be paid nine months after the year end so the accounting entries are:

Debit Profit and loss account
Credit Corporation tax creditor (shown as a current liability in the balance sheet)

In the next year, when the tax is likely to be paid, the entry will be:

Debit Corporation tax creditor
Credit Cash

DIVIDENDS

The actual amount of dividend to be paid by a company will be determined by many factors, the main one being the need to retain sufficient profits to provide for the future working capital and fixed asset requirements of the company.

Some companies pay an amount on account of the total dividend before the end of the year. This is known as an *interim dividend* – the bookkeeping entry is:

Debit Dividend account
Credit Cash

(The dividend account is closed off to the profit and loss account at the year-end.)

It will only be at the end of the year, when the company's results for the whole accounting period are known, that the directors can declare a final dividend.

As the payment of the final dividend takes place after the year-end, the figure in the accounts will again represent a provision. The entries are therefore:

Debit Profit and loss account
Credit Dividends proposed account (shown as current liability)

Hence we will have two debits for dividends in the profit and loss account – one paid and one proposed.

PRO FORMA COMPANY BALANCE SHEET

	Cost £	Dep'n £	£
Fixed assets			
Land and buildings	X	X	X
Plant and machinery	X	X	X
Fixtures, fittings, tools and equipment	X	X	X
Current assets			
Stocks		X	
Debtors		X	
Cash at bank and in hand		X	
		X	
Creditors: amounts falling due within one year			
Trade creditors		X	
Accruals and deferred income		X	
		X	
Net current assets			X
Total assets less current liabilities			X
Creditors: amounts falling due after more than one year			
Debenture loans			(X)
			X
Capital and reserves			
Share capital			X
Share premium account			X
Other reserves			X
Profit and loss account			X
Shareholders' funds			X

SHARE CAPITAL

When a company is formed, it usually raises its initial capital by issuing a number of shares.

The people who buy the shares and are the owners of the company are known as its *members* or *shareholders*.

Shareholders

The proportion of the company which each member owns can thus be calculated by reference to the number of shares he holds. For example, if a member holds 750 shares in a company which has 1,000 shares in issue, he has a 75% stake in the company.

The advantage of the share system is that members can easily transfer their interest in the company by selling their shares and the company can raise new capital by issuing more shares.

Shares have a face value which is also called the *nominal value* or *par value*. This is distinct from their *market value*.

Suppose a company issues 100 shares with a nominal value of £1 for £100 in total.

Mrs X 25 shares
Mrs Y 75 shares

The double entry is:

Debit Cash   100
Credit Share capital   100

If Mrs Y sells her shares to Mrs Z, this has no effect on the amount of share capital received by the company, so no entry is made in the share capital account.

If the stock market decides that the shares are worth only 80p each, no entry is made in the share capital account because, again, this has no effect on the capital received by the company.

Types of share capital

A company may issue different types (classes) of shares, by far the most important of which are:

● *Ordinary shares*

   The majority of companies will only have this type of share, whose holders usually have a right to vote at meetings and are therefore effectively the owners of the company.

● *Preference shares*

   'Preference' in this context means that the owners of these shares will have priority over the ordinary shareholders in the payment of their dividend, which is usually of a fixed amount.

   In addition, if the company winds up (ceases to exist) the preference shareholders will normally be repaid their capital before the ordinary shareholders.

The difference between these two classes of shares is in essence the difference between the risk-takers (the ordinary shareholders), whose reward will be geared to how well the company performs, and the non-risk-takers (the preference shareholders) whose entitlement is fixed.

Other terms

Authorised share capital

A company's Memorandum of Association states the amount of shares which it is allowed to issue to its shareholders. This is the *authorised share capital* of the company. A company does not necessarily issue all of the shares which it is authorised to issue.

Issued share capital

The number of shares actually issued is known as the *issued share capital*.

Called up share capital and paid up share capital

Once the company has asked its shareholders to pay for the shares it has issued to them, the shares are said to be *called up*. Once those shareholders have paid the company for the shares they are said to be *paid up*.

RESERVES

Reserves are the cumulative total of the company's retained profits.

A company may if it wishes, set aside some of its profits for a specific purpose. For example:

	£
Called-up share capital	1,000
Profit and loss account	1,000
	2,000

The company wishes to set aside £500 for replacement of fixed assets.

	£
Called-up share capital	1,000
Fixed asset replacement reserve	500
Profit and loss account	500
	2,000

This does not affect its total reserves, which remain at £1,000.

SHARE PREMIUM ACCOUNT

This arises when a company issues shares for more than their nominal value. The *premium* over this amount must be credited to a *share premium* account.

Example

Enterprise Ltd makes an issue of 10,000 £1 ordinary shares for £1.60 each. The entries are:

Debit	Cash account	£16,000	
Credit	Share capital account		£10,000
	Share premium account		£6,000

Note that a share premium account does *not* arise if the market value subsequently increases to more than the nominal value.

The share premium account cannot be distributed to shareholders. One of the few permitted uses of this reserve is to make a bonus issue (see below).

BONUS ISSUES

Introduction

Sometimes, extra shares may be issued to existing shareholders without any more money having to be paid for them. Such an issue of share is known as a *bonus* issue or a *scrip* or *capitalisation* issue. The extra shares are issued to existing shareholders in proportion to their present shareholdings. Since no cash changes hands, the exercise is merely a bookkeeping one.

The accounting entries are as follows:

Debit	Reserves
Credit	Ordinary share capital.

With the nominal value of the bonus shares issued.

Example

A public limited company has an authorised share capital of 2,000,000 ordinary shares of £1 each, and an issued and fully paid share capital of 600,000 ordinary £1 shares. At 30 June 19X1 its reserves amounted to £900,000. The company proposes to make a bonus issue of one share for every share held (a one for one bonus issue).

Required

Prepare an extract of A plc's balance sheet (a) immediately before; and (b) immediately after the issue of the bonus shares.

Solution

A plc
Balance sheet at 30 June 19X1

		(a) Before £'000	(b) After £'000
Net assets		1,500	1,500
Share capital			
Authorised:	ordinary shares £1 each	2,000	2,000
Issued and fully paid:	ordinary shares £1 each	600	1,200
Reserves		900	300
Shareholders' funds		1,500	1,500

Commentary

It can be seen from the above illustration that shareholders' funds are not changed by the bonus issue. However, the number of shares in issue and their total nominal value has increased by £600,000 (from £600,000 to £1,200,000), but the reserves have decreased by an equivalent amount (from £900,000 to £300,000). No change has taken place in the total value of the net assets.

RIGHTS ISSUES

A rights issue differs from a bonus issue in that the company actually raises cash through an additional issue of shares at a favourable price to the existing shareholders. Existing shareholders are given the exclusive right to take up a new issue of shares at a specific price. The number of shares that they are entitled to take up is in proportion to their existing holdings; for example, with a one for five rights issue, a shareholder with 100 shares has the right to subscribe for twenty shares. The issue price is normally below the market price.

Example

XYZ plc has 2,000,000 25p ordinary shares in issue and its summarised balance sheet is given below:

	£'000
Net assets	2,300
Share capital	500
Reserves	1,800
	2,300

The company decides to make a rights issue of one for every five held at £1 each.

Show the balance sheet after the rights issue is complete.

Solution

The rights issue is 400,000 shares @ £1 each and will raise cash of £400,000 which can be split between nominal value and premium as follows:

Nominal value 400,000 × 25p	100,000
Share premium (75p each)	300,000
Cash	400,000

The balance sheet is as follows:

	£'000
Net assets (2,300 + 400)	2,700
Share capital	600
Share premium	300
Reserves	1,800
	2,700

Shareholders' options

A shareholder who receives a rights offer has three options open to him. These are as follows:

(a) Take up rights and pay the required amount to the company, increasing his shareholding.
(b) Sell his rights to a third party who may then buy the shares from the company.
(c) Do nothing and let his rights lapse.

Option (a) above may be considered the normal course for a shareholder to follow, but some shareholders may not wish to take up the offer, or may not be in a position to do so. In this case they would adopt (b) or (c) as their course of action.

DEBENTURES

Debentures are a long-term loan. They are named after the legal agreement detailing the loan.

It is likely that there will be a number of debenture-holders in the same way that there are a number of shareholders. In other words, the company may well be borrowing from a number of people or organisations rather than just one.

CAPITAL INSTRUMENTS

FRS4 *Capital instruments* defines capital instruments as 'all instruments issued as a means of raising finance'.

Limited companies have more scope for raising finance than other forms of business organisation. We have seen that finance can be raised in two main ways:

* share capital (ordinary shares are sometimes referred to as 'equity')
* debentures (sometimes referred to as 'loan capital' or 'debt').

Until quite recently, and in the majority of cases, finance was capable of being fairly easily classified as share capital or loan capital. However, during the 1980's, some companies began to raise capital using more complex capital instruments, which grant rights other than simple interest or dividend participation. Many of these capital instruments have the characteristics of both debt and equity and it is often difficult to decide how to classify them and how to treat them in the accounts.

FRS4 states that capital instruments should be presented in financial statements in a way that reflects the *obligations of the issuer*:

* capital instruments should be classified as liabilities if they contain an obligation to transfer economic benefits

* capital instruments should be classified as shareholders' funds if they do not contain an obligation to transfer economic benefits.

If a company issues a debenture, it must pay interest to the debenture holders; therefore a debenture is a liability. If a company issues ordinary shares, members pay cash to the company for the right to be a member. The company may pay dividends to shareholders, but it is not obliged to do so. Therefore ordinary shares are classed as shareholders' funds. (Preference shares are classed as shareholders' funds because preference dividends may only be paid if there are distributable profits available whereas debt interest must be paid in all circumstances.)

Detailed accounting for, and disclosure of, complex capital instruments is beyond the scope of this Unit. You are merely required to have an appreciation of the definition of a capital instrument.

TYPES OF COMPANY

There are two types of limited company, public and private. A public company must include in its name the letters 'plc' standing for public limited company. Private companies must include 'Limited' ('Ltd') in their name.

The main difference is that a private company may not offer its shares or debentures to the public and so all companies listed on the Stock Exchange are public companies.

THE DUTIES OF COMPANIES REGARDING ACCOUNTING RECORDS

By S221 CA 1985, every company must keep accounting records which are sufficient to show and explain the company's transactions to disclose, with reasonable accuracy, the financial position of the company at any time.

Any officer who knowingly or wilfully authorises or permits his company to keep inadequate accounting records commits an offence.

Private company accounting records must be preserved by the company for three years from the date on which they were made; those of public companies must be preserved for six years.

The accounting records of a company must contain:

–   a day book or journal;

–   a record of assets and liabilities of the company;

–   if the company's business involves dealing with goods:

    –   statements of stock held by the company at the end of each financial year;

    –   the stocktaking records from which those statements are derived; and

    –   statements of all goods sold other than by ordinary retail trade and of all goods purchased, in sufficient detail to enable the goods, the buyers and the sellers to be identified.

ANNUAL ACCOUNTS

Contents of annual accounts

Profit and loss account and balance sheet

The directors of every company must prepare:

–   a profit and loss account for each financial year; and
–   a balance sheet as at the end of that financial year.

Directors' report

The balance sheet must be accompanied by a directors' report which details certain matters in relation to the company including:

–   a review of the development of the business over the year;
–   directors' recommendations for appropriation of profits to dividends and reserves;
–   details of changes in fixed assets;
–   political and charitable donations exceeding £200;
–   details of directors; and
–   if the company employs more than 250 people, its policy regarding disabled employees.

Auditors' report

The company's auditors must report to the members on the accounts examined by them and the report must state whether the accounts give a true and fair view of the state of the company's affairs and of its results for the period ending on the accounting date. The auditors' report must be signed by them and must state their names.

Normally, each year, the directors must lay copies of the balance sheet, profit and loss account, directors' report and auditors' report before the annual general meeting of the company. However, a private company may pass an elective resolution to dispense with the requirement to lay accounts and reports before general meetings.

A copy of these accounts must usually be sent to every member of the company not less than 21 days before the general meeting at which they will be considered.

However, listed companies can now send their shareholders summary financial statements instead of the full audited accounts. Shareholders have a right to ask for a full set of accounts.

Accounting reference periods

The key factor in arriving at the time limits for the preparation of annual accounts is the accounting reference period – the company's financial year.

The day on which the accounting reference period ends is known as the *accounting reference date*. A company has nine months from the date of incorporation to notify the Registrar of its accounting reference date. The first accounting reference date cannot be more than eighteen months after incorporation.

If a company does nothing to establish its own accounting reference date, this date will be the end of the month in which the anniversary of incorporation falls.

In the case of a private company, its annual accounts must be laid before a general meeting and filed with the Registrar within ten months after the end of the accounting reference period. In the case of a public company, the time limit is seven months.

QUESTIONS

1   **Regis Ltd**

Regis Ltd commenced trading on 1 February 19X0 as a sportswear manufacturer. The company has prepared its first trial balance as at 30 April 19X1 as shown below:

	£	£
Sales		799,701
Purchases	564,532	
Wages	43,271	
Rent and rates	97,000	
Light and heat	35,382	
Depreciation expense	20,500	
Bank interest paid	1,225	
Land (cost)	300,000	
Buildings	196,000	
Debtors ledger control account	253,211	
Creditors ledger control account		332,379
Share capital		200,000
Bad debt expense	25,000	
10% debentures 19X5		300,000
Cash at bank	23,572	
Cash in hand	150	
Commission paid	43,125	
Postage	4,112	
Motor vehicles	45,000	
Office equipment	13,500	
Share premium	20,000	
	1,685,580	1,632,080

You are given the following information:

(1)   The fixed assets, which were all purchased on the first day of trading, are stated at net book value. A full year's depreciation has been charged on the original cost at the following rates:

Motor vehicles – 25% straight line
Office equipment – 10% straight line
Buildings – 2% straight line

The directors have now decided that:

(a)   depreciation should be strictly time-apportioned; and
(b)   office equipment should now be depreciated over five years.

(2)   The original cost of the motor vehicles represents four vehicles.

They were all purchased for equal amounts. One of the vehicles was sold on 1 August 19X0 for £12,000, the only entry being made in the cash account.

(3)   The purchase day book has been overcast by £36,371 and the sales day book undercast by £89,371.

(4)   Sales returns totalling £414 have been omitted from the day book.

(5)   The debtors balance is stated net of a draft provision of £16,431. This provision represents 50% of Drinkell Ltd's debt of £12,450 and 100% of Smith Ltd's debt of £10,206. On further review of the ledger accounts the following adjustments are to be made to debtors:

   (a)   Speedie Ltd has gone bankrupt and the amount owing of £47,000 should be written off.

   (b)   Borrows Ltd is arguing about the quality of certain goods supplied and the directors feel it would be prudent to write off £16,671 relating to these goods.

   (c)   It has been decided that the provision against Smith Ltd's debt is no longer required. The provision against Drinkell Ltd's debt is to be maintained and a provision of 80% of Edward Ltd's debt of £8,000 is required. The directors, in addition, wish to provide against 2% of all other debts.

(6)   The balance per the bank statement does not agree to the trial balance figure by £571, being bank charges not recorded by the company.

(7)   A contra of £1,500 has been entered in the creditors control account but no corresponding entry has been made in the debtors control account.

(8)   No interest has been paid on the debentures.

(9)   Closing stock is valued at £77,971.

(10)   Corporation tax is estimated at £23,712 and will be paid nine months after the accounting period end.

(11)   The share capital of the company comprises of 200,000 £1 shares. The directors wish to propose a dividend of 10 pence per share.

Required

Prepare a profit and loss account in a format suitable for presentation to *management* for the first period of trading ending 30 April 19X1 and a balance sheet as at that date.

2   Withers Ltd

The trial balance of Withers Ltd at 30 September 19X6 (after some year-end adjustments) is as follows:

	Dr £	Cr £
100,000 25p ordinary shares		25,000
£1 preference shares		30,000
Bank loan		15,000
Profit and loss account at 1 October 19X5		18,500
Plant at cost at 30 September 19X6	71,500	
Plant – total depreciation at 30 September 19X6		31,800
Bank loan interest	1,500	
Directors' salaries	18,500	
Stock at cost at 30 September 19X6	28,650	
Trade debtors/creditors	52,430	27,920
Investment: Ordinary shares in Z Ltd		
(quoted value at 30 September 19X6 £18,000)	13,000	
Corporation tax for year ended 30 September 19X5		4,550
Bank balance	3,215	
Sales		290,000
Cost of sales	217,500	
Net operating expenses (before adjustment)	36,475	
	442,770	442,770

The following information is relevant:

(1)   Corporation tax for the year ended 30 September 19X6 is computed at £6,860. The corporation tax liability in respect of 30 September 19X5 is still outstanding.

(2)   Provision is to be made for:

(a)   Preference dividend of 7p per share.

(b)   Final ordinary dividend of 2p per share.

(c)   Directors' fees of £1,500 (£500 for each director).

(d)   Audit fee of £900 plus £75 expenses.

(e)   Pension to the widow of a director £1,000.

Required

Prepare a profit and loss account for the year ended 30 September 19X6 and a balance sheet at that date, in a format suitable for publication.

3   Billesley Ltd

Billesley Ltd has authorised share capital of 500,000 50 pence ordinary shares and 300,000 6% £1 preference shares.

The trial balance of Billesley Ltd at 30 June 19X2 was as follows:

	£	£
Land and buildings (cost and depreciation)	500,000	80,000
Plant (cost and depreciation)	180,000	105,000
Vehicles (cost and depreciation)	150,000	90,000
Issued share capital		
Ordinary shares		200,000
Preference shares		200,000
Share premium account		25,000
General reserve		10,000
Capital redemption reserve		20,000
Sales		500,000
Administrative expenses	110,000	
Selling expenses	65,000	
Provision for doubtful debts		12,000
12% Debentures		150,000
Creditors and accruals		74,000
Debtors and prepayments	116,000	
Purchases	280,000	
Stock	46,000	
Investment	75,000	
Profit and loss account		135,000
Interim dividends paid		
– ordinary	10,000	
– preference	6,000	
Cash at bank	63,000	
	1,601,000	1,601,000

The stock at 30 June amounted to £52,000 and the investment, which was a short-term use of surplus cash, had a market value of £79,000 at that date.

The directors wish to provide for a final ordinary dividend of 4% and the final preference dividend together with a transfer to the general reserve of £5,000.

Corporation tax of £12,000 is to be provided for.

The debenture loans were issued on 30 June 19X2.

Required

(a)   Prepare the profit and loss account for Billesley Ltd for the year ended 30 June 19X2 together with a balance sheet at that date, in a format suitable for publication.

(b)   One of your clients is a small shareholder in Billesley Ltd and has the following concerns about items in the accounts that he has received. Write a short response to each of his questions.

1   How many ordinary shares does Billesley actually have in issue at 30 June 19X2?

2   How and why was the share premium account created?

3   What are the company's management accounts and will they be the same as the accounts produced here?

SUMMARY

- Differences between sole traders' and companies' accounts:

    - treatment of profit;

    - composition of capital in the balance sheet; and

    - requirements of the Companies Acts 1985 and 1989 (note a company is a separate legal entity).

- Corporation tax:

    - a tax based on profits for a year; and
    - amount due shown as a current liability.

- Dividends:

    - amounts paid by the company to its shareholders, corresponding to drawings by a sole trader.

- Shares:

    - Ordinary

        - give control of the company; and
        - dividend dependent upon profitability.

    - Preference

        - do not give control; and

        - priority over ordinary shares in payment of dividend and (normally) on winding up.

- Reserves:

    - cumulative total of a company's retained profits – there may be several different reserves intended for specific purposes.

- Share premium account:

    - amount paid for shares over and above their nominal value.

- Debenture:

    - an acknowledgement by a company of a long-term loan made to it.

- Public company:

    - name has suffix 'plc'; and
    - may issue shares to the public.

- Private company

    - name has suffix 'Ltd'; and
    - may not issue shares to the public.

- Accounting records

    - must be kept by every company; and
    - must be preserved for three years (private company) or six years (public company).

- The directors of every company must prepare:

    - a profit and loss account for each financial year; and
    - a balance sheet at the end of that financial year.

Manufacturing accounts

INTRODUCTION

So far we have worked with trading accounts of the form:

	£	£
Sales		X
Opening stock	X	
Purchases	X	
	X	
Closing stock	(X)	
Cost of sales		(X)
Gross profit		X

This is perfectly satisfactory for a retail organisation that purchases and resells goods. A manufacturing company will need further details of the cost of manufacturing its products and these details can be set out in the form of a manufacturing account.

Definitions

- *Direct costs* are those which can be attributed to a particular unit of production and will normally include raw materials, productive wages and other expenses capable of direct identification with production. These three are often called *direct materials, direct wages* and *direct expenses*.

- *Indirect expenses* are production expenses which cannot be attributed to a particular unit of production. They are often called *manufacturing* or *works overheads* and will include such items as factory power, plant repairs etc.

- *Prime cost* is the total of the direct expenses.

- *Factory cost or works cost* is prime cost plus a share of the factory indirect expenses.

Stocks

A trading firm has stocks in only one form (ie. goods held for resale), but a manufacturing firm will have three forms of stocks:

- *direct materials* – items of raw materials which have not yet been issued to production;

- *work in progress* – items of partly completed goods;

- *finished goods* – items which are completed but unsold.

THE PRO FORMA

Basic format

The manufacturing account summarises the costs of production in the factory:

	£
Direct materials	X
Direct labour	X
Direct expenses	X
Prime cost	X
Manufacturing overheads	X
Factory cost	X

Detailed layout of manufacturing account

Pro forma manufacturing account

	£	£
Materials consumed		
Opening stock of raw materials	X	
Purchases of raw materials	X	
	X	
Less: Closing stock of raw materials	(X)	
		X
Direct wages		X
Direct expenses		X
		X
Prime cost		
Works indirect expenses		
Factory power	X	
Factory rent/rates	X	
Factory insurance	X	
Factory light and heat	X	
Plant repairs	X	
Plant depreciation	X	
		X
		X
Add: Opening work in progress		X
Less: Closing work in progress		(X)
Factory cost of goods produced – transfers to warehouse		X

Trading and profit and loss account

The trading and profit and loss account, which takes account of selling and distribution costs and administration expenses, will be in a reasonably familiar format:

Trading and profit and loss account

	£	£
Sales		X
Less: Cost of goods sold		
Opening stock of finished goods	X	
Transfers from factory	X	
	X	
Less: Closing stock of finished goods	(X)	
		(X)
Gross profit		X
Less: Distribution costs	X	
Administrative expenses	X	
		(X)
Net profit		X

PREPARATION OF THE MANUFACTURING ACCOUNT

Illustration 1

The following represent details of the factory costs of J White for the year ended 31 December 19X7.

	£
Opening stock of raw materials	1,000
Raw materials purchased	12,000
Direct (manufacturing) wages	24,000
Factory rent	800
Depreciation of plant in factory	850
General indirect expenses	550
Closing stock of raw materials	1,200
Work in progress	
1 January 19X6	4,000
31 December 19X6	6,000

Given that we have a basic format, we can now use the above information to demonstrate a developed layout.

J White
Manufacturing account for the year ended 31 December 19X7

	£	£
Direct materials		
Opening stock	1,000	
Purchases	12,000	
Carriage inwards	–	
Less: Returns	–	
	13,000	
Less: Closing stock	(1,200)	
		11,800
Direct wages		24,000
Direct expenses		–
Prime cost		35,800
Factory overhead		
Rent	800	
Plant depreciation	850	
General expenses	550	
		2,200
		38,000
Add: Opening work in progress		4,000
		42,000
Less: Closing work in progress		(6,000)
Manufacturing cost of goods completed		36,000

Note that opening and closing stocks of raw materials and work in progress are included in the manufacturing account. Stocks of finished goods are dealt with in the trading account, as is normal.

Certain overhead costs may require apportionment amongst these functional headings. For example, rent of premises may be £1,000 per annum. How should this be split between manufacturing, administration and selling? In such a case, the likely answer is on the basis of floorspace used. Thus the apportionment might be:

	Area (m^2)	*Apportionment* £	
Factory	6,000	500	Manufacturing account
Administration offices	3,600	300)	Profit and loss account
Sales offices	2,400	200)	
	12,000	1,000	

If you are required to apportion expenses, you will be told which basis to use.

The double-entry

In the trading account the manufacturing cost of goods completed will appear in the place of purchases as shown below. Thus a credit has been made to manufacturing account and a debit to trading account.

J White
Trading account for the year ended 31 December 19X7

	£	£
Sales (say)		60,000
Less: Cost of sales		
Opening stock (say)	6,000	
Cost of manufacture	36,000	
	42,000	
Less: Closing stock (say)	(5,000)	
		(37,000)
Gross profit		23,000

QUESTIONS

1   Punch

Punch is a sole trader engaged in the manufacture of toys. The following trial balance was extracted from the books at 31 March 19X1.

	Debit £	Credit £
Capital		39,390
Freehold land and buildings at cost	45,000	
Plant and machinery at cost	36,500	
Motor vans at cost	19,800	
Provision for depreciation – Land and buildings		2,700
– Plant and machinery		4,500
– Motor vans		3,700
Stocks at 1.4.X0 – Raw materials	12,725	
– WIP	18,000	
– Finished goods	20,500	
Purchases	82,550	
Sales		362,720
Wages – Factory	64,750	
– Administration	24,360	
– Sales	26,920	
Rent (nine months to 31.12.X0)	22,000	
Repairs to buildings	5,500	
Sales expenses	22,000	
Electricity and power	17,600	
Administration expenses	5,900	
Provision for doubtful debts		1,560
Debtors	38,970	
Creditors		42,230
Bank		6,320
Cash in hand	45	
	463,120	463,120

You are given the following information.

(1)   Provision is to be made for commission due to the sales manager. The commission is 20% of his own department's net profit after charging such commission.

(2)   Closing stocks on 31 March 19X1:

	£
Raw materials	9,650
WIP	21,000
Finished goods	24,500

(3)   Annual depreciation is to be provided at the following rates on the straight-line basis:

Land and buildings	2%
Plant and machinery	10%
Motor vans	25%

(4)   Debtors include an amount of £700 due from Sonic Ltd. Punch does not expect to be paid and has decided to write it off.

A general provision of 5% is to be maintained on remaining debts.

(5)   Factory rent for the 12 months to 31.12.X1 is £26,500.

(6)   Expenses are to be allocated as follows:

	Factory	Administration
Rent	7/10	3/10
Repairs	4/5	1/5
Electricity and power	2/3	1/3
Buildings depreciation	8/10	2/10

(7)   The following amounts were outstanding at the year-end:

	£
Electricity	960
Telephone (60% Sales, 40% Admin.)	240
Accountancy fees (Admin.)	850

Required

Prepare the manufacturing, trading and profit and loss accounts for the year ended 31 March 19X1 and the balance sheet at that date.

2   Gnome Ltd

The following trial balance was prepared by Gnome Ltd, plastics manufacturers, on 31 May 19X5.

	£	£
Share capital		
300,000 ordinary shares of £1 each fully paid		300,000
100,000 12% cumulative preference shares of £1 each fully paid		100,000
Capital redemption reserve		50,000
Share premium account		100,000
General reserve		150,000
Profit and loss account, 31 May 19X4		359,350
Goodwill	165,500	
Freehold land and buildings at cost	300,000	
Leasehold property at cost	75,000	
Amortisation of leasehold property, 31 May 19X4		15,000
Plant and machinery at cost	150,000	
Accumulated depreciation, 31 May 19X4		68,500
Fixtures and fittings at cost	50,000	
Accumulated depreciation, 31 May 19X4		15,750
Motor vehicles at cost	75,000	
Accumulated depreciation, 31 May 19X4		25,000
10% debentures		100,000
Debtors/Creditors	177,630	97,500
Bank overdraft		51,250
Stock of raw materials, 31 May 19X4	108,400	
Purchases of raw materials	750,600	
Carriage inwards (raw materials)	10,500	
Manufacturing wages	250,000	
Manufacturing overheads	125,000	
Cash	1,520	
Work in progress, 31 May 19X4	32,750	
Sales		1,347,300
Administrative expenses	158,100	
Selling and distribution expenses	116,800	
Financial, legal and professional expenses	54,100	
Provision for doubtful debts, 31 May 19X5		5,750
Stock of finished goods, 31 May 19X4	184,500	
	2,785,400	2,785,400

You discover the following information:

(1)   Stocks at 31 May 19X5

	£
Raw materials	112,600
Finished goods	275,350
Work in progress	37,800

(2)   Depreciation for the year is to be charged as follows:

Plant and machinery	8%	on cost
Fixtures and fittings	10%	on cost
Motor vehicles	20%	on reducing balance

(3)   Provision is to be made for a full year's interest on the debentures.

(4)   The leasehold land and buildings are held on a 50-year lease.

(5)   The goodwill arose from the purchase of an unincorporated business on 31 May 19X5.

Required

(a)   Prepare manufacturing, trading and profit and loss accounts for the year ended 31 May 19X5.

(b)   Prepare a balance sheet at that date.

SUMMARY

Manufacturing accounts provide a detailed analysis of the *cost of goods produced*.

For a manufacturing business, cost of goods sold includes:

*   raw materials;

*   production labour; and

*   production overheads (direct and indirect).

Production overheads need to be distinguished from selling and administrative expenses.

Limited company accounts: the balance sheet

INTRODUCTION

The financial statements of a company comprise:

- balance sheet and notes;

- profit and loss account and notes;

- statement of total recognised gains and losses;

- cash flow statement and notes;

- accounting policies note; and

- comparative figures.

In this session and the following session we will study the form and content of the balance sheet and profit and loss account which are required by the Companies Acts. In later sessions we will look at the detailed accounting and disclosure requirements of the various accounting standards.

FORM OF ACCOUNTS

The Companies Act 1985 requires that published accounts follow certain prescribed formats.

A number of different layouts are given in the Act for both the balance sheet and the profit and loss account, but once a company has adopted one of these formats it cannot be changed in future years unless the directors consider there are special reasons for doing so.

The formats given are only those which are most commonly used.

In reading the formats, you should be aware of the following points:

- Although only one year's figures are indicated on the pro forma, corresponding amounts for the previous year must be shown (these are not normally required by assessment questions).

- Headings are prefixed by a letter A, B, C or a number, I, II, III (Roman numerals), 1, 2, 3, 4 (Arabic numerals). These letters and numbers are not required in published statements or in assessment answers.

- Items prefixed by letters A, B, C etc. and by Roman numerals I, III, III, IV etc. may be omitted but not changed.

- Items prefixed by Arabic numerals 1, 2, 3, 4 etc. may be omitted, combined or described differently if necessary. If Arabic items are combined on the face of the balance sheet or profit and loss account, an analysis should be given in the notes to the accounts.

- Any item for which there is no amount to be shown for both the current and preceding years may be omitted.

BALANCE SHEET – FORMATS

Two formats exist for the balance sheet. Format 1, often referred to as the *vertical format*, is the most common and is normally used in practice. Format 2 is often referred to as the *horizontal format* and is not very common in practice.

Balance sheet – Format 1

				£	£	£
A	**Called-up share capital not paid***					X
B	**Fixed assets**					
	I	Intangible assets				
		1	Development costs	X		
		2	Concessions, patents,			
			licences, trade marks and similar rights and assets	X		
		3	Goodwill	X		
		4	Payments on account	X		
					X	
	II	Tangible assets				
		1	Land and buildings	X		
		2	Plant and machinery	X		
		3	Fixtures, fittings, tools and equipment	X		
		4	Payments on account and assets in course of construction	X		
					X	

				£	£	£
III		Investments				
	1	Shares in group undertakings	X		
	2	Loans to group undertakings	X		
	3	Participating interests	X		
	4	Loans to undertakings in which the company has a participating interest	X		
	5	Other investments other than loans	X		
	6	Other loans	X		
	7	Own shares	X		
			X		
				X	
		(Total of B)			X

C   **Current assets**

				£	£	£
I		Stocks				
	1	Raw materials and consumables	X		
	2	Work in progress	X		
	3	Finished goods and goods for resale	X		
	4	Payments on account	X		
			X		

				£	£	£
II		Debtors				
	1	Trade debtors	X		
	2	Amounts owed by group undertakings	X		
	3	Amounts owed by undertakings in which the group has a participating interest	X		
	4	Other debtors	X		
	5	Called-up share capital not paid*	X		
	6	Prepayments and accrued income*	X		
			X		

				£	£	£
III		Investments				
	1	Shares in group undertakings	X		
	2	Own shares	X		
	3	Other investments	X		
			X		

				£	£	£
IV		Cash at bank and in hand	X		
		(Total of C)		X	

D   **Prepayments and accrued income***   X

(Total of C + D)   X

			£	£	£
E	**Creditors: Amounts falling due within one year**				
	1	Debenture loans	X		
	2	Bank loans and overdrafts	X		
	3	Payments received on account	X		
	4	Trade creditors	X		
	5	Bills of exchange payable	X		
	6	Amounts owed to group undertakings	X		
	7	Amounts owed to undertakings in which the group has a participating interest	X		
	8	Other creditors including taxation and social security	X		
	9	Accruals and deferred income*	X		
					(X)
F	**Net current assets (liabilities) (C + D – E)**				X
G	**Total assets less current liabilities (A + B + F)**				X
H	**Creditors: Amounts falling due after more than one year**				
	1	Debenture loans	X		
	2	Bank loans and overdrafts	X		
	3	Payments received on account	X		
	4	Trade creditors	X		
	5	Bills of exchange payable	X		
	6	Amounts owed to group undertakings	X		
	7	Amounts owed to undertakings in which the group has a participating interest	X		
	8	Other creditors including taxation and social security	X		
	9	Accruals and deferred income*	X		
					(X)
I	**Provisions for liabilities and charges**				
	1	Pensions and similar obligations	X		
	2	Taxation, including deferred taxation	X		
	3	Other provisions	X		
					(X)
J	**Accruals and deferred income***				(X)
					X

			£	£
K	**Capital and reserves**			
	I	Called-up share capital		X
	II	Share premium account		X
	III	Revaluation reserve		X
	IV	Other reserves		
		1 Capital redemption reserve	X	
		2 Reserve for own shares	X	
		3 Reserves provided for by the articles of association	X	
				X
	V	Profit and loss account		X
				X

* alternative positions for the items marked

BALANCE SHEET – DISCLOSURES

Fixed assets

Note that tangible assets are just one of the three categories of fixed assets. Remember that assets are classified as fixed assets 'if they are intended for use on a continuing basis in the company's activities'.

The disclosures required in respect of fixed assets may be broken down into:

(a)   *General movements*

For each item under fixed assets, state the following (comparatives not required):

(i)   The aggregate purchase price or production cost, or valuation as at the beginning and end of the financial year.

(ii)   The effect on any amount shown in the balance sheet in respect of each fixed asset item as a result of any:

-    revaluation made during the year;
-    acquisitions during the year;
-    disposals during the year;
-    transfers (between category of fixed asset) during the year.

(iii)   In respect of provisions for depreciation or diminution in value:

-    the cumulative amount of such provisions as at the beginning and end of the year;

-    the amount provided during the year;

-    the amount of any adjustments made during the year in consequence of the disposal of any asset.

Example

The following extracts from the trial balance of Alpine Athletic Training plc relate to tangible fixed assets.

Trial balance at 31 December 19X7

	£	£
Premises at cost	600,000	
Plant and machinery at cost	135,000	
Provision for depreciation on plant and machinery at 1.1.X7		60,000
Motor vehicles at cost	54,000	
Provision for depreciation on motor vehicles at 1.1.X7		24,000

The following information is relevant to the year ended 31 December 19X7.

Depreciation is to be provided for the year as follows:

Buildings	2% on cost
Plant and machinery	10% on cost
Motor vehicles	25% on written down value

The only changes in fixed assets during the year were an addition to plant and machinery in early January 19X7 costing £30,000 and the purchase of premises for £600,000 comprising £150,000 for buildings and £450,000 for land.

Required

Produce in a form suitable for publication, the required information for fixed assets.

Solution

The first step is to work out the depreciation charge for the current year as follows:

Freehold premises
$$2\% \times 150,000 \qquad = \qquad £3,000$$

Plant and machinery
$$10\% \times 135,000 \qquad = \qquad £13,500$$

Motor vehicles
$$25\% \times (54,000 - 24,000) \qquad = \qquad £7,500$$

We can now construct a suitable note for inclusion in the notes to the accounts which would appear as follows.

Notes to the accounts (extract)

Note 1

Tangible fixed assets

	Freehold land and buildings £	Plant and machinery £	Motor vehicles £	Total £
Cost 1.1.X7	–	105,000	54,000	159,000
Addition during year	600,000	30,000	–	630,000
Cost 31.12.X7	600,000	135,000	54,000	789,000
Accumulated depreciation at 1.1.X7	–	60,000	24,000	84,000
Charge for year	3,000	13,500	7,500	24,000
Accumulated depreciation at 31.12.X7	3,000	73,500	31,500	108,000
Net book value at 31.12.X7	597,000	61,500	22,500	681,000
1.1.X7	–	45,000	30,000	75,000

The straight-line method of depreciation is applied to buildings and plant and machinery using 2% and 10% respectively. Vehicles are depreciated according to the reducing balance method at 25%.

Balance sheet (extract)

	19X7 £	19X6 £
Fixed assets		
Tangible assets (Note 1)	681,000	75,000

(b) *When fixed assets are stated at a valuation*

State

(i) the dates and amounts of the last revaluation;

(ii) the corresponding historical cost amounts;

(iii) where the revaluation has been made during the year, the names or qualifications of the valuers and the basis of valuation used.

(c) *Analysis of land and buildings*

Analyse net book amount of land and buildings under:

(i) freehold;

(ii) long leasehold (ie. not less than 50 years remaining unexpired at the end of the financial year); and

(iii) short leasehold.

Illustration

The analysis of land and buildings is achieved by creating separate headings in our fixed asset note for each group that exists. Our example of a fixed asset note above contained £600,000 in respect of freehold premises. Had this amount in fact been split between freehold and leasehold, our note might have appeared as follows.

Tangible fixed assets

	Freehold premises	Long leasehold	Plant & machinery	Motor vehicles	Total
	£	£	£	£	£
Cost 1.1.X7	–	–	105,000	54,000	159,000
Addition during year	400,000	200,000	30,000	–	630,000
Cost 31.12.X7	400,000	200,000	135,000	54,000	789,000
Accumulated depreciation 1.1.X7	–	–	60,000	24,000	84,000
Charge for year	1,000	2,000	13,500	7,500	24,000
Accumulated depreciation 31.12.X7	1,000	2,000	73,500	31,500	108,000
Net book value 31.12.X7	399,000	198,000	61,500	22,500	681,000
1.1.X7	–	–	45,000	30,000	75,000

Where such an analysis is too cumbersome, a note as follows will suffice.

The net book value of land and buildings is made up as follows:

	£
Freehold premises	399,000
Long leasehold	198,000
Total per original analysis	597,000

(d) *Investments (both fixed asset and current asset)*

(1) Aggregate amount of listed investments.

(2)   For each item which includes listed investments disclose:

- the aggregate market value of the listed investments where it differs from their balance sheet amount;

- both the market value and stock exchange value where the market value is taken as being higher than the stock exchange value.

Illustration

Such information will be given in a note to the accounts which may appear as follows:

Note: Investments

The total of investments of £400,000 given on the balance sheet comprises:

	£
Listed investments	250,000
Other investments	150,000
	400,000

The market value of the listed investments at 31.12.X7 was £284,000.

(3)   Details of each investment where the investing company holds 20% or more of the nominal value of any class of share or where the investment represents 20% of the book value of investing company's assets:

- name;
- country of incorporation (if outside Great Britain) ;
- description and proportion of each class of shares held.

Current assets

The additional requirements in respect of current assets are considerably simpler than those for fixed assets.

Note that current assets are those not intended for use on a continuing basis in the company's activities, ie. all assets are either fixed or current.

(a)   *Stocks*

(i)   Sub-classify the main categories of stock and work in progress in a manner appropriate to the business. This would normally comprise the following:

- finished goods and goods for resale;
- raw materials and consumables;
- work in progress.

(ii)   Where the purchase price or production cost of any item of stock is materially different from the replacement cost of that item, state the amount of the difference by way of a note.

(b)   *Debtors*

For each item under debtors, show separately the amount falling due after more than one year.

Debtors falling due after more than one year should be disclosed on the face of the balance sheet, rather than in the notes to the accounts if they are so material that readers might otherwise misinterpret the accounts.

Liabilities and provisions

(a)   *Creditors – general*

For each balance sheet item shown under creditors, disclose by way of a note the following:

   (i)   amounts falling due within one year or after more than one year:

   –   the aggregate amount of secured liabilities;
   –   an indication of the nature of the security given;

   (ii)   amounts falling due after more than one year:

   –   amount due for repayment after more than five years from the balance sheet date;

   –   terms of repayment and rate of interest for any such amounts.

(b)   *Debentures*

   (i)   Where the company has issued any debentures during the financial year, disclose by way of a note:

   –   the classes of debenture issued;
   –   in respect of each class, the amount issued and the consideration received.

   (ii)   Show separately the amount of any convertible loans.

(c)   *Taxation*

Identify separately amounts payable in respect of mainstream corporation tax and other tax and social security.

Illustration

This merely requires a note giving an analysis of the items included under the heading 'Other creditors including taxation and social security'. Typically this analysis for creditors falling due within one year would be:

	£
Corporation tax (mainstream)	64,000
Advance corporation tax	17,000
Social security	4,300
Other creditors	23,000
	108,300

(d)   *Advance corporation tax (ACT)*

   (i)   Include ACT on proposed dividends as current tax liability.

   (ii)   Deduct recoverable ACT on dividends paid in period from appropriate mainstream corporation tax liability.

(e)   *Dividends*

   (i)   Amount of proposed dividends (excluding related ACT), which should be included as a current liability.

   (ii)   Amount of any arrears of fixed cumulative dividends and the period for which each class is in arrears. Note that these are not provided for in the accounts and are only a contingent liability.

(f)   *Provisions – general*

   (i)   Disclose by way of a note particulars of each material provision included under 'other provisions' in the balance sheet (comparatives not required).

   (ii)   Where there is any movement on provisions, disclose (comparatives not required):

   –   the amount of the provision as at the beginning and end of the financial year,
   –   the amount transferred to or from the provisions during the year.

   The above information is not required where the movement consists of the application of a provision for the purpose for which it was established.

(g)   *Contingent liabilities*

For possible material contingent losses not provided against and which are not remote (and for material contingent gains if it is probable that the gain will be realised), disclose:

   –   the nature of the contingency,

   –   the uncertainties which are expected to affect the ultimate outcome,

   –   a prudent estimate of the net pre-tax financial effect (at date of approval of accounts by directors) or a statement that estimate is not practicable,

   –   an explanation of the taxation implications.

(h)   *Commitments*

    (i)   Disclose by way of a note aggregate or estimated amounts of capital commitments not provided for.

    (ii)   Particulars of any other financial commitments which:

        –   have not been provided for,
        –   are relevant to assessing the company's state of affairs.

    (iii)   Distinguish separately any commitments made on behalf of:

        –   any parent company or fellow subsidiary of the company,
        –   any subsidiary of the company.

Capital and reserves

The disclosures in respect of capital and reserves are straightforward and should present few problems.

(a)   *Share capital*

    (i)   Authorised share capital.

    (ii)   Amount of allotted share capital and amount of called-up share capital which has been paid up.

    (iii)   Number and aggregate nominal value of allotted shares of each class where more than one class of shares have been allotted.

    (iv)   Where the company has allotted any shares during the financial year:

        –   the classes of shares allotted, and

        –   for each class of shares, the number allotted, their aggregate nominal value and the consideration received by the company.

    (v)   Particulars of debentures which may be converted to shares:

        –   the number, description and amount of the shares in question,
        –   the period during which the right is exercisable, and
        –   the price to be paid for the shares allotted.

    (vi)   Number, description and amount of shares in the company held by its subsidiaries or their nominees.

(b)   *Redeemable shares*

    (i)   Earliest and latest dates of redemption by company.
    (ii)   Whether redemption at company's option or in any event.
    (iii)   Whether any (and if so what) premium is payable on redemption.

(c) *Reserves*

Where there is any movement on reserves, disclose (comparatives not required):

(i)   the amount of the reserves as at the beginning and end of the financial year,

(ii)   any amount transferred to or from the reserves during the year.

(d) *Revaluation reserve*

If assets are revalued, the revaluation surplus must be credited to a revaluation reserve (shown separately as item K III in balance sheet: format 1).

An amount may only be transferred from the revaluation reserve:

(i)   if the revalued asset is disposed of, when the revaluation credit may be transferred to the profit and loss account;

(ii)   on capitalisation.

Illustration

A typical note showing movements on reserves might appear as follows:

	Share premium £	*Revaluation reserve* £	*Profit and loss account* £
Balance at 1 January 19X7	160,000	122,000	614,000
Share issue during year	84,000	–	–
Capitalised on bonus issue	(125,000)	–	–
Revaluation during year	–	60,000	–
Retained profit	–	–	47,000
Balance at 31 December 19X7	119,000	182,000	661,000

QUESTIONS

1   Austen plc

You are presented with the following information for Austen plc for the year to 31 December 19X2.

Trial balance as at 31 December 19X2

	Dr £'000	Cr £'000
Debenture loans repayable 19X8		100
Provision for taxation		20
Stock of raw materials	20	
Trade debtors	60	
Investment (long term)	30	
Fixture and fittings (NBV)	55	
Cash at bank	10	
Goodwill (NBV)	25	
Plant and machinery (NBV)	95	
Prepayments	5	
Land and buildings (NBV)	150	
Trade creditors		50
Bank overdraft		35
Share capital		250
Profit and loss account		20
Value added tax payable		22
Accruals		3
Stock of finished goods	25	
Work in progress	25	
	500	500

The following additional information is provided in respect of Austen plc:

(1)   Fixed assets

	Balance at 1 January 19X2 £'000	Relating to purchases during year £'000	Relating to sales during year £'000
Cost			
Land and buildings	200	–	–
Plant and machinery	280	20	10
Fixtures and fittings	100	10	–
Depreciation			
Land and buildings	46	4	–
Plant and machinery	142	58	5
Fixtures and fittings	44	11	–

(2)   Investments

The investments are listed on the Stock Exchange. They cost £30,000 and their value at 31 December 19X2 was £45,000.

(3)   The bank overdraft is repayable on demand.

(4)   The debentures are repayable in 19X8 at par. The rate of interest on them is 12% and they are secured by a floating charge over all the assets.

(5)   The share capital consists of the following:

	Authorised £'000	Issued £'000
8% preference £1 shares	200	50
Ordinary £1 shares	400	200
	600	250

(6)   The debtors fall due within one year.

(7)   Taxation

The corporation tax is due on 1 October 19X3.

(8)   Goodwill at cost was £60,000.

Amortisation at 1 January 19X2 was £30,000.
£5,000 was written off during the year to 31 December 19X2.

Required

Prepare the balance sheet and notes thereto at 31 December 19X2, in a form suitable for publication.

2   Radical Ltd

After closing off the profit and loss account for the year ended 30 September 19X2, the following trial balance was extracted from the nominal ledger of Radical Ltd:

	£	£
Stocks on hand, at cost	192,734	
Debtors	172,062	
Cash in hand	2,431	
Balance at bank	42,735	
Freehold property, at cost	131,000	
Motor vehicles, at cost	406,795	
Ordinary shares in Midland Bank plc, at cost	22,632	
Prepayments	2,596	
Ordinary share capital		250,000
Preference share capital		100,000
9½% Loan stock		150,000
Creditors		64,700
Aggregate depreciation		
Freehold property		5,000
Motor vehicles		196,530
Provision for bad debts		13,420
Profit and loss account		89,185
Share premium account		52,400
Corporation tax at 33%		26,750
Proposed ordinary dividend		25,000
	972,985	972,985

You also obtain the following information:

(1)   The company has an authorised and issued share capital of £350,000 divided into 200,000 8% cumulative preference shares of 50p each and 1,000,000 ordinary shares of 25p each.

(2)   The 9½% loan stock is unsecured and repayable on 1 October 19Y9.

(3)   The balance on corporation tax account was due for payment nine months after the year-end.

(4)   Additional motor vehicles were purchased during the year at a cost of £40,450 and additions to freehold property were £26,000.

(5)   Depreciation has been charged during the year as follows:

Freehold buildings	£2,500
Motor vehicles	£84,000

Required

Prepare the company's balance sheet as at 30 September 19X2, in a form suitable for presentation to members. Ignore the requirement to produce a statement of accounting policies.

Corresponding figures are not required and the information given may be taken as if it included all that is necessary to satisfy the requirements of the Companies Act 1985.

Ignore ACT and income tax.

SUMMARY

In this session we have covered:

- the format of the balance sheet;

- the additional disclosures required by the Companies Acts.

You will need to use this session and the next as reference material when you begin to practise drafting detailed company accounts.

Limited company accounts: the profit and loss account

PROFIT AND LOSS ACCOUNT – FORMATS

The Act permits a choice of four profit and loss account formats. Format 1 is the most commonly used in practice.

The vertical profit and loss account – Format 1

		£	£
1	Turnover		X
2	Cost of sales		(X)
			—
3	Gross profit or loss		X
4	Distribution costs		(X)
5	Administrative expenses		(X)
6	Other operating income		X
7	Income from shares in group undertakings		X
8	Income from participating interests		X
9	Income from other fixed asset investments		X
10	Other interest receivable and similar income		X
11	Amounts written off investments		(X)
12	Interest payable and similar charges		(X)
13	Tax on profit or loss on ordinary activities		(X)
			—
14	Profit (or loss) on ordinary activities after taxation		X
15	Extraordinary income	X	
16	Extraordinary charges	(X)	
		—	
17	Extraordinary profit or loss		X
18	Tax on extraordinary profit or loss		(X)
19	Other taxes not shown under the above items		(X)
			—
20	Profit (or loss) for the financial year		X
			—

Note: All the lines in the profit and loss account are given Arabic numerals; this means that technically all of this information could be included in the notes to the accounts rather than on the face of the profit and loss account! The following items *must* be shown on the face of the profit and loss account:

(a) profit (or loss) on ordinary activities before taxation – a subtotal between lines 12 and 13;

(b) dividends paid and proposed; and

(c) transfers to or from reserves.

PROFIT AND LOSS ACCOUNT – DISCLOSURES

Analyses of turnover and profit before tax

Disclose by way of a note, an analysis of turnover by:

(i)   class of business,
(ii)   geographical market,

where, in the opinion of the directors, there is more than one class and/or market.

Illustration

A typical note covering these requirements may be as follows.

Analysis of turnover and operating profit

An analysis of the group's activities shows:

	Turnover £
Wholesaling	694,000
Retailing	276,000
	970,000

Turnover was distributed as follows:

	£
United Kingdom	846,000
Europe	115,000
Other	9,000
	970,000

Note: Further analysis of this nature may be required under SSAP25 if the company is large enough (see Session 17).

Particulars of staff

Disclose by way of a note:

(a)   average number of persons employed by the company and (in the group accounts) by its subsidiaries during the financial year, analysed by category;

(b)   (i)   wages and salaries paid/payable in respect of those persons,
       (ii)   social security costs thereon,
       (iii) other pension costs thereon.

Directors' emoluments

Disclose by way of a note:

(a)   Aggregate amounts of:

  –   emoluments (including benefits in kind, 'golden hellos', pension contributions) distinguishing those for services as director and other,

  –   amounts paid to third parties to secure the services of a director,

  –   pensions, distinguishing those for services as director and other,

  –   compensation for loss of office, distinguishing amounts for office of director and other offices.

include amounts in respect of past directors

(b)   In respect of the chairman of the company, his emoluments and those of highest paid director, if paid more than the chairman (in both cases excluding pension contributions by the company).

(c)   Number of directors whose emoluments (excluding pension contributions by the company) fall within each bracket of £5,000.

The individual disclosures in (b) and (c) are not required for a company which is not a member of a group and where its directors' emoluments are not more than £60,000. The individual disclosures in (b) and (c) are not required in respect of persons working wholly or mainly overseas.

Illustration

A typical note covering the above can be constructed from the following information.

Waugh plc has three directors whose emoluments are as follows:

Name	Fees as directors £	Remuneration as executives £	Pension contributions £
X (chairman)	2,000	47,000	7,000
Y	2,000	68,000	10,500
Z	1,000	22,000	3,500

Note to accounts

Directors' remuneration

The amounts paid to directors were:

	£
Fees as directors	5,000
Other emoluments (including pension contributions)	158,000

Emoluments of the chairman (excluding pension contributions) amounted to £49,000 and those of the highest paid director to £70,000. Other directors' emoluments were within the following ranges:

£20,001 – £25,000   1

Sundry charges

Disclose by way of a note:

(a)   Amounts of provisions made for depreciation or diminution in value of tangible and intangible fixed assets.

(b)   Effect on depreciation charge of any change from one method of depreciation to another, in year of change, if material.

(c)   Effect on depreciation charge of any revaluation of assets, in year of revaluation, if material.

(d)   Hire of plant and machinery.

(e)   Auditors' remuneration, including audit expenses.

(f)   Exceptional items.

Income from listed investments

Should be disclosed by way of a note.

Rents receivable

Rents receivable from land, after deduction of ground rents, rates and other outgoings, if a substantial part of revenue, should be disclosed by way of a note.

Interest payable

Disclose by way of a note:

The amount of the interest on:

(a)   bank loans and overdrafts, and loans made by the company (other than bank loans and overdrafts) which fall due for repayment within five years; and

(b)   all other loans.

Taxation

Disclose by way of a note:

(a)   Tax charge divided between:

    (i)   UK corporation tax,
    (ii)   tax attributable to franked investment income,
    (iii)   irrecoverable ACT,
    (iv)   deferred taxation.

(b)   Where applicable, distinguish the amounts attributable to taxation on ordinary and extraordinary activities.

(c)   If corporation tax rate not known for any part of period, use and disclose latest known rate.

See the session on taxation in company accounts for examples of this disclosure.

Extraordinary and exceptional items

(a)   Particulars of extraordinary income and charges, including separate disclosure of any related taxation.

(b)   Amount of profit or loss after extraordinary items.

   Note: Following the publication of FRS3, extraordinary items are now very rare.

(c)   Exceptional items are disclosed within the sundry items note (other than those shown on the face of the profit and loss account per FRS3 – see Session 9).

Dividends

(a)   Aggregate dividends paid   } in respect

(b)   Aggregate dividends proposed   } of each class of share

(c)   (Disclosure of the dividend per share is **desirable**.)

SUNDRY MATTERS

• **Disclosure of accounting policies**

   The accounting policies used by the company must be disclosed by note.

• **Compliance with accounting standards**

   It must be stated whether the accounts have been prepared in accordance with accounting standards. If not, details of material departures from the standards must be given, with reasons.

SSAP3: EARNINGS PER SHARE

The price-earnings ratio is an indicator used by investment analysts. It is therefore important that the figure for earnings per share, which is used in calculating that ratio, should be calculated and disclosed on a comparable basis between one company and another.

Scope of SSAP3

The standard applies only to companies which are listed on a recognised stock exchange.

Requirements of SSAP3

Listed companies should show, on the face of their profit and loss account, earnings per share both for the period under review and the corresponding previous period.

Calculation of EPS

The basic calculation is:

$$\text{Earnings per share} = \frac{\text{Profit attributable to equity shareholders}}{\text{Number of equity shares in issue and ranking for dividend}}$$

Example

Given below is the summarised profit and loss account of ABC plc, a listed company.

	19X5 £	19X4 £
Operating profit	6,420,000	5,680,000
Interest payable	(780,000)	(780,000)
Profit before taxation	5,640,000	4,900,000
Taxation	(2,440,000)	(1,980,000)
Profit after taxation	3,200,000	2,920,000
Dividends		
Preference dividend – paid	52,500	52,500
– proposed	52,500	52,500
Ordinary dividend – paid	160,000	130,000
– proposed	920,000	720,000
Retained profit for the year	2,015,000	1,965,000

The company's capital is as follows:

Authorised share capital	£
40,000,00 Ordinary shares 25p each	10,000,000
10,000,000 7% Preference shares 25p each	2,500,000
	12,500,000

Issued and fully paid	£
20,000,000 Ordinary shares 25p each	5,000,000
6,000,000 7% Preference shares 25p each	1,500,000
	6,500,000

Required

Calculate, for disclosure, the earnings per share for 19X5 on the face of the company's profit and loss account.

Solution

Earnings	*19X5*	*19X4*
	£	£
Profit after tax	3,200,000	2,920,000
Deduct: Preference dividend	105,000	105,000
Earnings	3,095,000	2,815,000
Number of equity (ordinary) shares in issue	20,000,000	20,000,000

$$\text{EPS 19X5} = \frac{3,095,000 \times 100}{20,000,000} = 15.475\text{p}$$

Comparative figure (also required):

$$\text{EPS 19X4} = \frac{2,815,000 \times 100}{20,000,000} = 14.075\text{p}$$

ACCOUNTS FOR SMALL AND MEDIUM-SIZED COMPANIES

Introduction

Certain small and medium-sized companies can take advantage of accounting exemptions in section 247 of Companies Act 1985 permitting them to prepare two sets of accounts, normal full accounts for their shareholders and abbreviated accounts which are filed at Companies House.

These exemptions are optional.

Small and medium sized companies are exempt from the requirement to state whether their accounts have been prepared in accordance with applicable accounting policies, regardless of whether they choose to file abbreviated accounts.

Conditions for exemption

- A company 'qualifies' as small or medium-sized if it meets two out of the following three size criteria in a particular year:

	Small	*Medium-sized*
Turnover not more than	£2,800,000	£11,200,000
Fixed and current assets not more than	£1,400,000	£5,600,000
Average number of employees not more than	50	250

Note that this does not on its own entitle a company to file abbreviated accounts (see below).

- A company is entitled to file abbreviated accounts for a particular year if it satisfies two of the following three criteria:

  - 'qualifies' this year;
  - 'qualified' last year;
  - was entitled to file abbreviated accounts last year.

Thus, we need to look at two years together to see if the conditions are met.

- If the qualifying conditions are met in the company's first financial year, it can file abbreviated accounts in that year.

- Whatever their size, there are some companies which can never file abbreviated accounts. These are as follows:

    - public companies;

    - banking and insurance companies;

    - companies authorised to carry out investment business;

    - companies in a group which contains a public company, a banking or insurance company, or a company authorised to carry out investment business.

Exemptions permitted for medium-sized companies

- In the profit and loss account, turnover, cost of sales, gross profit and other operating income are combined as one figure.

- No analysis of turnover by class of business or geographical destination.

Exemptions permitted for small-sized companies

- **Profit and loss account**

    Not required.

- **Balance sheet**

    Only items which bear a letter or Roman numeral (ie. the main headings).

- **Notes to the accounts**

    Only the following notes are required:
    (i)   accounting policies;
    (ii)   share capital;
    (iii)   debtors recoverable after more than one year;
    (iv)   creditors due after more than five years;
    (v)   secured creditors;
    (vi)   the movements (in total) on intangible fixed assets, tangible fixed assets and fixed asset investments.

Advantages and disadvantages of filing abbreviated accounts

Abbreviated accounts enable a company to maintain a certain degree of confidentiality. Information which might be of interest to competitors is not made public. This is particularly true of abbreviated accounts for small companies, which do not contain a profit and loss account. Accounts for medium sized companies do not disclose turnover or profit margins.

The main disadvantage of filing abbreviated accounts is the additional cost and work required since the company still has to prepare full audited accounts for the members.

OTHER EXEMPTIONS FOR SMALL COMPANIES

Regardless of whether a small company (as previously defined) has chosen to *file* abbreviated accounts, it may take advantage of certain additional exemptions when *preparing* full accounts for distribution to shareholders.

These exemptions result in a simplified balance sheet format, with some of the items bearing an Arabic numeral being combined. For example:

- Tangible assets have only two categories: 'land and buildings' and 'plant and machinery, etc.'.

- All categories of stock are combined, with the exception of payments on account.

- The nine separate headings under creditors in the full format are reduced to four.

The profit and loss account remains the same.

There is also a considerable reduction in the number of notes required; for example, security of creditors, particulars of staff, emoluments of directors, taxation notes are all not required.

SUMMARY FINANCIAL STATEMENTS

The Companies Act 1989 introduced summary financial statements. These may be produced by public limited companies which have a full Stock Exchange Listing (not USM companies) as an alternative to producing full accounts.

This recognises that the vast amount of detail as required by full Companies Act formats and disclosures may not be of relevance or interest to all shareholders.

Requirements

Companies must always file a full set of accounts with the Registrar of Companies.

The company must ascertain whether its shareholders wish to receive full or summary financial statements. This will usually be achieved by writing to each shareholder. Once a shareholder's preference has been ascertained, it will be up to the shareholders to notify the company of any change in future years. The shareholders will always have the right to demand a full set of accounts.

The contents of the summary financial statements must be derived from the full accounts. No additional information can be included which is not in the full accounts.

The summary financial statements will carry a 'health warning' to advise shareholders not to take investment decisions based on the contents of these statements.

Contents

Profit and loss account

	£
Turnover	X
Aggregate of income from shares in investments held	X
Net aggregate of interest receivable and payable	X
Profit or loss on ordinary activities before tax	X
Tax on profit on ordinary activities	(X)
Net aggregate of extraordinary income and charges after tax	X
Profit or loss for the financial year	X
Aggregate dividends paid and proposed	(X)
Aggregate directors' emoluments	X

Balance sheet

	£	£
Fixed assets		X
Current assets	X	
Prepayments and accrued income	X	
Creditors: Amounts falling due within one year	(X)	
Net current assets (liabilities)		X
Total assets less current liabilities		X
Creditors: Amounts falling due after more than one year		(X)
Provisions for liabilities and charges		(X)
Accruals and deferred income		(X)
		X
Capital and reserves		X

QUESTIONS

1   Bronte plc

Bronte plc is a retailer. The following (selected) balances have been extracted from the ledger on 31 December 19X2.

	Dr £'000	Cr £'000
Stock at 1 January 19X2	109	
Salaries – office	60	
Salaries – distribution	55	
Expenses – office (see (5))	17	
Expenses – distribution (see (5))	31	
Turnover		1,515
Purchases	884	
Bank interest received		10
Income from fixed asset investments		20
Depreciation written off: Office equipment	5	
Motor vehicles	10	
Property	40	
Debenture interest paid	65	
Interim dividend paid	20	
Retained profits 1 January 19X2		1,190

The following information is relevant:

(1)   Stocks at 31 December 19X2 are £121,000.

(2)   Tax on the profit from ordinary activities is estimated at £141,000.

(3)   Depreciation on property is to be allocated as follows:

Cost of sales	70%
Distribution	10%
Administration	20%

(4)   Wages and salaries include the following in respect of directors:

	£
Mr Anne (Finance Director)	25,000
Mrs Jane (Sales Director)	34,000
Ms Emily (Chairman)	12,000

In addition to the three directors, six employees work in distribution and the office maintains a staff of eight.

(5)   The amounts for office and distribution expenses include the following costs:

	£
Audit fee	3,000
Hire of plant	1,000

(6)   The current rate of corporation tax is 33%.

(7)   Debentures are repayable in 19X9.

(8)   The called-up share capital is 200,000 ordinary shares of £1 each.   The directors propose a final dividend of 20p per share.

Required

Prepare in a form suitable for publication the profit and loss account and relevant notes for Bronte plc, for the year ended 31 December 19X2.   Ignore advance corporation tax and income tax.

2   **Church's Ltd**

Church's Ltd, a company which manufactures footwear, makes up its accounts to 31 December in each year.   The company has an authorised share capital of £300,000, divided into 150,000 6½% preference shares of £1 each and 300,000 ordinary shares of 50p each. It is not a member of a group.

The following balances have been extracted from the ledger for the year ended 31 December 19X0.

Debit	£	**Credit**	£
Cost of sales	349,996	Sales	595,932
Motor expenses	79,842	Discounts received	420
Depreciation of motor vehicles	5,290	Investment income received:	
Other distribution costs	39,420	Unlisted	546
Wages and salaries	62,917	Listed	780
Other administrative costs	5,746		
Audit fee	700		
Depreciation of fixtures and fittings	520		
Depreciation of buildings	1,000		
Pension to former director's widow	750		
Superannuation scheme	4,250		
Corporation tax	12,410		
Debenture interest	800		
Preference dividend paid on 30 September 19X0	6,500		

You are given the following additional information:

(1)   Wages, salaries, pension and superannuation are to be broken down as follows:

	Distribution £	Administration £
Wages and salaries	34,715	28,202
Pension to former director's widow	–	750
Superannuation scheme	2,250	2,000

The charge for wages and salaries includes the salaries of the managing director £13,500 and sales director £13,000.   Superannuation scheme also includes £858 on their behalf. Provision is to be made for directors' fees of £7,500, being £2,500 for each director, including the chairman, who does not receive a salary.   The company has employed an average of 10 people in the year.

(2)   The charge for corporation tax in the profit and loss account is the amount estimated to be payable on the profits for the year at 33%.

(3)   The directors recommend payment of an ordinary dividend of 5.2p per share. The ordinary share capital in the balance sheet is £100,000.

(4)   The debentures are repayable in 19Z9.

Required

Prepare the company's profit and loss account and associated notes for the year ended 31 December 19X0 in accordance with generally accepted accounting principles and in a form suitable for presentation to members. (An accounting policies note is not required.)

Ignore income tax.

SUMMARY

In this session we have covered:

•   the format of the profit and loss account;

•   the additional disclosures required by the Companies Acts.

In order to become proficient at drafting limited company financial statements, you must practise whenever possible.

You should also try to look at as many sets of published accounts as you can.

Reporting financial performance

INTRODUCTION

FRS3 is intended to provide users of financial statements with information about important components of financial performance. It achieves this in two ways:

- by requiring companies to make detailed disclosures of a range of items included in the profit and loss account; and

- by setting out the permitted accounting treatment for these items so that all companies are required to account for them in the same way.

The term *reporting entity* is used throughout the FRS. A reporting entity is any business which prepares financial statements which are intended to show a true and fair view. A reporting entity need not be a limited company. However, the requirements of FRS3 are most likely to apply to limited companies.

CONTINUING OPERATIONS, ACQUISITIONS AND DISCONTINUED OPERATIONS

FRS3 requires businesses to analyse their results between continuing operations, acquisitions (as a component of continuing operations) and discontinued operations.

An operation may be represented by a separate class of business within a single company or, if group accounts are prepared, a company or companies within a group. The requirements of the FRS apply to both these situations.

An *acquisition* is an operation that is acquired in the period.

A *discontinued operation* is an operation that is sold or terminated.

Disclosures

FRS3 requires all the standard profit and loss account headings to be analysed between continuing operations, acquisitions (as a component of continuing operations) and discontinued operations, down to the level of operating profit.

Operating profit is not a term used in the Companies Act formats and the FRS does not formally define it. However, operating profit is normally profit before income from shares in group undertakings, ie. gross profit and other operating income less distribution costs and administrative expenses.

Turnover and operating profit must be analysed on the face of the profit and loss account. The analysis of the other headings may be shown either on the face of the profit and loss account or in the notes.

Obviously, where a company has no acquisitions and no discontinued operations there is no need for the additional analysis.

Illustration

Profit and loss account

	£'000	£'000
Turnover		
Continuing operations		550
Acquisitions		50
		600
Discontinued operations		175
		775
Cost of sales		(620)
Gross profit		155
Distribution costs		(44)
Administrative expenses		(80)
Other operating income		10
Operating profit		
Continuing operations	20	
Acquisitions	6	
	26	
Discontinued operations	15	
		41
Profit on sale of fixed assets in continuing operations		22
Profit on ordinary activities before interest		63
Other interest receivable and similar income		2
Interest payable		(20)
Profit on ordinary activities before taxation		45
Tax on profit on ordinary activities		(14)
		31
[Extraordinary items] (included only to show positioning)		–
Profit for the financial year		31
Dividends		(8)
Retained profit for the financial year		23

Notes to the financial statements

	Continuing £'000	Discontinued £'000	Total £'000
Cost of sales	485	135	620
Distribution costs	31	13	44
Administrative expenses	68	12	80
Other operating income	10	–	10

The total figures for continuing operations include the following amounts relating to acquisitions: cost of sales £40,000, distribution costs £3,000, administrative expenses £3,000 and other operating income £2,000.

EXCEPTIONAL ITEMS

Definition

Exceptional items are defined as those which:

(a)   are material;

(b)   derive from events or transactions that fall within the ordinary activities of the business;

(c)   need to be disclosed separately by virtue of their size or incidence if the financial statements are to give a true and fair view.

All three criteria must be present for an item to be classed as exceptional.

Examples

FRS3 does not give examples of exceptional items other than to specify three types of exceptional item which should be separately disclosed on the face of the profit and loss account (see below).

Exceptional items might include:

- redundancy costs;
- amounts transferred to employee share schemes;
- profits or losses on the disposal of fixed assets;
- abnormal charges for bad debts and write-offs of stock and work in progress;
- abnormal provisions for losses on long-term contracts; and
- surpluses arising on the settlement of insurance claims.

Accounting entries

Exceptional items are accounted for in the normal way. For example, an exceptionally large bad debt is debited to profit and loss account, with the corresponding credit entry being made in the provision for bad debts account or the individual debtors account as appropriate.

Disclosure

In published accounts, exceptional items are normally included under the statutory headings of 'cost of sales' 'administrative expenses' or 'distribution costs' in line with a company's policy, but because they are material items further information must be given.

Normally, exceptional items will be disclosed as separate items in the note to the published accounts which discloses the other items required to be shown by the Companies Act. For example:

Operating profit has been arrived at after charging:

	£
Depreciation	3,714,000
Audit fee	162,000
Directors' remuneration	732,000
Exceptional item – bad debt arising on liquidation of major customer	1,680,000

FRS3 specifies that there are three types of exceptional item which must always be disclosed on the face of the profit and loss account. These are:

- Profits or losses on the sale or termination of an operation.

- Costs of a fundamental reorganisation or restructuring, having a material effect on the nature and focus of the reporting entity's operations.

- Profits or losses on the disposal of fixed assets.

Other types of exceptional item should be shown on the face of the profit and loss account if they are so material that it is thought necessary for the accounts to show a true and fair view.

If exceptional items are shown on the face of the profit and loss account, they are disclosed separately after operating profit and before interest. Look at the formats shown earlier in the session.

Exceptional items must be included under the appropriate heading of continuing or discontinued operations.

Illustration

Consider an investment that is held by a company that occasionally deals in investments (although this is not its main area of operation). Assume that it purchases the investment for £600,000 and sells it for £1,400,000, making a profit of £800,000 which is considered to be exceptional.

The profit and loss account extract would be as follows.

	£
Operating profit (say)	4,000,000
Profit on sale of investments (1,400,000 – 600,000)	800,000
Profit on ordinary activities before interest	4,800,000

The vital point to understand is that the exceptional item is charged against profit before taxation. This differentiates the treatment of exceptional and extraordinary items.

EXTRAORDINARY ITEMS

Definition

Extraordinary items are defined as those which:

- are material;
- possess a high degree of abnormality;
- arise from events or transactions that fall outside the ordinary activities of the business;
- are not expected to recur.

Again, all four criteria must be present for an item to be classed as extraordinary.

FRS3 also defines ordinary activities. Ordinary activities are any activities which are undertaken by a reporting entity (for example, a company) as part of its business. They include:

- Such related activities in which the reporting entity engages in furtherance of, incidental to, or arising from its main activities.

- The effects on the reporting entity of any event in the various environments in which it operates, including the political, regulatory, economic and geographical environments, irrespective of the frequency or unusual nature of the events. (Examples of these would include changes in the law, which might mean that a particular item could no longer be produced, or an economic recession resulting in closures and redundancies.)

This definition of 'ordinary activities' is extremely wide. Virtually all activities are ordinary activities.

This in turn means that in practice extraordinary items are extremely rare. The FRS does not give any examples of extraordinary items.

PRIOR-PERIOD ADJUSTMENTS

Definition

Prior-period adjustments are those material adjustments applicable to prior periods arising from

(a)   changes in accounting policies; or
(b)   the correction of fundamental errors.

A fundamental error is one of such significance as to destroy the true and fair view and hence the validity of a set of accounts, and which would have led to their withdrawal had the error been recognised at the time.

Normal recurring corrections and adjustments of accounting estimates made in prior years do not constitute prior-year adjustments.

Examples

Examples of changes in accounting policies which are likely to give rise to prior-year adjustments are:

(a)   method of valuing stock;
(b)   method of accounting for development costs.

Fundamental errors are particularly unique events but size is of considerable importance and the amount involved should be judged not only by reference to its impact on the assets of the enterprise but also by its effect upon profits.

Accounting entries

When a change in basis of accounting occurs, it is important that the accounts are prepared on a consistent basis. It therefore follows that the new accounting policy must be applied to those assets or liabilities standing in the books at the commencement of the current year, thereby adjusting the opening figures to the new basis.

Illustration

A company decides that, given the current situation in the business and the likely future trend, a new basis of accounting is more appropriate to the valuation of their stock than the method previously adopted. It changes from the average method of valuation to a first in, first out basis.

The profits retained at the last balance sheet date amount to £16,483,000 and the stock at that time and the current stock at the end of our financial year have been valued on both the old and new basis as follows:

	Old basis £	New basis £
Opening stock brought forward from last year	946,000	998,000
Closing stock at the end of the current year	1,117,000	1,206,000

Before the accounts relating to the current year are prepared, the stock account will contain only the amount brought forward from the previous year.

Stock account

	£	
Balance b/f		
– Opening stock at old value	946,000	

This stock should now be adjusted to the new method of valuation by a prior-period adjustment of £52,000 (£998,000 – £946,000)

Stock account

	£	
Balance b/f	946,000	
Period-period adjustment	52,000	
	998,000	

The retained profits brought forward will reflect this adjustment.

	£
Profits retained in previous years	16,483,000
Prior-period adjustment on change in basis of accounting	52,000
New retained profit brought forward	16,535,000

The accounts for the current year can now be prepared, using the new method of valuation consistently.

Stock account			
	£		£
Balance b/f	946,000	Trading account (current year)	
Prior-year adjustment		– Opening stock at new value	998,000
– Retained profit	52,000	Balance c/f	1,206,000
Trading account (current year)			
– Closing stock at new value	1,206,000		
	2,204,000		2,204,000

Disclosure

Prior-period adjustments should be accounted for by restating the prior period profit, with the result that the opening balance of retained profits is altered (as shown above). The effect of the change should be disclosed, where practicable, by showing separately, the restatement of the previous period profit and the amount involved.

This restatement must immediately follow the profit and loss account, or alternatively be shown by way of note with a reference to its location on the face of the profit and loss account.

An illustration of this restatement, with the figures from the previous section, is as follows:

Statement of retained profits

	£'000
Retained profits brought forward	
– as previously reported	16,483
– prior-period adjustment	52
– as restated	16,535
Retained profits for the financial year	X
Retained profits carried forward	X

STATEMENT OF TOTAL RECOGNISED GAINS AND LOSSES

Introduction

FRS3 requires all reporting entities to prepare a statement of total recognised gains and losses. This must be presented with the same prominence as the other primary statements.

Recognised gains and losses include the following:

- the profit or loss for the period;
- surpluses or deficits on revaluation of properties;
- changes in the value of an investment property;
- prior-period adjustments.

Some of these items may be taken directly to reserves, rather than pass through the profit and loss account. The purpose of the statement of total recognised gains and losses is to show all the gains and losses which have been recognised in a period and which are available to shareholders.

If there are no recognised gains and losses other than the profit or loss for the period, there should be a statement to that effect immediately below the profit and loss account.

Realised and unrealised gains – an example

A common example of a recognised gain which does not pass through the profit and loss account is an unrealised surplus on revaluation of fixed assets.

The double entry for revaluing a fixed asset upward is

		£	£
Dr	Fixed asset (at cost)	X	
Dr	Accumulated depreciation	X	
	Cr Revaluation reserve		X

It is not prudent to recognise the increase in value in the profit and loss account since it is unrealised. However, when the fixed asset is sold and the gain becomes realised it cannot then be reversed out of the statement of recognised gains and losses and included in the profit and loss account. The profit or loss on disposal must be calculated on the revalued amount.

Illustration

Bell Ltd revalued land costing £20,000 to £30,000. Three years later, it sold the land for £25,000.

The initial double-entry is:

Dr	Land at cost	£10,000	
	Cr Revaluation reserve		£10,000

at the time the revaluation takes place.

The unrealised gain of £10,000 is included in the statement of recognised gains and losses in the period in which the revaluation takes place.

The subsequent double-entry is :

Dr	Cash	£25,000	
Dr	Loss on disposal	£5,000	
	Cr Fixed assets		£30,000

at the time the disposal takes place. The £5,000 loss is recognised in the profit and loss account for the period in which the disposal takes place (as an exceptional item, if material).

The previous revaluation surplus of £10,000 will be transferred from the revaluation reserve to the profit and loss *reserve* as it is now realised. This will have no net effect on the statement of recognised gains and losses.

Without FRS3 it would be possible to account for the disposal as follows:

Dr	Cash	£25,000	
Dr	Revaluation reserve	£10,000	
	Cr	Fixed assets	£30,000
	Cr	Disposals	£5,000

which would give rise to a realised profit of £5,000 which would be included in the profit and loss account (this will, in fact, be disclosed in the note of historical cost profits).

Under FRS3 a net 'recognised gain' of £5,000 has been included in the statement of recognised gains and losses instead:

	£
Unrealised gain (when revalued)	10,000
Loss on disposal (through profit and loss)	(5,000)
	5,000

Disclosure

Pro forma statement of total recognised gains and losses

	19X3 £	19X2 (as restated) £
Profit for the financial year	X	X
Unrealised surplus on revaluation of properties	X	
Unrealised (loss)/gain on trade investment	(X)	X
Total recognised gains and losses relating to the year	X	X
Prior-period adjustment (as explained in note X)	(X)	
Total gains and losses recognised since last annual report	X	

There are two things to note:

- profit for the financial year is before dividends; and
- the disclosure of the prior-period adjustment.

Note also that the write-off of purchased goodwill to reserves is not a recognised gain or loss and should not be included in the statement.

NOTE OF HISTORICAL COST PROFITS AND LOSSES

FRS3 requires this note to be prepared where there is a material difference between an entity's result as disclosed in the profit and loss account and its result on the historical cost basis.

In practice, the note will normally be required where the accounts contain properties included at a valuation rather than at cost.

The note should include a reconciliation of the reported profit on ordinary activities before taxation to the historical cost profit on ordinary activities before taxation. The note should also show the retained profit for the financial year reported on the historical cost basis.

The note should be presented immediately following the profit and loss account or the statement of total recognised gains and losses.

Pro forma note of historical cost profits and losses

	£
Reported profit on ordinary activities before taxation	X
Realisation of property revaluation gains of previous years	X
Difference between a historical cost depreciation charge and the actual depreciation charge for the year calculated on the revalued amount	X
Historical cost profit on ordinary activities before taxation	X
Historical cost profit for the year retained after taxation, minority interests, extraordinary items and dividends	X

RECONCILIATION OF MOVEMENTS IN SHAREHOLDERS' FUNDS AND STATEMENT OF RESERVES

FRS3 requires a reconciliation of the opening and closing totals of shareholders' funds of the period.

Shareholders' funds include share capital and share premium as well as all reserves.

The purpose of this statement is to summarise all changes in net assets between the opening and closing balance sheets, including items which are not recognised gains and losses (eg. issues of shares).

The Companies Act requires a statement of reserves showing all movements on reserves in the year.

Reconciliation of movements in shareholders' funds

	£
Profit for the financial year	X
Dividends	(X)
	X
Other recognised gains and losses relating to the year (net) [#]	X
New share capital subscribed	X
Goodwill written off	(X)
Net addition to shareholders' funds	X
Opening shareholders' funds (£Y before prior year adjustment of £Z)	X
Closing shareholders' funds	X

[#] From the statement of total recognised gains and losses.

Statement of reserves (required by the Companies Act)

	Share premium account £	Revaluation reserve £	Profit and loss account £	Total* £
At beginning of year:				
As previously stated	X	X	X	X
Prior year adjustment			(X)	(X)
	—	—	—	—
As restated	X	X	X	X
Premium on issue of shares (nominal value £X)	X			X
Goodwill written off			(X)	(X)
Transfer from profit and loss account for the year			X	X
Decrease in value of trade investment		(X)		(X)
Surplus on property revaluations		X		X
Transfer of realised profits		(X)	X	
	—	—	—	—
At end of year	X	X	X	X
	—	—	—	—

* This is not strictly necessary under the Companies Act. Also, the Act does not require comparatives for the statement of reserves. FRS3 does however require a comparative for the reconciliation of movements in shareholders' funds.

Tutorial note: You will not be required to draft either the note of historical cost profits/losses or the statement of movements in shareholders' funds in the central assessment.

COMPREHENSIVE EXAMPLE

Extracts from the accounts of Lincoln Ltd for the year ended 31 December 19X7 are as follows:

Profit and loss account

	£'000
Profit on ordinary activities before taxation	50
Taxation	(10)
	—
Profit on ordinary activities after taxation	40
Dividends	(10)
	—
Retained profit for the year	30
	—

During the year, goodwill of £25,000 was written off directly to reserves. The profit and loss account reserve has been reduced by a prior year adjustment of £30,000.

Balance sheet

		19X7 £'000	19X6 £'000
Share capital		100	100
Revaluation reserve		335	235
Profit and loss account	(19X6 figure is after dealing with prior year adjustment)	145	70
		580	405

Fixed assets – land and buildings

	Valuation £'000	Historical Cost £'000
Cost/valuation		
At 1 January 19X7	500	250
Additions	75	75
Disposals	(130)	(55)
Revaluations	120	–
At 31 December 19X7	565	270
Depreciation		
At 1 January 19X7	45	40
Charge 15	5	
Disposals	(10)	(5)
Revaluations	(50)	–
At 31 December 19X7	–	40
Net book value at 31 December 19X7	565	230

Disposal proceeds amounted to £135,000.

Required

Prepare a statement of total recognised gains and losses, a note of historical cost profits and losses, a reconciliation of movements in shareholders' funds and a statement of reserves for the year ended 31 December 19X7.

Solution

Statement of total recognised gains and losses for the year ended 31 December 19X7

	£'000
Profit for the financial year	40
Unrealised surplus on revaluation of properties (120 + 50)	170
Total recognised gains and losses relating to the year	210
Prior year adjustment	(30)
Total gains and loss recognised since last annual report	180

Note of historical cost profits and losses

	19X7 £'000
Reported profit on ordinary activities before taxation	50
Realisation of property revaluation gains of previous years (W)	70
Difference between historical cost depreciation charge and the actual depreciation charge for the year calculated on the revalued amount (15 – 5)	10
Historical cost profit on ordinary activities before taxation	130
Historical cost profit for the year retained after taxation, minority interests and dividends	110

Reconciliation of movements in shareholders' funds

	19X7 £'000
Profit for the financial year	40
Dividends	(10)
	30
Other recognised gains and losses relating to the year	170
Goodwill written off	(25)
Net addition to shareholders' funds	175
Shareholders' funds at 1 January 19X7 (originally £435,000 before deducting prior year adjustment of £30,000)	405
Shareholders' funds at 31 December 19X7	580

Statement of reserves

	Revaluation reserve £'000	Profit and loss account £'000	Total £'000
At 1 January 19X7			
As previously stated	235	100	335
Prior year adjustment	–	(30)	(30)
As restated	235	70	305
Goodwill written off	–	(25)	(25)
Transfer from profit and loss account for the year	–	30	30
Surplus on property revaluations	170	–	170
Transfer of realised profits	(70)	70	–
At 31 December 19X7	335	145	480

Working

Realisation of property revaluation gains

	£'000
Valuation NBV (130 – 10)	120
Historic cost NBV (55 – 5)	50
	70

QUESTIONS

1 Collins plc

Collins plc, an established engineering company, has extracted the following trial balance at 31 March 19X2.

	£'000	£'000
Share capital: £1 ordinary shares		500
Share premium account		150
Profit and loss at 1 April 19X1		1,523
Capital redemption reserve		50
10% debentures, redeemable 19X9 (secured by floating charge)		300
Freehold land and buildings		
Cost	2,010	
Accumulated depreciation		60
Plant and machinery		
Cost	500	
Accumulated depreciation		210
Motor vehicles		
Cost	120	
Accumulated depreciation		50
Goodwill		
Cost	150	
Accumulated depreciation		10
Investment 25,000 £1 ordinary shares in Hollywood plc		
(a listed company)	30	
Stocks at 1 April 19X1		
Raw materials	50	
Work in progress	75	
Finished goods	150	
Creditors ledger control		210
Debtors ledger control	300	
Rates prepayment	4	
Cash in hand	2	
Bank overdraft		41
Wages accrual		2
Expenses accrual		6
Bank loan, repayable 19X5 (interest at 2% above base rate)		75
Sales		5,125
Purchases and factory wages	4,100	
Distribution costs	200	
Administrative expenses (including £300 political		
donation to Conservative Party)	610	
Debenture interest	30	
Dividend income		8
Bank interest		
Overdraft	5	
Loan	7	
Surplus on disposal of investment		30
Corporation tax	2	
Auditors' fees	5	
	8,350	8,350

The following additional information is relevant.

(1)   Stocks at 31 March 19X2 were:

	£
Raw materials	45,000
Work in progress	79,000
Finished goods	170,000

(2)   The directors received the following remuneration:

	£
Mr A (Chairman)	35,000
Mr B	22,000
Mr C	41,000
Mr D	15,000
Mr E	Nil

All the directors were additionally paid fees of £1,500 each and had pension contributions paid by the company on their behalf of £2,000 each. Mr D worked for the company overseas during the year, returning only for the monthly board meetings.

All emoluments have already been charged to the appropriate expense account.

(3)   Corporation tax of £25,000 is to be provided (calculated at 33%); the existing balance is due to an underprovision in the previous year.

(4)   Depreciation has already been provided as follows:

	£	Estimated useful economic life
Land	Nil	–
Buildings	10,000	50 years
Plant and machinery	35,000	20 years
Motor vehicles	20,000	5 years
Goodwill	7,500	20 years

(5)   During the year, plant was purchased for £20,000, and freehold land and buildings for £1,000,000. A holding of Dynasty plc, a listed company, classified as a fixed asset investment was bought for £42,000 and sold for £72,000 during the year. Tax of £9,000 is payable on the surplus. This is in addition to that provided in (3) above.

(6)   Staff (including directors) were employed during the year as follows:

	Factory	Distribution	Administrative
Average number employed	120	10	35
Wages and salaries	£1,140,000	£82,000	£267,000
Pension contributions	£210,000	£16,000	£50,000

All staff costs have already been charged to the appropriate expense account.

(7)   All directors have held 20,000 shares in the company throughout the year.

(8)   There was an issue of 150,000 shares at £2 during the year to fund the purchase of land and buildings.

Required

(a)   Prepare the profit and loss account and related notes.
(b)   Prepare the balance sheet and related notes.
(c)   Prepare the accounting policies note.

Prepare the above in a form suitable for presentation to the members.

Ignore advance corporation tax and income tax.

2   Claret

Claret Ltd has an issued share capital of 2,000,000 50p ordinary shares all of which were issued at par on incorporation.

The balance on the profit and loss account at 1 January 19X8 was £20,658,000 and the draft retained profit for the year was £1,825,000.   The directors had decided to propose a dividend of £250,000 for the year.

At 1 January 19X8 the balance on the revaluation reserve was £83,000.   On 31 December 19X8 a property was revalued to £430,000.   It was purchased on 1 January 19X1 for £650,000 and is being depreciated over 20 years.

During the year the company issued 160,000 50p ordinary shares at a market price of 210p per share.   The share issue was to help finance the purchase of an unincorporated business. The total purchase consideration was £370,000 and the business had the following net assets at the date of acquisition:

	£'000
Tangible fixed assets	165
Net current assets	95
	260

The directors of Claret Ltd feel that the business had £10,000 of doubtful debts at the date of acquisition which had not been provided for.

After the preparation of the draft accounts had been completed, it was discovered that the method of valuing closing stock had been incorrectly applied for the last three years resulting in the following overvaluations of stock.

	£'000
At 31 December 19X6	40
At 31 December 19X7	55
At 31 December 19X8	62

Required

Prepare the following extracts from the financial statements of Claret Ltd as at 31 December 19X8:

(a)   statement of total recognised gains and losses;

(b)   note on reconciliation of shareholders' funds.

Ignore the requirement to produce comparative figures.

SUMMARY

The key points to learn are:

- Exceptional items arise from the ordinary activities of the business, whereas extraordinary items do not. Extraordinary items are extremely rare.

- Prior period adjustments are necessary in only two situations:

    –   changes in accounting policies; and
    –   correction of fundamental errors.

- Items must be material.

You must learn how to prepare the following:

- Statement of total recognised gains and losses (a primary statement)

- Statement of reserves

You must also be aware of the nature and content of the following:

- Note of historical cost profits and losses

- Reconciliation of movements in shareholders' funds

Fixed assets: tangible assets

SSAP12: ACCOUNTING FOR DEPRECIATION

Introduction

Fixed assets are those assets which are intended for use on a continuing basis in the enterprise's activities.

SSAP12 covers all fixed assets other than:

- investment properties, which are dealt with in SSAP19;
- goodwill, which is dealt with in SSAP22;
- development costs, which are dealt with in SSAP13;
- investments.

Most fixed assets wear out or become obsolete. The purpose of depreciation is to reflect this wearing out by making a charge against income for a business, thereby matching the cost of the asset with the revenue it generates. This is an example of the *accruals concept*, which is one of the four fundamental accounting concepts contained in SSAP2.

Definitions

Depreciation is the measure of the wearing out, consumption or other reduction in the useful economic life of a fixed asset whether arising from use, effluxion of time or obsolescence through technological or market changes.

The useful economic life of an asset is the period over which the present owner will derive economic benefits from its use.

Allocation

Depreciation should be allocated to accounting periods so as to charge a fair proportion of the cost of the asset to each accounting period expected to benefit from its use.

In practice, it is necessary to consider:

- The carrying amount of the asset.

  This could be historic cost or a valuation.

- The length of an asset's expected useful economic life to the business.
  This life may be:

– predetermined, as with a lease;
– directly governed by extraction or consumption, as in a mine or quarry;
– dependent on its physical deterioration through use or age;
– reduced by economic or technological obsolescence.

- The estimated residual value of the asset at the end of its useful economic life.

The annual depreciation charge for a fixed asset would then be obtained by allocating the **depreciable amount** over the useful economic life of the asset, where;

Depreciable amount = Cost (or valuation) less estimated residual value

It might be expected that, at this stage, the standard would consider the various accounting bases for depreciation: for example, straight-line, reducing-balance, machine-hours and unit depletion. However, there is no such consideration, the task being imposed upon management to 'select the method regarded as most appropriate to the type of asset and its use in the business'.

The methods of depreciation most commonly used in practice are:

- straight-line;
- reducing balance.

Asset lives

The length of a fixed asset's life is clearly a very important number in a depreciation calculation. However it is an estimate, as it is necessary to make predictions about the future.

SSAP12 states that asset lives must be estimated on a *realistic* basis.

Asset lives should be reviewed regularly and, when necessary, revised. If an asset life is changed, the accounting treatment is to write off the net book amount over the revised remaining useful economic life.

Illustration

A moulding machine cost £50,000 on 1 January 19X1 and at the date of purchase had an estimated useful economic life of ten years. Its estimated residual value is £Nil.

Initially the annual depreciation charge is:

$$\frac{£50,000}{10 \text{ years}} = £5,000 \text{ pa}$$

At 31 December 19X4 the machine would be stated in the accounts at:

	£
Cost	50,000
Less: Accumulated depreciation (four years @ £5,000)	(20,000)
Net book value	30,000

It has a remaining useful economic life of six years.
In 19X5 the management decided that the machine was wearing out more rapidly than expected and revised its remaining useful life down to three years.

Therefore, the new annual depreciation charge is:

$$\frac{£30,000}{3 \text{ years}} = £10,000 \text{ pa}$$

At 31 December 19X5 the machine would be included in the accounts at:

	£
Cost	50,000
Less: Accumulated depreciation (£20,000 + £10,000)	(30,000)
Net book value	20,000

Permanent diminution in value

If there is a permanent diminution in the value of a fixed asset and the net book amount is considered not to be recoverable in full, the net book amount should be written down immediately to the estimated recoverable amount.

Having written off the fall in value, continue to depreciate the remaining balance over the asset's remaining useful economic life.

Recoverable amount is defined as the greater of the net realisable value of an asset and, where appropriate, the amount recoverable from its further use.

Change in method of depreciation

A change of method, say from machine-hour rate to straight-line, is only allowed where the 'new method will give a fairer presentation of the results and of the financial position'.

While this seems reasonable, the accounting treatment of the change of method does not. Following FRS3 (see Session 9) you would expect that the effect of the change of method on the amount of the depreciation accumulated up to the beginning of the accounting period in which the change is made, would be treated as a change of accounting policy and therefore as a prior-year adjustment and adjusted against the reserves brought forward. This is *not* the case, since SSAP12 requires that only the year in which the change is made and later years should be affected by the change, with disclosure in the year of change of the effect, if material.

Illustration

Ford plc makes up its accounts to 31 December each year. On 1 January 19X0, it bought a machine for £100,000, and started depreciating it at 15% per annum, on the reducing-balance basis. On 31 December 19X3 the machine would be included in Ford plc's accounts at:

	£
Cost	100,000
Accumulated depreciation	47,800
Net book value	52,200

During 19X4, the company decided to change the basis of depreciation to straight-line, over 10 years.

In accordance with SSAP12 the unamortised cost at 1 January 19X4 of £52,200 must be written off over the six years remaining of the ten-year life.

The new annual charge will be:

$$\frac{£52,200}{6 \text{ years}} = £8,700 \text{ per annum}$$

- Balance sheet presentation would be:

	19X4	19X3 (not restated)
	£	£
Cost	100,000	100,000
Accumulated depreciation	56,500	47,800
Net book value	43,500	52,200

- Profit and loss account would show:

(i) Charge for the year   £8,700

(ii) **Note:** As a result of the change in depreciation policy from 15% reducing balance to 10% straight-line, the charge for depreciation is £870 (£8,700 – 15% × £52,200) higher than it would otherwise have been.

Revaluations

It is common practice for companies to include fixed assets in their historical cost accounts at their current values, rather than original cost.

Depreciation of such assets should be based on the revalued amounts and the remaining useful economic lives.

Illustration

Ferrari plc bought an office building with a 50-year lease, on 1 January 19X1, for £3 million. The company's accounting policy is that depreciation is provided for on the straight-line method over the useful lives of the assets.

Five years later, on 1 January 19X6, the office block has a market value of £4.5 million. Ferrari plc decide to incorporate this into their financial statements. At 31 December 19X5 the office building would be stated in the accounts at historical cost less related depreciation.

	£
Cost	3,000,000
Accumulated depreciation (3,000,000 ÷ 50 for 5 years)	300,000
Net book value	2,700,000

If the revaluation takes place on 1 January 19X6, to incorporate the valuation in the company's books it is necessary to increase the cost of the building to valuation and write back any accumulated depreciation. The corresponding credit entries are to a revaluation reserve. The double-entry is:

		£	£
Dr	Fixed assets – cost	1,500,000	
Dr	Fixed assets – accumulated depreciation	300,000	
Cr	Revaluation reserve		1,800,000

If accounts are prepared on 1 January 19X6, the building will be included at £4,500,000.

The depreciation charge for 19X6 will be based on this value and the remaining useful life of the building, ie:

$$\frac{£4,500,000}{45 \text{ years}} = £100,000$$

Buildings and land

It was common accounting practice prior to the issue of the standard for no depreciation to be provided on buildings on the grounds that market value exceeded net book value in the balance sheet. The standard takes the view that because buildings are no different from other fixed assets in that they have a limited useful economic life, albeit usually significantly longer than that of other types of assets, they should be depreciated having regard to the same criteria.

Freehold land does not normally require a provision for depreciation, unless it is subject to depletion, for example by the extraction of minerals.

Disclosure requirements of SSAP12

- An accounting policy note giving details of the depreciation methods used and useful economic lives or depreciation rates, for each major class of fixed asset.

  A typical depreciation note:

  Depreciation on property and equipment, excluding freehold land, is provided for on the straight-line method based upon the estimated useful lives of the various assets as follows:

	Estimated useful life
Freehold buildings	60 years
Short leasehold property	life of lease
Plant and machinery	5 to 10 years
Fixtures and fittings	5 to 10 years
Motor vehicles	5 years

- Total depreciation charged for the year. This information is normally shown in the note:

  Operating profit is stated after charging:

	£
Depreciation on tangible fixed assets	X

- The gross amount of depreciable assets and the related accumulated depreciation. This information is included in the standard fixed asset note to the balance sheet which is required by the Companies Act 1985.

- A note explaining the reason and effect of a change in the method of depreciation.

- Where assets have been revalued, the effect of the revaluation on the depreciation charge should be disclosed in the year of revaluation.

Where fixed assets have been revalued, the financial statements are prepared under the **alternative accounting rules** rather than the historical cost accounting rules. Under these rules CA 1985 requires the following extra disclosures in the notes to the balance sheet:

- the corresponding historical cost amount and, if relevant, accumulated depreciation, or the difference between the historical cost amount and the amount included in the balance sheet;

- the years in which the assets were valued and the various values;

- in the case of assets valued during the year, the names of the valuers or particulars of their qualifications and the bases of valuation used.

SSAP19: ACCOUNTING FOR INVESTMENT PROPERTIES

It has been seen that property held for its investment potential was exempted from the SSAP12 requirement of depreciation. SSAP19 was developed to cover the specific problem of investment properties.

Definition

An investment property is an interest in land and/or buildings:

- in respect of which construction work and development have been *completed*; and
- which is held for its *investment potential*, any rental income being negotiated at arm's length.

The following are exceptions from the definition:

- a property which is owned and occupied by a company for its own purposes is not an investment property;

- a property let to and occupied by another group company is not an investment property for the purposes of its own accounts or the group accounts.

Principles

In broad terms, the standard requires investment properties to be included in the balance sheet at their open market value and any surplus or deficit on revaluation to be reported as a movement on an 'investment revaluation reserve'. In practice this means that investment properties are revalued annually.

Treatment of revaluation surpluses and deficits

The period's net revaluation surplus (deficit) should be credited (debited) to an investment revaluation reserve. It should not be dealt with in the profit and loss account. Changes in market value are shown in the statement of total recognised gains and losses. The exception to this is where a revaluation deficit on an individual property is expected to be permanent. In this case, the full amount of the deficit should be charged in the profit and loss account for the period. This would be disclosed as an exceptional item in accordance with FRS3, if material.

Depreciation

SSAP19 requires that investment properties should not be depreciated. The exception is that properties held on lease with an unexpired period not exceeding 20 years should be amortised over the remaining useful life. This is because shorter leases lose value through the effluxion of time and therefore should be depreciated through the profit and loss account in accordance with SSAP12. This would additionally mean that the rents receivable from the property are matched with the associated cost (loss in value of the property) in the profit and loss account in accordance with SSAP2.

Example

Centreblock plc has three freehold investment properties, each of which originally cost £1m. At 31 December 19X1, the open market value of the properties was as follows:

	£'000
Property 1	*1,250*
Property 2	*1,100*
Property 3	*750*
	3,100

Before accounting for these valuations, the carrying value of the properties was £3,150,000 and the credit balance on the investment revaluation reserve was £150,000. The fall in value of property 3 has arisen because of technical obsolescence and is expected to be permanent. Prior to this valuation, property 3 had been included in the balance sheet at £1,050,000.

Required

Show the journal to incorporate the valuations into the accounts for the year ending 31 December 19X1.

Solution

			£'000	£'000
Dr	Profit and loss account for year (750 – 1,050) (permanent diminution for property 3)		300	
Cr	Investment revaluation reserve (2,350 – 2,100) (gain on properties 1 and 2)			250*
Cr	Fixed assets: Investment properties (3,100 – 3,150)			50

* = included in statement of total recognised gains and losses

Previous surplus on property 3 can be transferred to the profit and loss reserve as a reserve movement (not affecting earnings):

		£'000	£'000
Dr	Investment revaluation reserve	50	
Cr	Profit and loss reserve		50

Key disclosures

- Names or qualifications of valuers and basis of valuation used.

- If the valuer is an employee or officer of the company or group, the notes must state this.

- Display prominently in the accounts:

  - the carrying value of investment properties; and
  - the investment revaluation reserve.

Investment properties are usually shown as a separate category of tangible fixed asset.

Companies Act 1985 and SSAP19

The Companies Act 1985 requires that all fixed assets with a limited useful economic life should be systematically depreciated over that life. The application of SSAP19 obviously is a departure from this requirement in order to give a true and fair view, which is permissible under the Act. However, particulars of the departure, the reasons for it and its effect should be given in a note to the accounts.

Additionally, since investment properties are not carried at a figure based on cost, the Act requires that the following be disclosed by way of note:

- the corresponding historical cost amount and, if relevant, accumulated depreciation; or

- the difference between the historical cost amount and the amount included in the balance sheet.

SSAP4: ACCOUNTING FOR GOVERNMENT GRANTS

Introduction

Government grants are available in various forms. The two most common are:

- grants to cover all or part of the cost of specific capital expenditure, for example, on particular fixed assets (capital-based grants);

- grants to cover all or part of specific expenses, for example, on a particular project (revenue-based grants)

Government grants include grants from local government agencies and EC bodies.

Accounting for grants (particularly capital-based grants) may present two problems:

- the grant must be matched with the expenditure towards which it is intended to contribute (applying the accruals concept);

- the grant should not be recognised until the business has complied with any conditions for its receipt (applying the prudence concept).

Capital-based grants

Grants must be matched with the expenditure to which they are intended to contribute. Expenditure on fixed assets appears in the profit and loss account as depreciation. This means that a grant received to finance the purchase of a fixed asset must be matched with the depreciation charged in respect of that asset.

Illustration

Nissan plc purchases a fixed asset for £6,000 in 19X5 and receives a 20% government grant. The asset has an expected life of three years at the end of which it is expected to have nil scrap value.

Solution

Treat the amount of the grant as a deferred credit, a portion of which is transferred to revenue annually. The deferred credit is shown under accruals and deferred income in the balance sheet.

Profit and loss account	*19X5*	*19X6*	*19X7*
	£	£	£
Depreciation charge	2,000	2,000	2,000
Related government grant credit	(400)	(400)	(400)

Balance sheet at end of year	*19X5*	*19X6*	*19X7*
	£	£	£
Fixed assets: Cost	6,000	6,000	6,000
Less: Accumulated depreciation	2,000	4,000	6,000
Net book value	4,000	2,000	–
Accruals and deferred income			
Government grants	(800)	(400)	–

Revenue-based grants

The general principle is that the grant must be matched, as far as possible, with the expenditure to which it relates.

Grants made:

- to give immediate financial support or assistance to an enterprise; or
- to reimburse costs previously incurred

should be recognised in the profit and loss account of the period in which they become *receivable*.

Grants made:

- to finance the general activities of an enterprise over a specific period; or
- to compensate for a loss of current or future income

should be recognised in the profit and loss account of the period in respect of which they are *paid*.

In practice, this may mean that a debtor or creditor must be set up if the grant is actually received in a different period from the one in which the expenditure is incurred.

Prudence

A grant should not be recognised in the profit and loss account until all conditions for its receipt have been complied with and there is reasonable assurance that the grant will be received.

Occasionally, there may still be a potential liability to repay a grant in the future. For example, if a grant is received in respect of building work, one of the conditions might be that the building should not be sold within a certain period of time. A provision should be made where repayment is probable. This should be set off against any unamortised deferred credit and any excess charged in the profit and loss account immediately.

Disclosure

Disclosure of the following matters is required by SSAP4 (revised):

- the accounting policy adopted for government grants;

- the effects of government grants on the results for the period and the financial position of the enterprise;

- where material assistance has been received by forms of government assistance other than grants, details of that assistance;

- potential liabilities to repay grants, in accordance with SSAP18.

QUESTIONS

1 Ford plc

The following fixed asset balances have been extracted from the books of Ford plc as at 31 December 19X7.

	£'000	£'000
Freehold factory cost at 1 January 19X7	1,440	
Freehold factory revaluation	760	
Freehold factory additions	500	
Freehold factory depreciation at 1 January 19X7		144
Freehold factory revaluation adjustment	144	
Freehold factory depreciation charge		60
Plant and machinery cost at 1 January 19X7	1,968	
Plant and machinery additions	75	
Plant and machinery depreciation at 1 January 19X7		257
Plant and machinery depreciation charge		233
Motor vehicles cost at 1 January 19X7	449	
Motor vehicles additions	35	
Motor vehicles depreciation at 1 January 19X7		194
Motor vehicles depreciation charge		87
Office equipment and fixtures cost at 1 January 19X7	888	
Office equipment and fixtures additions	22	
Office equipment and fixtures depreciation at 1 January 19X7		583
Office equipment and fixtures depreciation charge		182

You are given the following information for the year ended 31 December 19X7:

(1) The factory was acquired in March 19X2 and is being depreciated over 50 years.

(2) At 1 January 19X7, depreciation was provided on cost on a straight-line basis. The rates used were 20% for office equipment and fixtures, 25% for motor vehicles and 10% for plant and machinery.

(3) Early in the year the factory was revalued to an open market value of £2.2 million and an extension was built costing £500,000.

(4) During the year the directors decided to change the method of depreciating motor vehicles to 30% reducing balance to give a fairer presentation of the results and of the financial position. The effect of this change was to reduce the depreciation charge for the year by £34,000.

(5) It is the company's policy to charge a full year's depreciation in the year of acquisition.

Required

Prepare the disclosure notes for fixed assets for the year ended 31 December 19X7 required by SSAP12 and CA 1985.

2 Cribbage plc

On 31 December 19X0, Cribbage plc bought two freehold properties, Bramley Rise and Bramley Towers, which it intends to hold as investment properties. The cost of Bramley Rise was £500,000 and of Bramley Towers £700,000.

In subsequent years, the valuation of the two properties was as follows:

At 31 December	19X1 £'000	19X2 £'000	19X3 £'000
Bramley Rise	560	580	540
Bramley Towers	750	680	640

Required

Show how the above properties and revaluation surpluses/deficits would be reflected in the financial statements for the years ended 31 December 19X1– 19X3. Assume that any diminutions in value are to be treated as temporary.

SUMMARY

SSAP12

- Annual depreciation charge is calculated by allocating cost less residual value over a fixed asset's useful economic life.

- If the life of an asset is revised, you must write off the existing net book amount over the revised remaining useful life.

- Where there is a permanent diminution in the value of a fixed asset, the net book amount should be written down immediately to the estimated recoverable amount.

- A change in the method of depreciation is permitted, if it presents a fairer picture. It is not treated as a prior-year adjustment.

- When assets are revalued, the depreciation charge should be based on the revalued amount.

- Land is not normally depreciated.

SSAP19

- Investment properties should be revalued each year to their open market value.

- Any surplus or deficit on revaluation is to be reported as a movement on an 'investment revaluation reserve'.

SSAP4

- Grants should be recognised in the profit and loss account in order to match them with the expenditure towards which they are intended to contribute.

- A capital-based grant should be credited to revenue over the useful life of the asset concerned, usually by setting up a deferred credit, which is transferred to revenue over the same length of time as the asset is depreciated.

Fixed assets: intangible assets

SSAP13: ACCOUNTING FOR RESEARCH AND DEVELOPMENT

Introduction

It has proved extremely difficult to standardise the accounting treatment of research and development (R & D) expenditure, because this is an area where two fundamental accounting concepts, accruals and prudence, come into head-on conflict.

From one point of view, R & D expenditure is incurred for the future development of business, with a view to decreasing future costs or increasing future revenue. The accruals concept would therefore have R & D expenditure which leads to reduced costs or increased sales carried forward and written off over all the accounting periods which benefit from that expenditure.

On the other hand, it can be argued that it is impossible to be certain of the future benefits of R & D expenditure, since some projects may be abortive and others may result in lower than anticipated benefits. Therefore, in accordance with the prudence concept, all such expenditure should be written off in the year in which it is incurred.

SSAP13 gives guidance regarding the appropriate accounting treatment for R & D expenditure and sets out disclosure requirements.

Definitions

The SSAP classifies R & D expenditure in the following broad categories:

- *Pure (or basic) research* – experimental or theoretical work undertaken primarily to acquire new scientific or technical knowledge for its own sake rather than directed towards any specific aim or application.

- *Applied research* – original or critical investigation undertaken in order to gain new scientific or technical knowledge and directed towards a specific practical aim or objective.

- *Development* – use of scientific or technical knowledge in order to produce new or substantially improved materials, devices, products or services, to install new processes or systems prior to the commencement of commercial applications, or to improve substantially those already produced or installed.

Exceptions

Research and development expenditure as defined by SSAP13 does *not* include:

- Expenditure incurred in locating and exploiting oil, gas and mineral deposits in the extractive industries.

- Situations where companies enter into a firm contract:

  - to carry out development work on behalf of third parties on such terms that the related expenditure is to be fully reimbursed; or

  - to develop and manufacture at an agreed price calculated to reimburse expenditure on development as well as on manufacture.

Accounting treatment

- *Fixed assets* – The cost of fixed assets acquired or constructed in order to provide facilities for research and development activities over a number of accounting periods should be capitalised and written off through the profit and loss account over their useful economic lives. Depreciation will be calculated in accordance with SSAP12 and such depreciation may itself form part of development expenditure (covered below) which could be carried forward to later periods.

- *Other expenditure* – Expenditure on pure and applied research (other than on fixed assets) should be written off through the profit and loss account in the year of expenditure.

In general, the standard requires that development expenditure should also be written off in the year of expenditure. However, development expenditure can be deferred to future periods if *all* the following criteria are met:

- There is a clearly defined project.

- The related expenditure is separately identifiable.

- The outcome of such a project has been assessed with reasonable certainty as to:

  - its technical feasibility;

  - its ultimate commercial viability considered in the light of factors such as likely market conditions (including competing products), public opinion, consumer and environmental legislation.

- The aggregate of the deferred development costs, any further development costs and related production, selling and administration costs is reasonably expected to be exceeded by related future sales or other revenues.

- Adequate resources exist, or are reasonably expected to be available, to enable the project to be completed and to provide any consequential increases in working capital.

Development expenditure which has been deferred is included in the balance sheet as an intangible fixed asset and amortised.

Amortisation

SSAP13 states that, if development costs are deferred to future periods, they should be amortised. The amortisation should start with the commercial production or application of the product, service, process or system and should be allocated on a systematic basis to each accounting period, by reference to either (i) the sale or use of the product, service, process or system, or (ii) the period over which these are expected to be sold or used.

Illustration

A company has incurred development expenditure of £250,000 in relation to product X. This development expenditure meets all the criteria for deferral laid down in SSAP13.

Production of product X has now commenced and sales are expected to take place as follows:

	Number of units
19X1	75,000
19X2	150,000
19X3	75,000

After 19X3 sales are expected to decline dramatically.

The deferred development expenditure will be amortised as follows:

	Charge £
19X1 (75/300 × £250,000)	62,500
19X2 (150/300 × £250,000)	125,000
19X3 (75/300 × £250,000)	62,500

The note to the balance sheet will appear as follows:

Intangible fixed assets – development costs

	19X1 £	*19X2* £	*19X3* £
Cost at beginning and end of year	250,000	250,000	250,000
Amortisation			
At beginning of year	–	62,500	187,500
Charge for year	62,500	125,000	62,500
At end of year	62,500	187,500	250,000
Net book value at end of year	187,500	62,500	–
Net book value at beginning of year	250,000	187,500	62,500

Deferred development expenditure for each project should be reviewed at the end of each accounting period and, where the circumstances which have justified the deferral of the expenditure no longer apply or are considered doubtful, the expenditure should be written off immediately, project by project, to the extent to which it is considered to be irrecoverable .

Disclosure

- The accounting policy on R & D expenditure should be stated and explained.

- The total amount of R & D expenditure charged in the profit and loss account should be disclosed, analysed between the current year's expenditure and amounts amortised from deferred expenditure.

- Movements on deferred development expenditure and the amount carried forward at the beginning and the end of the period should be disclosed.

- Deferred development expenditure should be disclosed under intangible fixed assets in the balance sheet.

Scope

The disclosure requirement outlined above applies only to the following:

- public limited companies; special category companies (ie. banking, insurance, shipping companies); holding companies with a plc or special category company as a subsidiary;

- companies that exceed the criteria, multiplied by 10, for defining a medium-sized company (S248 CA 1985).

All the other requirements of SSAP13 apply to all financial statements intended to give a true and fair view.

SSAP22: ACCOUNTING FOR GOODWILL

Nature and meaning of goodwill

The value of a business as a whole will often be different from the total value of its individual net assets. The difference, which may be positive or negative, is described as *goodwill*.

Goodwill is therefore, by definition, incapable of realisation separately from the business as a whole; that is, you cannot sell off pieces of goodwill in a business. This characteristic of goodwill distinguishes it from all other items in the accounts.

Definitions

Goodwill is the difference between the value of a business as a whole and the aggregate of the fair values of its separable net assets.

Separable net assets are those assets (and liabilities) which can be identified and sold (or discharged) separately without necessarily disposing of the business as a whole.

Separable net assets are not purely tangible assets; they can include identifiable intangibles such as concessions, patents, licences and trade marks.

There are two types of goodwill:

- *purchased goodwill* is goodwill which is established as a result of the purchase of a business;
- *non-purchased goodwill* is any goodwill other than purchased goodwill.

Other phrases which you need to understand are:

Fair value – the amount for which an asset (or liability) could be exchanged in an arm's length transaction.

Useful economic life of purchased goodwill – the best estimate of the life of such goodwill at the date of purchase.

Other points to consider are that:

- the value of goodwill has no reliable or predictable relationship to any costs which may have been incurred;

- individual intangible factors which may contribute to goodwill cannot be valued;

- the value of goodwill may fluctuate widely according to internal and external circumstances over relatively short periods of time; and

- the assessment of the value of goodwill is highly subjective.

Therefore, any amount attributed to goodwill is unique to the valuer and to the specific point in time at which it is measured, and is only valid at that time and in the circumstances then prevailing.

There is no difference in character between purchased goodwill and non-purchased goodwill. However, the value of purchased goodwill, although arising from a subjective valuation of the business, is established as a fact at a particular point in time by a market transaction; this is not true of non-purchased goodwill which, while it may be presumed to exist, has not been evidenced in a purchase transaction.

Factors which may contribute to goodwill

There are many practical reasons why positive goodwill arises such as:

- market dominance arising from the purchase;
- superior management;
- strategic location;
- excellent reputation of products or service.

Accounting treatment of goodwill

- *Non-purchased goodwill*: No amount should be attributed to non-purchased goodwill in the balance sheets of companies or groups. This has always been the case. SSAP22 was issued to standardise the treatment of purchased goodwill.

- *Purchased goodwill*: Two alternative treatments are permissible here. We can examine these by means of an illustration.

Illustration

Suppose that Harvey acquires the business of Wallbanger for £250,000 in cash. Immediately prior to the purchase, the balance sheets of the two businesses can be summarised as follows:

	Harvey £	*Wallbanger* £
Tangible fixed assets	750,000	130,000
Net current assets	350,000	70,000
Capital and reserves	1,100,000	200,000

We can also assume that the book values of Wallbanger's assets are equal to their current market value (or fair value).

Therefore Harvey has paid £250,000 for a business whose separable net assets reach a total of just £200,000. It is clear that the difference paid represents goodwill of £50,000.

If Harvey now pools the Wallbanger assets in its balance sheet, it should appear as follows:

	£
Purchased goodwill	50,000
Tangible fixed assets £(750,000 + 130,000)	880,000
Net current assets £(350,000 + 70,000 – 250,000)	170,000
Capital and reserves	1,100,000

Clearly Harvey has acquired purchased goodwill from Wallbanger. It is also probable that Harvey's business contains some goodwill, but this cannot be disclosed in the balance sheet, since it represents non-purchased goodwill.

How should this purchased goodwill which Harvey has bought be dealt with in its accounts?

Option 1

One method is to adopt the approach used in the above example. The purchased goodwill bought by Harvey is carried in the balance sheet, just like any other capital asset. It is argued that Harvey has paid cash in exchange for an asset and, as such, the goodwill represents a real asset. However, should the goodwill not be depreciated in Harvey's balance sheet just like other fixed assets?

SSAP22 allows this treatment, providing that the company writes off the goodwill through its profit and loss account over its useful economic life. It is certainly not permissible to carry goodwill in the balance sheet for an indefinite period as a permanent item.

Option 2

Another method is to eliminate goodwill from the accounts by immediately writing it off, which is consistent with the accepted practice of excluding non-purchased goodwill from the accounts. The immediate write-off of purchased goodwill should be made against reserves, *not* as a charge to the profit and loss account. This follows the concept of prudence, particularly given the characteristics of goodwill, as an asset which is often difficult to measure.

This is the treatment preferred by SSAP22.

In our illustration, the balance sheet of Harvey after the acquisition of Wallbanger would have looked as follows:

	£
Tangible fixed assets (as before)	880,000
Net current assets (as before)	170,000
Capital and reserves	1,050,000

Capital and reserves is made up as follows:

	£
Reserves brought forward	1,100,000
Less: Purchased goodwill written off	(50,000)
	1,050,000

- *Negative purchased goodwill*: Any excess of the aggregate of the fair values of the separable net assets acquired over the fair value of the consideration given (negative goodwill) should be credited directly to reserves. This could arise in practice where the vendor wanted a quick sale and therefore accepted a low price in return.

Disclosure

The accounting policy followed in respect of goodwill should be explained in the notes to the accounts. Goodwill arising on any acquisitions in the year should be shown separately for each acquisition if material.

Where positive goodwill is being amortised over its useful economic life, it should be shown as a separate item under intangible assets in the balance sheet until fully written off.

The following should also be disclosed:

- The movement on the goodwill account, showing cost, accumulated amortisation and net book value at the beginning and end of the year.

- The amount of goodwill amortised through the profit and loss account during the year.

- The period selected and the reasons for selecting that period for amortising the goodwill relating to each major acquisition.
- Separate disclosure of the fair value of the consideration and the amount of purchased goodwill arising on each acquisition during the period, including the method of dealing with goodwill.

- Provision of a table showing the book value of each major category of assets and liabilities as in the records of the acquired company. Any differences between these book values and the fair values should be explained and analysed between:

    - revaluations;
    - provisions for future trading losses;
    - other provisions;
    - adjustments to bring accounting policies into line with those of the acquiring group;

-   any other major item.

• Analysis of movements on provisions related to acquisitions, including details of the extent to which the provisions have proved unnecessary.

• When a business that has been acquired is sold, disclose:

-   the profit or loss on disposal;

-   the amount of purchased goodwill attributable to the business sold and how it has been treated in calculating the profit or loss on the disposal.

QUESTIONS

1   Newprods Ltd

During the course of a year, Newprods Ltd incurred expenditure on many research and development activities. Details of three of them are given below.

Project 3   To develop a new compound in view of the anticipated shortage of a raw material currently being used in one of the company's processes. Sufficient progress has been made to suggest that the new compound can be produced at a cost comparable to that of the existing raw material.

Project 4   To improve the yield of an important manufacturing operation of the company. At present, material input with a cost of £100,000 pa becomes contaminated in the operation and half is wasted. Sufficient progress has been made for the scientists to predict an improvement so that only 20% will be wasted.

Project 5   To carry out work, as specified by a creditworthy client, to attempt to bring a proposed aerospace product of that client into line with safety regulations.

Costs during the year

	Project		
	3	*4*	*5*
	£	£	£
Staff salaries	5,000	10,000	20,000
Overheads	6,000	12,000	24,000
Plant at cost (life of ten years)	10,000	20,000	5,000

Required

(a)   Define the following:

   (i)   pure research expenditure;
   (ii)   applied research expenditure;
   (iii)   development expenditure.

(b)   State the circumstances in which it may be appropriate to carry forward research and development expenditure to future periods.

(c)   Show how the expenditure on projects 3, 4 and 5 would be dealt with in the balance sheet and profit and loss account in accordance with SSAP13.

2   Gill Wood Ltd

During 19X7, Gill Wood Ltd made the acquisition of an unincorporated business (purchase price £40,000 cash and 60,000 £1 ordinary shares which at the date of issue are valued at £2.40 each). The fair value of the separable net assets of the business at the date of acquisition was:

	£
Land and buildings	80,000
Plant and machinery	70,000
Stocks	10,500
Debtors	8,090
	168,590

The liabilities were discharged by the previous proprietor.

Required

(a)   Define *purchased goodwill*.

(b)   Calculate the amount of goodwill which will arise in the accounts of Gill Wood Ltd in 19X7 and state how it will be dealt with.

3   Woodpecker Ltd   **(AAT Pilot CA D94)**

A client of your firm, Woodpecker Ltd, a wholesale builders' merchant, has recently lost its financial accountant and has asked the firm to provide assistance in drafting the financial statements of the company for the year ended 31 March 1994. The accountant who left the company has produced an extended trial balance, which includes some of the normal year-end adjustments and gathered some further information which may be relevant to the year-end accounts. You have been asked by one of the partners of the firm to take on the task.

The extended trial balance of Woodpecker Ltd is set out after the following further information:

(1)   The authorised share capital of the company is as follows:

    4,000,000 ordinary shares of 25p each
    500,000 10% preference shares of £1 each

At the beginning of the year 1,600,000 shares were in issue (all were fully paid). A further 800,000 shares were issued during the year at a price of 75p per share. The whole of the proceeds of the issue, which were received in full, was credited to the ordinary share capital account.

(2)   The directors decided that instead of paying a dividend to ordinary shareholders they would make a bonus issue of shares at the year-end. Ordinary shareholders received one ordinary share of 25p for every six ordinary shares held by them at the year-end. No entries have been made in the extended trial balance to reflect this issue.

(3)   The interim dividend in the trial balance represents a dividend paid to preference shareholders. It has been decided to provide for the full preference dividend in the year-end accounts but no entry has yet been made to reflect this decision.

(4) No interest on the debentures has been paid during the year or provided for in the extended trial balance.

(5) The investment property shown in the extended trial balance at a value of £800,000 represents an office building purchased by the company as an investment. It has been revalued by J Wheeler and Co, a firm of chartered surveyors, at £600,000 based on its value, given its current use. The valuation has not been reflected in the extended trial balance.

(6) Audit fees of £25,000 have not been paid or provided for in the extended trial balance.

(7) The corporation tax charge for the year has been calculated as £275,000.

(8) The balance on the goodwill account arose out of the purchase of an unincorporated business some years ago. The goodwill was purchased at a cost of £50,000 and is being amortised over ten years. No entry has been made for the amortisation of goodwill for the year ended 31 March 1994.

(9) The remuneration of the directors for the year was as follows:

	£
Chairman	31,000
Sales director	42,000
Executive director	56,000

The remuneration of the directors is included in the salaries and wages figure in the extended trial balance. The directors' fees and pension contribution made on behalf of the directors are made up as follows:

	Fees £	Pension contributions £
Chairman	2,000	4,000
Sales director	2,000	5,000
Executive director	3,000	6,000
	7,000	15,000

The two directors, other than the sales directors, work on general administration.

(10)   For the purposes of the published financial statements, the following allocation of expenses is to be made:

	Distribution costs £'000	Administrative expenses £'000
Motor expenses	47	31
Light and heat	20	6
Insurance	29	9
General expenses	186	48
Depreciation of motor vehicles	151	38
Depreciation of office equipment	22	15
Depreciation of buildings	16	5
Depreciation of fixtures and fittings	65	–

Salaries and wages, excluding directors' remuneration, are to be allocated on the basis of 75% to the distribution department and 25% to the administration department.

(11)   All of the operations of the company are continuing operations.

Woodpecker Ltd – Extended trial balance at 31 March 1994

Account	Ledger balances Dr £'000	Ledger balances Cr £'000	Adjustments Dr £'000	Adjustments Cr £'000	Profit and loss account Dr £'000	Profit and loss account Cr £'000	Balance sheet Dr £'000	Balance sheet Cr £'000
Salaries and wages	1,468				1,468			
Salesmen's commission	102		4		106			
Motor expenses	72		6		78			
Sales		8,086				8,086		
Buildings (accumulated depreciation)		117		21				138
Fixtures and fittings (accumulated depreciation)		176		65				241
Motor vehicles (accumulated depreciation)		219		189				408
Office equipment (accumulated depreciation)		51		37				88
Investment revaluation reserve		150						150
Directors' pension contributions	15				15			
Advertising	67			11	56			
Stock	731		937	937	731	937	937	
Trade debtors	840						840	
Provision for doubtful debts		20		17				37
Goodwill	20						20	
Purchases	5,035				5,035			
Land and buildings (cost)	1,267						1,267	
Fixtures and fittings (cost)	632						632	
Motor vehicles (cost)	745						745	
Office equipment (cost)	194						194	
Investment property	800						800	
Depreciation (motor vehicles)			189		189			
Depreciation (fixtures and fittings)			65		65			
Depreciation (office equipment)			37		37			
Depreciation (buildings)			21		21			

Account	Ledger balances Dr £'000	Ledger balances Cr £'000	Adjustments Dr £'000	Adjustments Cr £'000	Profit and loss account Dr £'000	Profit and loss account Cr £'000	Balance sheet Dr £'000	Balance sheet Cr £'000
Ordinary share capital		1,000						1,000
10% preference share capital		300						300
Directors' fees	7				7			
Share premium		250						250
Light and heat	19		7		26			
Interim dividend	15				15			
Increase in provision for doubtful debts			17		17			
General expenses	227		28	21	234			
Insurance	45			7	38			
Profit and loss account		778						778
Accruals				45				45
Prepayments			39				39	
Cash in hand	3						3	
Cash at bank		139						139
Trade creditors		568						568
8% debentures		450						450
Profit					885			885
	12,304	12,304	1,350	1,350	9,023	9,023	5,477	5,477

Assessment tasks

Task 1

Make any adjustments you feel to be necessary to the balances in the extended trial balance as a result of the matters set out in the further information above. Set out your adjustments in the form of journal entries. (Ignore any effect of these adjustments on the tax charge for the year as given above.) No narratives are required for the journal entries.

Task 2

(a)   Draft a profit and loss account for the year ended 31 March 1994 and a balance sheet as at that date in a form suitable for publication using Format 1 in accordance with the Companies Act 1985 as supplemented by FRS3 *Reporting financial performance*. (Students are *not* required to prepare a statement of total recognised gains and losses or the reconciliation of movements in shareholders' funds required under FRS3.)

(b)   Provide suitable notes to the accounts, in so far as the information given above allows, for the following accounting items:

(i)   share capital;
(ii)   directors' remuneration.

Task 3

The directors of the company are unclear as to the nature of goodwill. They have asked you to define goodwill and state whether they could have adopted any alternative accounting treatment to the one they have followed in the financial statements. Justify your answers, where appropriate, by reference to accounting concepts, SSAPs and/or FRSs.

SUMMARY

SSAP13

* Research and development expenditure falls into three categories:

    –   pure research
    –   applied research
    –   development expenditure

* Development expenditure (only) can be deferred to future periods if it meets the criteria laid down in the SSAP.

* If development expenditure is deferred, it should be amortised.

SSAP22

* Non-purchased goodwill should never appear in the balance sheet.

* To calculate goodwill we compare:

    –   the value of the business as a whole; with
    –   the aggregate of the fair values of the business's separable net assets.

● Purchased goodwill must not be carried as a permanent item. There are two possible treatments:

    – immediate write-off against the profit and loss account reserve;
    – amortisation over its useful economic life.

Review of Module One

You have now completed the first module of the Study Pack. You have now covered much of the knowledge and understanding required for Element 1 *Draft limited company final accounts* and all the specialist knowledge and understanding which is required for Element 2 *Draft sole trader and partnership final accounts*.

You have covered the following:

- the background to the drafting of final accounts, including the legal framework and accounting concepts

- drafting final accounts for sole traders;

- drafting final accounts for partnerships, including:

    - rights of partners
    - appropriation of profit
    - changes in a partnership
    - dissolution of a partnership.

- the requirements of the Companies Acts, including:

    - the format for the balance sheet and profit and loss account; and
    - disclosure requirements

- many of the requirements of Accounting Standards:

    - correct accounting treatments; and
    - disclosure requirements

- the preparation of a manufacturing account

You should now be able to use this knowledge and understanding to:

- prepare sole trader final accounts

- prepare partnership final accounts

in a format suitable for management or in a format suitable for publication.

You should remember that the *principles* of preparing accounts are the same for all organisations, whether they are limited companies, sole traders or partnerships. The format of sole trader and partnership accounts is not prescribed by law, but the accounts should be drawn up in accordance with current best practice. This may mean that the accounts should comply with applicable accounting standards. Look back at Session 3 for a list of the accounting standards which are most likely to apply to sole traders and partnerships.

You should now attempt Practice Central Assessment 1.

Stocks and long-term contracts

STOCK

Accounting treatment

Stocks should be stated at the lower of *cost* and *net realisable value*.

Cost

SSAP9 defines cost as: 'that expenditure which has been incurred in the *normal course of business* in bringing the product or service to its *present location and condition'*.

This means that two identical items may have different costs if they are in different locations. For example, the cost of an item which has been shipped to a distribution centre in France will include the normal transport costs to France and hence will have a higher cost than a similar item held in the factory in England.

Note that only costs incurred in the *normal* course of business should be included. If the lorry taking items to France broke down, the costs of the breakdown would not be included as part of the transport costs since they are considered abnormal.

Cost includes the following.

- *Cost of purchase* which comprises:

    - purchase price – including import duties, transport, handling costs and any other directly attributable costs; less

    - trade discounts, rebates and subsidies.

- *Cost of conversion* which comprises:

    - costs which are specifically attributable to units of production – direct labour, direct expenses and subcontracted work;

    - production overheads;

    - other overheads, if any, attributable in the particular circumstances of the business to bringing the product or service to its present location and condition.

Illustration

The Standard Company plc has stock at 31 December 19X7 and has gathered the following information together in order to determine its cost.

	£
Cost of original materials	16,000
Cost of work on material	
Labour 1,000 hours @ £2.50	2,500
Variable overhead	700
Fixed production overhead during the period 1 October to 31 December 19X7	40,000
Number of hours worked in the period 1 October to 31 December 19X7	18,000 hours

You also discovered that 2,000 hours of work were lost during December due to an industrial dispute over the holiday work programme.

Selling and distribution costs during the quarter were £10,000.

The value of the stock held at 31 December 19X7 is:

	£
Material cost	16,000
Labour cost	2,500
Variable overhead	700
Fixed overhead $\dfrac{£40,000}{20,000 \text{ hrs}} \times 1,000 \text{ hrs}$	2,000
	————
	21,200
	————

Fixed overheads are absorbed on a basis of the labour hours worked, 1,000 hours, as a proportion of normal working hours for the period, 20,000 hours.

The industrial dispute will not increase the value of the stock even though it reduced the number of hours actually worked in the quarter.

Selling and distribution overheads have been ignored as the goods in stock have not been sold or distributed.

Net realisable value

Net realisable value is defined as the actual or estimated selling price (net of trade but before settlement discounts) less:

- all further costs to completion;
- all costs to be incurred in marketing, selling and distributing the product.

Settlement discounts are those discounts which are offered as an inducement for early payment of an invoice; as such, they are more akin to an interest or finance expense than to a true discount and hence are not deducted in determining net realisable value.

Illustration

The Standard Mix Company plc has the following items in stock at its year-end:

	Cost £	Selling price £
Item A	7,000	10,000
Item B	8,400	10,200
Item C	9,200	10,400

Item A is ready for immediate sale.

Item B is also ready for sale but, due to falling demand, a 25% special discount will be needed to encourage a buyer to come forward.

Item C requires packaging before it can be sold and this cost is estimated at £1,800.

The net realisable values of these items are:

		£	£
Item A	NRV		10,000
Item B	Selling price	10,200	
	Discount 25%	(2,550)	
	NRV		7,650
Item C	Selling price	10,400	
	Packaging	(1,800)	
	NRV		8,600

For stock purposes, these items will be valued as follows:

Item	*Cost* £	*NRV* £	*Stock value* £
A	7,000	10,000	7,000
B	8,400	7,650	7,650
C	9,200	8,600	8,600
Stock at lower of cost and net realisable value			23,250

The comparison of cost and net realisable value needs to be made in respect of each item of stock *separately*. If this is difficult in practice, similar groups or categories of stock should be taken together.

By comparing the total realisable value of stocks with the total cost, you could net off foreseeable losses against unrealised profits. This is not acceptable under SSAP9 and the Companies Act.

Methods of costing

In practice, it is often difficult to relate expenditure to specific units of stocks. This is because a number of identical items may have been purchased or made at different times.

SSAP9 permits the use of any of the following methods, consistently applied:

- *Unit cost* – The actual cost of purchasing or manufacturing identifiable units of stock.

- *Weighted average cost* – The calculation of the cost of stocks and work in progress on the basis of the application to the unit of stocks on hand of an average price computed by dividing the total cost of units by the total number of such units (this average price may be arrived at by means of a continuous calculation, a periodic calculation or a moving periodic calculation).

- *FIFO (first in, first out)* – The calculation of the cost of stocks and work in progress on the basis that the quantities in hand represent the latest purchases or production.

- *Standard cost* – The calculation of the cost of stocks and work in progress on the basis of periodically predetermined costs calculated from management's estimates of expected levels of costs, operations, operational efficiency and the related expenditure.

  There is a proviso. Standards must be reviewed frequently to ensure that they bear a reasonable relationship to the actual costs of the period.

- *Selling price less an estimated profit margin* – This is acceptable only if it can be clearly shown that it gives a reasonable approximation of the actual cost.

The following methods should *not* normally be used:

- *LIFO (last in, first out)* – The calculation of stocks and work in progress on the basis that the quantities in hand represent the earliest purchases or production.

- *Base stock* – The calculation of the cost of stocks and work in progress on the basis that a fixed unit value is ascribed to a predetermined number of units of stock, any excess over this number being valued on the basis of some other method. If the number of units in stock is less than the predetermined minimum, the fixed unit value is applied to the number in stock.

- *Replacement cost* – The cost at which an identical asset could be purchased or manufactured at the balance sheet date.

The Companies Act 1985 states that the following methods are acceptable:

- first in, first out (FIFO);
- last in, first out (LIFO);
- a weighted average price;
- any other method similar to the methods mentioned above.

The method of valuation used should provide the fairest practicable approximation to actual cost. You should be familiar with most of these methods of valuation from your earlier studies.

LONG-TERM CONTRACT WORK IN PROGRESS

Introduction

Long-term contracts (for example, building a dam or constructing a road) generally extend over a number of years. The length of time taken to complete such projects presents a special problem in accounting terms. If we wait for completion of the contract before taking any of the profit it earns, we will find that the first years of a contract show no return on the investment made in it. A very large profit will arise, however, when the project is completed. In order to overcome this problem, part of the contract's turnover and profit is recognised each year as it proceeds.

Definitions

- *Long-term contracts* are contracts entered into for the design, manufacture or construction of a single substantial asset or the provision of a service where the time taken substantially to complete the contract is such that the contract activity falls into different accounting periods.

  A contract that is required to be accounted for as long-term by this Accounting Standard will usually extend for a period exceeding one year. However, a duration exceeding one year is not an essential feature of a long-term contract. Some contracts with a shorter duration than one year should be accounted for as long-term contracts if they are sufficiently material to the activity of the period that not to record turnover and attributable profit would lead to a distortion of the period's turnover and results such that the financial statements would not give a true and fair view, provided that the policy is applied consistently within the reporting entity and from year to year.

- *Attributable profit* is that part of the total profit currently estimated to arise over the duration of the contract, after allowing for estimated remedial and maintenance costs and increases in costs so far as not recoverable under the terms of the contract, that fairly reflects the profit attributable to that part of the work performed at the accounting date.

- *Foreseeable losses* are those which are currently estimated to arise over the duration of the contract (after allowing for estimated remedial and maintenance costs and increases in costs so far as not recoverable under the terms of the contract). This estimate is required irrespective of:

  - whether or not work has yet commenced on such contracts;
  - the proportion of work carried out at the accounting date;
  - the amount of profits expected to arise on other contracts.

- *Payments on account* are all amounts received and receivable at the accounting date in respect of contracts in progress.

Accounting treatment

Attributable profit is that part of the total contract profit which has been earned to date. By including such profit in its accounts, a company could be anticipating unrealised profits. This treatment is not prudent unless the company is reasonably certain in advance about the contract's outcome.

Where the outcome of a contract can be foreseen with reasonable certainty, SSAP9 states that attributable profit should be calculated on a prudent basis and included in the accounts. The amount of profit taken up should reflect the proportion of work carried out at the accounting date.

Where the outcome of a contract cannot be assessed with reasonable certainty, no profit should be reflected in the profit and loss account in respect of that contract.

If an ultimate loss on the contract is expected, all the loss should be recognised as soon as it is foreseen.

Illustration

You will not be assessed on detailed accounting for long term contracts. However, it is useful to have an appreciation of the technique in order to understand the issues involved.

Spade Ltd has one long-term contract in progress in the year ending 30 June 19X4, the details of which are as follows:

	£'000
Contract price	2,000
Costs incurred to date	1,200
Estimated further costs to complete	600
Value of work done (work certified)	1,400
Amounts invoiced	1,250

The contract commenced in the current year.

We begin by identifying whether the contract is expected to make a profit or loss overall, as this is crucial to the rest of the workings. We calculate the total estimated profit or loss as follows:

		£'000	£'000
Contract price			2,000
Less:	Costs incurred to date	1,200	
	All further costs to completion	600	
			(1,800)
Total estimated profit			200

At the year-end, we calculate turnover and attributable profit, or foreseeable loss, for each contract, giving cost of sales as the balancing figure.

Turnover

As this is the first year of the contract, turnover for the year is the value of work certified, £1,400. (If this were the second or subsequent year of the contract, turnover for the year would be the cumulative value of work certified less turnover previously recognised in the profit and loss account.)

Gross profit

The contract is expected to make a profit overall. We calculate the *attributable profit* from the start of the contract to the balance sheet date and deduct any amounts included in the profit and loss account in earlier years to obtain the current year's gross profit figure. However, if the contract is not far enough advanced to assess the outcome with reasonable certainty, we cannot recognise any profit.

Methods of calculating attributable profit

SSAP9 does not specify how to calculate attributable profit but does state that it should reflect the proportion of work carried out at the balance sheet date and take account of any known inequalities of profitability in the various stages of the contract. There are three possible methods:

(i)   Using: $\dfrac{\text{Work certified}}{\text{Contract price}} \times$ Total estimated profit

Attributable profit $= \dfrac{1,400}{2,000} \times 200 = £140,000$

(ii)   Using: $\dfrac{\text{Cost to date}}{\text{Total estimated cost}} \times$ Total estimated profit

Attributable profit $= \dfrac{1,200}{1,800} \times 200 = £133,333$

(iii)   Using: Turnover to date – Cost to date

Attributable profit $= 1,400,000 - 1,200,000 = £200,000$

In this case, method (iii) is not likely to be appropriate as it is unlikely to be prudent to recognise the whole profit before the contract is finished.

Note: If the contract is expected to make a loss overall, we must recognise the full loss in the profit and loss account immediately, less any amounts already recognised in earlier years. This applies even if we have not yet started work and even if other contracts are profitable. We include in cost of sales whatever figure is needed to make gross profit for the contract equal the foreseeable loss, whether or not the relevant costs have been incurred yet (if they have not, we will set up a provision).

Cost of sales

The easiest way to deal with this figure is to treat it as the balancing figure in the profit and loss account workings. For the purpose of this example, we will assume that attributable profit is to be calculated using work certified as a proportion of total contract price [Method (i)].

This gives us the profit and loss account figures:

	£'000
Turnover (work certified)	1,400
Cost of sales (β)	(1,260)
Gross profit	140

The balance sheet

The figures which appear in the balance sheet arise from the matching process that we have just carried out in order to determine turnover and attributable profit.

We have earned more revenue than we have billed, and we include the balance in:

	£
Debtors: Amounts recoverable on contracts	**150**

The balance is calculated as follows:

	£
Cumulative turnover from start of contract to balance sheet date (Dr)	1,400
Less: Amounts invoiced (SSAP9 calls this *payments on account*)(Cr)	(1,250)
	150

We have charged more costs to the profit and loss account than we have so far incurred. Hence, we make an accrual or provision (the distinction is not significant):

	£
Provisions for liabilities and charges	**60**

OR

	£
Accruals and deferred income	**60**

The balance is calculated as follows:

	£
Costs incurred from start of contract to balance sheet date (Dr)	1,200
Less: Cumulative cost of sales to date (Cr)	(1,260)
	(60)

DISCLOSURE REQUIREMENTS

Accounting policies

Accounting policies adopted in calculating the following must be disclosed:

- cost;
- net realisable value;
- turnover;
- attributable profit;
- foreseeable losses.

Stocks and work in progress

Total stocks and work in progress should be subclassified in a manner appropriate to the business so as to indicate the amount held in each of the main categories. This is usually achieved by giving the analysis required in the balance sheet formats by CA 1985.

	£
Raw materials and consumables	X
Work in progress	X
Finished goods and goods for resale	X
Payments on account	X
	X

QUESTION

1   Jackson Ltd

Jackson manufactures one product, a filing cabinet. The costs of making a cabinet have been established as follows:

Per unit	£
Raw materials	10
Import duties on above	1
Direct labour	15

In addition, the following costs are also incurred every month:

	£
Factory power	3,000
Foremen's salaries	2,000
Depreciation of plant	7,000
Sales department costs	6,000
Administration costs	2,000
	20,000

The normal activity level is 5,000 units produced per month. The selling price is £50 per unit.

The directors are arguing about the valuation of stocks produced during May. The differing views are as follows:

(1)   The company manufactures only one product, and therefore all of the costs incurred by the company should be shared equally by each unit and stocks should be valued at £30 per unit.

(2)   During May, only 4,000 units were produced. The overheads should therefore be shared out between those units. However, the sales department costs should be ignored as the units are still in stock. Therefore a valuation of £29.50 is suggested.

(3)   It would be imprudent to include any overheads in the valuation of stocks and that a conservative valuation would be £26 per unit.

Required

(a)   Briefly explain the significance of the FIFO and LIFO valuation methods in measuring profit and in valuing stock.

(b)   Define the terms 'cost' and 'net realisable value' as used in SSAP9.

(c)   Set out the circumstances in which you consider that net realisable value is likely to be less than cost.

(d)   Discuss the views expressed by the directors and recommend a valuation of the units produced during May.

SUMMARY

Stock and short-term WIP

- Remember the key phrase is *lower of cost and net realisable value*.

    (i)   Determine costs (purchase price of goods plus attributable overheads).

    (ii)   Compare costs with net realisable value (usually selling price less additional costs to complete or sell).

- Disclosure requirements:

    (i)   accounting policies;
    (ii)   stocks and work in progress note.

Long-term contract WIP

- Long-term contracts should be assessed on a contract by contract basis and reflected in the profit and loss account by recording turnover and related costs as contract activity progresses.

- Attributable profit should be recognised in the profit and loss account where it is considered that the outcome of the contract can be assessed with reasonable certainty.

Accounting for leases and hire purchase contracts

TYPES OF TRANSACTION

Legally, there are three main types of 'extended credit' transaction:

- credit sale
- hire purchase
- lease

Traditionally, they have been accounted for in accordance with their legal form as shown in the following table:

	Credit sale	Hire purchase	Lease
Title	Passes to buyer immediately	Passes to buyer at the end of the agreement	Never passes to the lessee (buyer)
Buyer/lessee	Asset capitalised Liability recognised Interest and depreciation charged to profit and loss	Asset capitalised Liability recognised Interest and depreciation charged to profit and loss	Rentals charged to profit and loss account
Seller/lessor	Debtor recognised Finance income spread over agreement	Debtor recognised Finance income and gross profit spread over agreement	Asset capitalised Rental income credited to profit and loss account

The problem

Similar transactions may be accounted for in different ways. A leasing transaction may be very similar in substance to a hire purchase transaction.

The solution

Transactions should be accounted for in accordance with their *commercial substance* and not merely their *legal form*.

TYPES OF LEASE

Finance lease

A lease that transfers substantially all the risks and rewards of ownership of an asset to the lessee.

Operating lease

A lease other than a finance lease.

Commercial substance of finance and operating leases

A *finance lease* is similar in substance to the ownership of an asset, financed by a loan repayable by instalments over the period of the lease. The lessee would normally have sole use of the asset and would be responsible for its maintenance, repair and insurance even though legal title to the asset remains with the lessor. An *operating lease*, on the other hand, is the 'short-term' hire of an asset.

FINANCE LEASE

SSAP21 requires that finance leases (or equivalent agreements) are capitalised in the lessee's balance sheet by including both the

- value of the asset in fixed assets;
- the outstanding leases commitments in creditors.

The profit and loss account is charged with depreciation on the asset and an appropriate share of the finance charge.

The problems

The two critical questions to be answered are:

(a) At what value should the asset be capitalised?
(b) What finance charge should be made in the profit and loss account?

The capitalised value in the balance sheet

At the start of the lease, the sum to be recorded both as an asset and as a liability should be *the present value of the minimum lease payments*, derived by discounting them at the interest rate implicit in the lease.

In practice, in the case of a finance lease the *fair value* of the asset will often be a sufficiently close approximation to the present value of the minimum lease payments and may in these circumstances be substituted for it.

The finance charge

The excess of the minimum lease payments over the initial capitalised value represents the finance charge. The total finance charge should be allocated to accounting periods during the lease term so as to produce a constant periodic rate of charge on the remaining balance of the obligation for each accounting period (ie. the actuarial method), or a reasonable approximation thereto.

Although you will not be assessed on detailed accounting for leases, the following numerical example will help you to understand the issues involved.

The lessor will account for future amounts receivable under finance leases as a debtor, which are then allocated to the profit and loss over the term of the lease.

OPERATING LEASE

An operating lease is effectively a short-term rental agreement, with no option to purchase the goods. The supplier retains title throughout and usually undertakes to keep them in good working order. The domestic rental of a television or video recorder would generally constitute such an agreement.

In this case, it is the lessor that records the asset as a fixed asset and depreciates it. Rental is recognised on a straight-line basis in both the lessee's and lessor's books over the lease term.

Hire purchase

Hire purchase could fall into either of these categories, depending upon the terms of the agreement, and SSAP21 requires that they be accounted for accordingly. It is usual that they are treated as a finance lease. A difference may be that the hire purchase seller takes credit not only for finance income, but also for gross profit on the actual sale of the asset.

SUMMARY

SSAP21 is an important contribution in the development of Accounting Standards since it represents the application of commercial substance as the solution to one form of off-balance sheet finance. The important matters which you must appreciate are:

- the problem of reflecting the commercial substance of a transaction over its strict legal form;

- the distinction between a finance lease and an operating lease.

Taxation in company accounts

INTRODUCTION

You will need to understand three major aspects of this topic:

(a)   the system whereby tax is paid;
(b)   the bookkeeping entries leading to the amounts which are disclosed in financial statements;
(c)   the standards which are a guide to best accounting practice.

You should work through this session carefully, ensuring you fully understand each step before progressing to the next. The session stresses the presentation of tax information in a company's statutory accounts.

CORPORATION TAX

The basics

Companies pay corporation tax on their profits. The current rate of corporation tax is 33%.

Clearly corporation tax cannot be paid until after the annual profit figure has been found; therefore, when preparing a profit and loss account, a provision must be made for the corporation tax payable on those profits.

Illustration 1

A company makes an operating profit before taxation of £300,000 in the year ended 31 December 19X7. Corporation tax is estimated at £99,000. (Note that in practice the tax will be 33% of *taxable* profits, which will not usually equal *operating* profits.)

Profit and loss account (extract) 19X7

	£
Profit on ordinary activities before taxation	300,000
Tax on profit on ordinary activities	
Corporation tax on income @ 33%	(99,000)
Profit on ordinary activities after taxation	201,000

Corporation tax account

	£		£
Balance c/f	99,000	Profit and loss account	99,000
	99,000		99,000
		Balance b/f	99,000

The balance on the corporation tax account is carried forward and will appear on the balance sheet under the creditors heading.

The full description given in the profit and loss account above is required either on the face of the profit and loss account as shown or in the notes to the accounts.

Due dates for payment

Corporation tax is payable nine months after the end of the company's accounting period.

In the profit and loss account above, being to 31 December 19X7, the corporation tax we have identified will be payable on 1 October 19X8.

In the statutory accounts the amount of £99,000 will be included in:

'Creditors : amounts falling due within one year'

Within that heading it will be included within the description:

'Other creditors including taxation and social security'

Adjustments relating to prior years

When the provision for corporation tax is made in the accounts, it is only an estimate of the actual liability which will eventually be agreed with HM Inspectors of Taxes. Any difference between the original estimate and the actual figure will be adjusted in the next year's charge. If material, this figure will be disclosed separately.

Illustration 1 (continued)

In 1 October 19X8 the company pays £93,000 corporation tax on the 19X7 profit, not the £99,000 as estimated. The profit for the year 19X8 is £400,000 and corporation tax is estimated at £132,000.

Profit and loss account (extract) 19X8

	£	£
Profit on ordinary activities before taxation		400,000
Tax on profit on ordinary activities		
Corporation tax on income @ 33%	132,000	
Adjustment for overprovision in previous year	(6,000)	
		(126,000)
Profit on ordinary activities after taxation		274,000

Corporation tax account

		£			£
1.10.X8	Cash – actual charge	93,000	1.1.X8	Balance b/f – provision	99,000
1.10.X8	Profit and loss account		31.12.X8	Profit and loss account	
	– overprovision	6,000		– 19X8 expected charge	132,000
31.12.X8	Balance c/f	132,000			
					231,000
		231,000			
			1.1.X9	Balance b/f	132,000

ADVANCE CORPORATION TAX (ACT)

The basics

Companies are sometimes required to pay part of their corporation tax earlier than the due dates. The factor which determines whether an 'advance' payment is necessary or not is whether a company pays a dividend.

When a dividend is paid, a company must also make a payment of 'advance corporation tax' equivalent to 20/80ths of the dividend. A dividend of £8,000 would mean that advance corporation tax (ACT) of £2,000 is payable.

This payment is not an extra tax charge. It is simply a prepayment of the tax charge for that year.

The rule of 'set-off'

Advance corporation tax paid in respect of a dividend paid during an accounting period may be set off against the corporation tax liability for the accounting period in which the dividend was paid.

Illustration 2

Vogue plc pays an interim dividend of £8,000 for the year ended 31 December 19X6 on 30 June 19X6.

The ACT of £2,000 (20/80 × £8,000) will be offset against the corporation tax liability for the year ended 31 December 19X6, because the dividend is paid in that accounting period.

Illustration 3

Harpers plc pays a final dividend of £15,000 for the year ended 31 December 19X6 on 1 February 19X7.

The ACT on the dividend of £3,750 (20/80 × £15,000) will be offset against the corporation tax liability of the year ended 31 December 19X7 because the dividend was paid in that year.

Note: The year in respect of which the dividend is payable is irrelevant; it is the year in which the dividend is actually paid that is important.

In illustrations 2 and 3, both dividends were in respect of the year ended 31 December 19X6; that is, both would appear in the profit and loss account of the year ended 31 December 19X6. The resulting ACT payments, however, offset against the corporation tax of different years; that is, the years in which the dividends are actually paid.

Illustration 4

Cosmopolitan plc made a trading profit of £700,000 in the year to 31 March 19X4. Corporation tax is estimated at £231,000. The 19X3 corporation tax of £202,000 was paid on the due date although the original provision was £210,000.

An interim dividend of £84,000 was paid in the year ended 31 March 19X4.

We will write up the relevant extracts of the profit and loss account and balance sheet.

Cosmopolitan plc

Profit and loss account (extract) 31 March 19X4

	£	£
Profit on ordinary activities before taxation		700,000
Tax on profit on ordinary activities		
Corporation tax on income @ 33%	231,000	
Overprovision in respect of prior year	(8,000)	
		(223,000)
Profit on ordinary activities after taxation		477,000
Dividend paid		(84,000)
Retained profit		393,000

Advance corporation tax account

	£			£
Cash	21,000	31.3.X4	Corporation tax a/c	21,000
	21,000			21,000

Corporation tax liability account

		£			£
1.1.X4	Cash – 19X3 actual charge	202,000	1.4.X3	Balance b/f – 19X3 provision	210,000
1.1.X4	Profit and loss a/c – overprovision	8,000	31.3.X4	Profit and loss a/c – 19X4 liability	231,000
31.3.X4	ACT account	21,000			
31.3.X4	Balance c/f	210,000			
		441,000			441,000
			1.4.X4	Balance b/f	210,000

Balance sheet (extract) 31 March 19X4

£

Creditors: Amounts falling due within one year
Other creditors including taxation and social security   210,000

Note that the ACT does not appear in the profit and loss account. The ACT simply affects the timing of the payment of part of the total corporation tax charge; therefore, at the year-end the amount of corporation tax payable is the total charge of £231,000 less the amount of £21,000 pre-paid as ACT.

ACT payable and recoverable

The ACT account we have just written up for Cosmopolitan plc contains only two entries:

(a)   Cash £21,000 (debit) – this is the amount paid as a result of the dividend, ie: 20/80 × £84,000.

This may be considered to be the ACT payable.

(b)   Corporation tax account £21,000 (credit) – this is setting the ACT against the corporation tax liability for the period in which the dividend was paid.

This effectively recovers the ACT paid by reducing the payment to be made on 1 January 19X5. This may be considered as ACT recoverable.

The bookkeeping can reflect these two aspects of the ACT and we could keep separate accounts for ACT payable and ACT recoverable. When the dividend is proposed for payment, we can credit ACT payable with the ACT related to the dividend and debit the same amount to ACT recoverable. ACT payable is then cleared by the payment and ACT recoverable is transferred to corporation tax liability account reducing the outstanding creditor.

The entries in our illustration would be:

ACT payable account

	£		£
Cash (2)	21,000	ACT recoverable a/c – ACT on the dividend (1)	21,000
	21,000		21,000

ACT recoverable account

	£		£
ACT payable a/c – ACT on the dividend (1)	21,000	Corporation tax liability account (3)	21,000
	21,000		21,000

The numbers in brackets indicate the order in which the entries occur.

Proposed dividends at year-end

When a company has a proposed dividend at its year-end, this means that when the dividend is paid (in the next year) ACT will also be payable at the same time. This ACT can be set against the corporation tax arising on the next year's profits (not against the tax on the current year's profits).

Illustration 5

Assume the same facts that we used in the Cosmopolitan plc illustration, but with a proposed final dividend of £27,000. The ACT accounts will be as follows:

ACT payable account

	£		£
Cash (2)	21,000	ACT recoverable a/c (paid dividend) (1)	21,000
Balance c/f – ACT payable	6,750	ACT recoverable a/c (proposed dividend) (4)	6,750
	27,750		27,750
		Balance b/f	6,750

ACT recoverable account

	£		£
ACT payable a/c (paid dividend (1)	21,000	Corporation tax account (3)	21,000
ACT payable a/c (proposed dividend (4)	6,750	Balance c/f – ACT recoverable	6,750
	27,750		27,750
Balance b/f	6,750		

Balance sheet (extract) 31 March 19X4

	£
Debtors	
Prepayments and accrued income	
ACT recoverable	6,750
Creditors: Amounts falling due within one year	
Other creditors including taxation and social security (Note)	243,750

Note

	£
Other creditors include	
Corporation tax (231,000 – 21,000)	210,000
ACT payable	6,750
Proposed dividend	27,000
	243,750

You should note that the proposed dividend at the year-end causes both a credit and a debit balance of £6,750 to be brought down in respect of the ACT. The credit balance is the liability that the company will incur when the dividend is paid. The debit balance on the ACT recoverable account will reduce the corporation tax payable in respect of the following accounting period by being transferred to the corporation tax liability account.

Dividends received

When a company receives a dividend from another company in the UK, this dividend is paid out of profits on which corporation tax has been paid. This income in the hands of the recipient company is therefore fully taxed and no further tax is payable on it.

SSAP8, however, requires that all investment income of a company be shown gross of tax in order to facilitate comparison between (i) this sort of income received by companies and other sorts of income that they receive and (ii) with income received by individuals.

Arising from this requirement to show 'gross' dividends received, we have a number of entries which will affect the tax charge shown in the accounts. The detail of these entries is dealt with below.

Remember that these rules only relate to dividends received by UK companies from other UK companies.

Tax credits

Dividends received by individuals in the UK are deemed to be received net of basic rate income tax. This means that the dividend is assumed to be the net amount of a gross payment from which basic rate income tax has been deducted.

Illustration 6

Dividend actually received £75.

This is treated as the net amount after deducting basic rate income tax, which is currently 25%. This 25% is referred to as the *tax credit* relating to the dividend and may be found by taking 25/75th of the amount received. In this case 25/75 × £75 = £25. The gross amount of the dividend is therefore £75 + £25 = £100.

Presentation in profit and loss account

Companies, as we have already stated, pay no tax on this form of income, nor are they normally allowed to reclaim the tax credit attaching to the dividend.

They are required to show this income plus its tax credit in their profit and loss account. Therefore, the tax credit is also brought in as part of the taxation charge in order to reduce the gross income back to the net amount, which was actually received. (Note that the rate of ACT, which is currently 20/80, applies when dealing with a company rather than with an individual.)

Illustration 7

A company receives a dividend of £80.

The tax credit is 20/80 × £80 = £20

The gross income is therefore £100.

The profit and loss account of the company will show the following:

Profit and loss account (extract)

	£	£
Operating profit		50,000
Income from other fixed asset investments (gross)		100
Profit on ordinary activities before taxation		50,100
Tax on profit on ordinary activities		
Corporation tax on income (say)	17,500	
Adjustment for under(over) provisions (say)	2,000	
Tax credits on UK dividends received	20	
		(19,520)
Profit on ordinary activities after taxation		30,580

Please note that the net effect on the profit and loss account is a credit of £80, being the dividend received. However, this is brought in in two steps: as gross income of £100 (credit) and the associated tax of £20 (debit). This is purely for presentation purposes; it is not part of the double-entry.

ACT and tax credits

So far, we have considered the payment and receipt of dividends separately. We must now consider the more realistic situation of a company receiving and paying dividends in the same year.

Offset of tax credits against ACT payable

The taxation rules governing the payment of ACT state that the amount of ACT to be paid as a result of a dividend payment will be reduced by the amount of any tax credit attaching to dividends received in the same accounting period.

Example

A company receives a dividend of £8,100.
It also decides to pay a dividend of £32,400 in the same year.

Required

Calculate the ACT that must be paid.

Solution

The normal way of making this calculation is to compare the 'gross' dividend figures. These are referred to as the *franked receipts and payments*.

	£
Franked payment (re dividend paid)	
$32,400 \times \dfrac{100}{80}$	40,500
Franked receipt (re dividend received)	
$8,100 \times \dfrac{100}{80}$	10,125
Difference	30,375

ACT payable is:

Difference × Rate of ACT	(30,375 × 20%)	£6,075

Effect on accounting for ACT paid

This calculation of ACT payable is carried out on standard Inland Revenue forms. It is in no way part of the bookkeeping. Once the amount of ACT payable has been calculated, it is entered in the books in the normal way. Following the figures in the above example, the entries would be:

ACT payable account

	£		£
Cash (2)	6,075	ACT recoverable a/c (1)	6,075

ACT recoverable account

	£		£
ACT recoverable a/c (1)	6,075	Corporation tax liability a/c (3)	6,075

Effect on accounting for dividends received

The rule regarding setting off ACT and tax credits has *no effect* whatsoever on the entries relating to the receipt of the dividend and its presentation in the profit and loss account.

The dividend received of £8,000 is grossed up and shown as dividend income of £10,000.

The tax credit of £2,000 associated with this dividend is shown as part of the corporation tax charge.

INCOME TAX

The basics

When a company makes certain payments (eg. debenture interest or royalty payments) it is required to deduct basic rate income tax, currently 24%, from these, paying the net amount to the payee and the tax deducted to the Inland Revenue.

For example, if the company Best Ltd pays £10,000 debenture interest gross, it will pay:

	£
To the payee	7,600
To the Revenue	2,400
	10,000

This is, of course, very similar to what a company does when it pays salaries; it pays the net amount to the employee and the tax is paid to the Revenue under PAYE.

Similarly, if a company receives these types of income, the paying company will have deducted basic rate income tax from the payment and paid it to the Revenue, so that the receiving company only receives the net amount.

Note that the paying company is simply acting as a collector of the tax which it then pays to the Revenue. Consider again the analogy with PAYE. When the company pays this tax to the Revenue, it is not paying part of its own liability; it is simply collecting that tax on behalf of the Revenue. The tax it pays over is the liability of the employee. It is exactly the same with the tax deducted by the company when making these payments. In the example above, when Best Ltd pays £2,400 income tax to the Revenue, it is not paying part of its own liability but paying the liability of those who receive the payments.

Accounting entries

The amounts paid and received as interest or royalties are grossed up by the amount of the tax deducted and shown in the profit and loss account at their *gross* amount.

Income tax on payments made is debited to the appropriate expense account and then credited to the income tax account to record the liability to the Inland Revenue. Income tax on amounts received is credited to the appropriate revenue account and debited to the income tax account, thus reducing the credit balance to be paid over to the Revenue.

Illustration 8

Company plc pays debenture interest of £41,040 (net) and receives a royalty of £32,832 (net). The amounts are grossed up for inclusion in the profit and loss account and the income tax suffered on the royalty is set off against tax deducted from debenture interest when payment is made to the Inland Revenue.

Debenture interest

	£		£
Cash – net interest	41,040	Profit and loss account –	
Income tax (24/76 × 41,040)	12,960	gross interest	54,000
	54,000		54,000

Royalties received

	£		£
Profit and loss account –		Cash – net royalty	32,832
gross royalties	43,200	Income tax (24/76 × 32,832)	10,368
	43,200		43,200

Income tax

	£		£
Royalties	10,368	Debenture interest	12,960
Cash – net amount due	2,592		
	12,960		12,960

Note that the income tax on these receipts and payments must be kept totally separate from ACT. There is no connection whatsoever between them.

Corporation tax on income received

We saw earlier that when a company receives dividends, it pays no corporation tax on these. You should recall that they are simply grossed up for presentation purposes in the profit and loss account, with the associated tax credit being shown as part of the taxation charge.

The position with interest and royalties is totally different!

Income from these is chargeable to corporation tax at the normal rate (33%) and this is part of the corporation tax charge in the accounts.

Naturally, credit must be given to the company for the tax deducted and paid by the paying company.

Illustration 9

Options plc receives debenture interest of £7,600 net from Accountancy Ltd. Its other taxable income is £40,000.

(a)   The profit and loss account would be as follows:

	£
Taxable income	40,000
Debenture interest received $7,600 \times \dfrac{100}{76}$	10,000
Taxable profits	50,000
Corporation tax thereon at 33%	(16,500)
Profit after tax	33,500

Note that the gross amount of interest received is included in taxable profits and therefore suffers corporation tax at 33%.

(b)   The books would be written up as follows:

Corporation tax liability

		£			£

(5)	Income tax a/c –
	   suffered at source
		2,400	(4)	Profit and loss –
				   charge for year
					16,500

	Balance c/f	14,100			16,500
		16,500			

Debenture interest received

		£			£
(2)	Profit and loss account – gross	10,000	(1) (3)	Cash – net Income tax account	7,600 2,400
		10,000			10,000

Income tax

		£			£
(3)	Debenture interest a/c	2,400	(5)	Corporation tax account	2,400
		2,400			2,400

Note that the company, Options plc, is given credit for the income tax paid at source, by the paying company, Accountancy Ltd. Remember that when Accountancy Ltd pays the £7,600 to Options plc and the related £2,400 tax to the Revenue, this £2,400 is Options' liability, not Accountancy's; Accountancy is simply acting as a collector on the Revenue's behalf.

If Options plc had had no corporation tax liability (perhaps because it had made a trading loss that offset this interest received), the Revenue would repay to Options plc the £2,400 tax paid by Accountancy Ltd.

Illustration 10

Economist plc pays £15,200 debenture interest (net) and received £7,600 royalty (net). Its other taxable income is £50,000.

(a)   The profit and loss account would be as follows:

	£
Other income	50,000
Debenture interest received (7,600 × 100/76)	10,000
Debenture interest paid (15,200 × 100/76)	(20,000)
Taxable profit	40,000
Corporation tax thereon (40,000 × 33%)	(13,200)
Profit after tax	26,800

(b)   The books would be written up as follows.

Corporation tax liability

	£		£
Balance c/f	13,200	Profit and loss	13,200
	13,200		13,200

Debenture interest received

	£		£
Profit and loss – gross	10,000	Cash – net	7,600
		Income tax	2,400
	10,000		10,000

Debenture interest paid

	£		£
Cash – net	15,200	Profit and loss – gross	20,000
Income tax	4,800		
	20,000		20,000

Income tax

	£		£
Debenture interest received	2,400	Debenture interest paid	4,800
Balance c/f	2,400		
	4,800		4,800
Cash – to Revenue	2,400	Balance b/f	2,400

Note that no income tax is offset against the corporation tax liability. The £2,400 income tax that remains to be paid is not Economist plc's liability; it is simply paying it on behalf of the payees.

DISCLOSURE REQUIREMENTS OF SSAP8

The purpose of SSAP8 is to standardise the treatment of taxation in company accounts and therefore the taxation disclosures in the profit and loss account and the balance sheet are very important.

Profit and loss account

Income
Dividends received from UK companies (grossed up by 100/80)	X
Royalties received (grossed up by 100/76)	X

Expenditure
Debenture interest paid (gross)	X
Tax on ordinary activities (Note)	X

Note: Tax on ordinary activities

Corporation tax on ordinary activities @ 33%	X
Under/(over) provision in previous year	X/(X)
Tax on franked investment income	
(20/80 × dividends received (cash amount) from UK companies)	X
	X

Balance sheet

Debtors
ACT recoverable (20/80 × proposed dividend)	X

Creditors: amounts falling due within one year
Proposed dividend (amount payable to shareholders)	X
ACT on proposed dividend (20/80 × proposed dividend)	X
Income tax due to Revenue (difference between IT deducted from debenture interest paid and IT suffered on royalty income)	X
Corporation tax payable (date) (this year's CT charge less any ACT set-off)	X

Note: The rule of 'set-off' is: ACT in respect of a dividend paid during the year may be set off against the corporation tax liability for the year in which the dividend was paid.

ACCOUNTING FOR VALUE ADDED TAX

Introduction

VAT is collected by businesses on behalf of the government. VAT is incurred by a business within the price paid for supplies purchased (an input tax) and levied by the business when it charges for goods sold to its customers (an output tax). The difference between the amount levied and the amount incurred is paid quarterly to HM Customs and Excise. The current rate is 17.5%. The eventual payer is the consumer who stands at the end of the manufacturing and distribution chain.

Illustration 11

Goods purchased for £117.50 – Debit purchases £100, VAT £17.50
Goods sold for £352.50 – Credit sales £300, VAT £52.50

Thus revenue and costs are not affected by VAT, but the net amount (£35) collected for value added by the business and owed to Customs and Excise is shown in the VAT account.

VAT account			
	£		£
Input tax on purchases	17.50	Output tax on sales	52.50
Balance due to HM Customs and Excise c/f	35.00		
	52.50		52.50
Cash	35	Balance b/f	35

The standard

SSAP5 deals with the very straightforward problem which raises no controversy at all. The Standard consists of two short paragraphs which are reproduced below, followed by a brief explanation.

Turnover

Turnover shown in the profit and loss account should exclude VAT on taxable outputs. If it is desirable to show the gross turnover also, the VAT relevant to that turnover should be shown as a deduction in arriving at the turnover exclusive of VAT.

Irrecoverable VAT

Irrecoverable VAT allocable to fixed assets and to other items disclosed separately in published accounts should be included in their cost where practicable and material.

Explanation

Turnover

Since the trader who is registered for VAT is merely acting as a tax collector by adding VAT to his prices and then paying it over to HM Customs and Excise, it is reasonable and correct to exclude the VAT from turnover.

Irrecoverable VAT

When a trader actually bears VAT, it is again reasonable and correct that capital revenue items affected should include that VAT. A trader is unable to offset VAT suffered on his purchases when, for example, he is not registered for VAT.

ACCOUNTING FOR DEFERRED TAX

Introduction

There are two types of difference between profits chargeable to corporation tax and profits as stated in the financial statements: permanent differences and timing differences.

Permanent differences

These arise from items of income and expenditure which are never included in arriving at taxable profits (eg. disallowed entertaining).

Timing differences

These arise from items of income and expenditure which are included in both financial statements and tax computations but in different years (eg. interest, royalties, capital allowances in excess of related depreciation charges). *Such differences may originate but must, by definition, reverse over a period of time.*

Because of these timing differences, the taxation charge as calculated by the tax authorities may not represent the charge on the accounting profits. For example, debenture interest payable is included in the accounts on an accruals basis, whereas it is included in the computations on a cash paid basis for tax purposes.

Illustration 12

Details of debenture interest paid and payable by a company:

	19X1 £	*19X2* £	*19X3* £
Interest payable (accounts)	10,000	10,000	10,000
Interest paid (tax computation)	8,000	10,000	12,000
Profit before taxation	50,000	50,000	50,000

The rate of corporation tax is 33%.

If the tax charge were computed on the unadjusted profit before taxation it would be £16,500 for each of the three years.

The actual tax charge for each of the three years is as follows:

	19X1 £	19X2 £	19X3 £
Profit before taxation	50,000	50,000	50,000
Add back interest payable	10,000	10,000	10,000
Deduct interest paid	(8,000)	(10,000)	(12,000)
	52,000	50,000	48,000
Corporation tax at 33%	(17,160)	(16,500)	(15,840)

The total amount of tax paid over the three year period is the same amount that would have been paid if the tax charge had been based on accounting profit. However, the timing differences give rise to fluctuations in the *annual* tax charge.

SSAP2 states that a company should match the expenses incurred in a period with profits earned in that period. In order to ensure that the total tax charge relates to accounting profits earned, extra tax can be charged or released through a deferred taxation account.

The calculation of deferred tax is beyond the scope of Unit 14. You are only required to understand the concept and to be able to make the accounting entries.

The accounting entries for deferred taxation

In periods when corporation tax is reduced by timing differences, a charge to deferred taxation is made in the profit and loss account and a provision is set up in the balance sheet. The double entry is:

Dr   Deferred tax charge (profit and loss account)
       Cr   Provision for deferred tax (balance sheet)

This increases the tax charge in the profit and loss account.

To reverse the provision, the entries are:

Dr   Provision for deferred tax
       Cr   Deferred tax charge

This has the effect of reducing the tax charge.

Illustration 13

Profit before taxation for the year ended 31 December 19X1 is £160,000. The corporation tax charge for the year has been estimated at £40,000. The provision for deferred tax brought forward at the start of the year was £60,000. The deferred tax provision is to be increased by £8,000.

How will this information appear in the accounts for the year ended 31 December 19X1?

To increase the deferred tax provision, the following adjustment is required:

Dr   Deferred tax charge   £8,000
       Cr   Provision for deferred tax   £8,000

The information will be disclosed as follows:

Profit and loss account (extract)

	£
Profit on ordinary activities before taxation	160,000
Tax on profit on ordinary activities	(48,000)
Profit on ordinary activities after taxation	112,000

Notes to the profit and loss account

Tax on profit on ordinary activities

	£
Corporation tax on profits	40,000
Deferred taxation	8,000
	48,000

Balance sheet (extract)

	£
Provisions for liabilities and charges	
Deferred taxation	68,000

Notes to the balance sheet

	£
Deferred taxation	
At 1 January 19X1	60,000
Profit and loss account	8,000
At 31 December 19X1	68,000

QUESTIONS

1   Times Ltd

Times Ltd was formed in 19X0 and prepares accounts to 30 June each year.

The following information relates to the year to 30 June 19X4:

(1)   A dividend of £4,320 was received on 20 January 19X4.

(2)   Corporation tax liability for the year ended 30 June 19X3 had been estimated at £50,000. However, £52,500 was finally paid.

(3)   Estimated corporation tax liability for the year ended 30 June 19X4 has been agreed at £75,000.

(4)   Times Ltd paid interim dividends of £8,100 on 31 March 19X4.

(5)   Proposed final dividend of £16,200 will be paid after the year-end.

(6)   Assume the rate of income tax to be 25%, the rate of ACT to be 20/80 and the rate of corporation tax to be 33%.

(7)   Assume that no dividends were paid or proposed prior to the current year.

Required

Prepare an extract of the profit and loss account for the year to 30 June 19X4 and a balance sheet extract as at the date to reflect how the above matters will be disclosed.

2   Fairbrother Ltd

The following trial balance was extracted from the books of Fairbrother Ltd at 30 June 19X6:

		£	£
£1 ordinary shares (authorised and fully paid)			250,000
Profit and loss at 30 June 19X6			348,380
8% debentures			100,000
Land and buildings	Cost	370,000	
	Accumulated depreciation		30,000
Plant and machinery	Cost	340,000	
	Accumulated depreciation		170,000
Motor vehicles	Cost	80,000	
	Accumulated depreciation		35,000
Trade debtors		130,000	
Trade creditors			97,000
Stocks at 30 June 19X6		97,862	
Cash balances		11,220	
Bank overdraft			53,500
100,000 ordinary shares in Fowler plc, a listed company (market value on 30 June 19X6: £73,000)		59,000	
ACT paid		350	
Sundry creditors			4,552
		1,088,432	1,088,432

You are also given the following information:

(1)   Depreciation has already been provided as follows:

	£
Land and buildings	5,000
Plant and machinery	42,500
Motor vehicles	7,000

Additions of fixed assets during the year were motor vehicles, £20,000 and plant and machinery £70,000.

(2)   The debentures are secured on the land and buildings and are redeemable at par in 19Y9.

(3)   The company paid an interim dividend of £10,000 in December 19X5 and received a dividend from Fowler plc of £8,600 in the same month.

(4)   Fees of £4,000 are to be provided for each of the three directors.

(5)   Corporation tax of £59,000 is to be provided in respect of the year.

(6)   Sundry creditors

		£
Accruals		9,832
Prepayments		(6,387)
Social security		1,107
		4,552

(7)   The directors wish to propose a final dividend of 10%.

Required

Prepare the company's balance sheet and related notes as at 30 June 19X6 in accordance with generally accepted accounting principles and in a form suitable for presentation to members.

Notes

Ignore the requirement to state the company's accounting policies. Comparative figures are not required.

Assume the basic rate of income tax to be 25% and the rate of ACT to be 20/80.

SUMMARY

SSAP8

- ACT paid in an accounting period is set against the corporation tax liability of that same period, regardless of what period the dividends relate to.

- Dividends received must be disclosed gross in the published accounts. The tax deducted at source is shown as part of the tax charge for the year.

- ACT on proposed dividends represents a current liability and a deferred asset.

It is important that you learn the disclosure requirements on pages 224–225.

SSAP5

Turnover should be disclosed in the published accounts net of VAT.

SSAP15

Deferred tax should be charged/(released) to/(from) the profit and loss account to match the tax charge for a period with profits earned in that period.

Post balance sheet events and contingencies

SSAP17: ACCOUNTING FOR POST BALANCE SHEET EVENTS

Introduction

Post balance sheet events are those events, both favourable and unfavourable, which occur between the balance sheet date and the date on which the financial statements are approved by the board of directors.

It is necessary to have a standard on the accounting treatment of post balance sheet events to provide sufficient information for the users of the financial statements.

The explanatory foreword to SSAP17 gives the following reasons for the standard:

'Events arising after the balance sheet date need to be reflected in financial statements if they provide additional evidence of conditions that existed at the balance sheet date and materially affect the amounts to be included.

'To prevent financial statements from being misleading, disclosure needs to be made by way of notes of other material events arising after the balance sheet date which provide evidence of conditions not existing at the balance sheet date. Disclosure is required where the information is necessary for a proper understanding of the financial position.'

Types of event

The standard distinguishes two types of post balance sheet event: *adjusting events* and *non-adjusting events*.

Adjusting events

These require the accounts to be adjusted to reflect their impact. They are defined as being 'post balance sheet events which provide additional evidence of conditions existing at the balance sheet date'.

Such events are relevant because they relate to items appearing in the accounts or transactions reported in them.

Examples of these, given in the appendix of SSAP17, are as follows.

- *Fixed assets* – The subsequent determination of the purchase price or of the proceeds of sale of assets purchased or sold before the year-end.

- *Property* – A valuation which provides evidence of a permanent diminution in value.

- *Investments* – The receipt of a copy of the financial statements or other information in respect of an unlisted company which provides evidence of a permanent diminution in the value of a long-term investment.

- *Stocks and work in progress*

  (i)   The receipt of proceeds of sales after the balance sheet date or other evidence concerning the realisable value of stocks.

  (ii) The receipt of evidence that the previous estimate of accrued profit on a long-term contract was materially inaccurate.

- *Debtors* – The renegotiation of amounts owing by debtors or the insolvency of a debtor.

- *Dividends receivable* – The declaration of dividends by subsidiaries relating to periods prior to the balance sheet date of the holding company.

- *Taxation* – The receipt of information regarding rates of taxation.

- *Claims* – Amounts received or receivable in respect of insurance claims which were in the course of negotiation at the balance sheet date.

- *Discoveries* – The discovery of errors or frauds which show that the financial statements were incorrect.

Non-adjusting events

These are merely noted in the accounts *if material*. They are post balance sheet events which concern conditions which did not exist at the balance sheet date. Consequently they do not result in changes in amounts in financial statements. They may, however, be of such materiality that their disclosure is required by way of notes to ensure that the financial statements are not misleading.

Examples of these, given in the appendix to SSAP17, are as follows.

- Mergers and acquisitions

- Reconstructions and proposed reconstructions

- Issues of shares and debentures

- Purchase and sale of fixed assets and investments

- Losses of fixed assets or stocks as a result of a catastrophe such as a fire or flood

- Opening new trading activities or extending existing trading activities

- Closing a significant part of the trading activities if this was not anticipated at the year-end

- Decline in the value of property and investments held as fixed assets, if it can be demonstrated that the decline occurred after the year-end

- Government action, such as nationalisation

- Strikes and other labour disputes

Window-dressing

The balance sheet is a 'snapshot' of the affairs of the business at a particular moment. This does not necessarily mean that it shows the typical financial position throughout the year. For example, if a business makes most of its sales in the period shortly before Christmas, debtors are likely to be at their highest and stocks are likely to be at their lowest on 31 December.

A business may enter into transactions which are *primarily undertaken* to improve the appearance of the balance sheet. After the year-end, these transactions may reverse. This practice is known as *window-dressing*.

Under SSAP17, a material post balance sheet event should be disclosed where it is the reversal or maturity of a transaction which was entered into primarily to alter the appearance of the company's balance sheet.

Disclosure requirements

- Financial statements should be prepared on the basis of conditions existing at the balance sheet date and should disclose the date they were approved by the board of directors.

- A material post balance sheet event requires changes in the amounts to be included in financial statements where:

  - it is an adjusting event; or

  - it indicates that application of the going concern concept to the whole or a material part of the company is not appropriate.

  This second point considers the situation where post year-end events indicate that the company is no longer a going concern. Clearly the accounts will need to be adjusted if they were originally prepared on a going concern basis.

- A material post balance sheet event should only be disclosed where:

  - it is a non-adjusting event of such materiality that its non-disclosure would affect the ability of the users of financial statements to reach a proper understanding of the financial position; or

  - it is the reversal or maturity after the year-end of a transaction entered into before the year-end, the substance of which was primarily to alter the appearance of the company's balance sheet (ie. a 'window-dressing' transaction).

  In respect of each post balance sheet event which is required to be disclosed, the following information should be stated by way of notes in financial statements:

  - the nature of the event; and

  - an estimate of the financial effect, or a statement that it is not practicable to make such an estimate.

Companies Act 1985

The Companies Act 1985 requires disclosure of particulars of any important events affecting the company or any of its subsidiaries which have occurred since the end of that year.

This disclosure required by the Act is to be contained in the directors' report; SSAP17 on the other hand requires that these items be shown as a note to the accounts. Accordingly, there is likely to be some duplication of disclosure and it will not be sufficient for the directors' report merely to refer to the appropriate note in the accounts.

The Companies Act makes no distinction between adjusting and non-adjusting events.

SSAP18: ACCOUNTING FOR CONTINGENCIES

Introduction

This SSAP deals with the accounting treatment and disclosure of contingent gains and losses. The treatment is partly determined by the application of SSAP2 and the concept of prudence, and partly by the accounting requirements of the Companies Act 1985.

Different treatments are required for gains and losses following the concept of prudence; that is, losses should be recognised when known but profits only when realised.

Definition

SSAP18 contains the following definition of a contingency:

'A contingency is a condition which exists at the balance sheet date, where the outcome will be confirmed only on the occurrence or non-occurrence of one or more uncertain future events. A contingent gain or loss is a gain or loss dependent on a contingency.'

Examples

Typical examples of contingencies are:

*   law suits or claims pending;

*   guarantees:

    –   of completion of contracts;
    –   for the borrowings of other group companies;

*   arrears of preference dividends.

Disclosure

Following SSAP18, different treatments are adopted for contingent gains and losses. These treatments may be summarised as follows:

	Contingent loss	Contingent gain
Where event is probable and quantifiable	Accrue	Note to accounts
Where event is possible	Note to accounts	Ignore
Where event is remote	Ignore	Ignore

Where a note to the financial statements is required, it should disclose the following:

- the nature of the contingency;

- the uncertainties which are expected to affect the ultimate outcome; and

- a prudent estimate of the financial effect, made at the date on which the financial statements are approved by the board of directors; or a statement that is not practicable to make such an estimate.

Companies Act 1985

The Companies Act 1985 requires information to be given with respect to the amount, or estimated amount, of any contingent liability not provided for, its legal nature and any valuable security provided.

QUESTIONS

1   Trunfair Ltd

The directors of Trunfair Ltd, a trading company, are about to approve the company's financial statements for the year ended 31 July 19X3.

Since the financial statements were originally prepared, the following material information has become available:

(1)   On 1 September 19X3, a major design fault was found in a new product and it was withdrawn from the market. Stocks of the product have been returned to Trunfair Ltd's supplier for a full refund. The company had committed itself to an advertising schedule for this new product involving total expenditure of £300,000 to be written off evenly over three years. £150,000 had been spent in the first year to 31 July 19X3.

(2)   On 15 September 19X3 torrential rain caused flooding at the company's riverside warehouse resulting in an uninsured stock loss totalling £200,000.

(3)   Year-end debtors included £120,000 owed by a customer who went into liquidation on 16 September 19X3. The invoice was dated 15 July 19X3.

Required

Advise the directors on the effect the above information should have on the financial statements for the year ended 31 July 19X3, giving your reasons.

2   Vacs Ltd

Vacs Ltd is a manufacturing company which prepares financial statements to 30 September each year. The draft financial statements for the year ended 30 September 19X3 show a decrease in turnover and profit to £1,650,000 and £182,000 respectively with net assets of £232,000 at the year-end. Before the financial statements can be finalised and approved by the directors, the following points need to be addressed.

(1)   Vacs Ltd has renewed the unlimited guarantee given in respect of the bank overdraft of another company.

(2)   A former director, who was dismissed from the company's service for acting outside his authority, has given notice of his intention to claim substantial damages for loss of office. On 1 September 19X3 a claim was received for £150,000. The company's legal advisers do not think he will succeed in any claim and have been negotiating with the former director, who has reduced his claim to £100,000. A provision of £50,000 has been made in the accounts.

(3)   Shortly after the year-end, the company's major competitor introduced its own version of Vacs' main product 'The Dust Buster'. The rival version has received excellent reviews because of its technological superiority. In an attempt to maintain their market share, the directors have cut the price by 50%. At the moment, stocks of the 'Dust Buster' are included in the draft accounts at £575,000 on which a normal mark-up of 30% would have been achieved.

Required

Draft a memorandum to the directors of Vacs Ltd advising them of the implications of the above items for the financial statements for the year ended 30 September 19X3, giving reasons where necessary for the views taken.

SUMMARY

Post balance sheet events

Does the event provide additional evidence of *conditions existing at the balance sheet date*?

- If so, you must *adjust* the financial statements.
- If not, you must *disclose* the event (if it is material).

Contingencies

Is the contingency:

- probable and quantifiable?
- possible?
- remote?

The treatment depends on the likelihood of the outcome. Look back at the table on page 155. Remember the prudence concept – you rarely include contingent gains but you must accrue for losses as soon as they are foreseen.

Disclosures

Finally, you must learn the correct disclosures for both post balance sheet events and contingencies.

Cash flow statements

THE PURPOSE OF THE CASH FLOW STATEMENT

Accruals accounting deliberately removes the effect of *cashflows* from the profit and loss account. It is important, however, for users of financial statements to get information about the amount of cash available to and required by an enterprise.

Cash is of great importance to the continuing existence of an enterprise. For instance, cash is needed to pay existing liabilities (including corporation tax) and to fund future investment (including the purchase of fixed assets).

The cash flow statement looks at the cash inflows and outflows of a business in a particular accounting period.

BASIC ILLUSTRATION

Let us consider Rathbone Ltd, a company which operates entirely on a cash basis.

The profit and loss account for the first year of trading was:

	£
Sales	500
Costs	300
	200

From this, we can assume that the cash balance of the company will have increased by £200 at the end of the year.

Let us now suppose that the sales had been made on credit and at the year-end there were debtors of £50. The cash balance would have increased by £150 [(500 – 50) – 300].

We could reconcile the profit for the year with the increase in cash.

	£
Profit for the year	200
Increase in debtors	(50)
Increase in cash (450 – 300)	150

In addition let us now suppose that the purchases had been made on credit and that £30 was outstanding at the year-end.

	£
Profit for the year	200
Increase in debtors	(50)
Increase in creditors	30
Increase in cash (450 – 270)	180

Finally let us suppose that there was stock of £20 on hand at the year-end, ie:

	£
Costs: Purchases	320
Closing stock	(20)
	300

The reconciliation would then be:

	£
Profit for the year	200
Increase in debtors	(50)
Increase in creditors	30
Increase in stock	(20)
Increase in cash (450 – 290)	160

There might, however, be other cash inflows and outflows. Suppose the company issued some share capital during the year and bought a fixed asset for cash. Our statement would then look like this:

	£
Profit for the year	200
Increase in debtors	(50)
Increase in creditors	30
Increase in stock	(20)
	160
Issue of share capital	150
Payments to purchase fixed assets	(80)
Increase in cash (450 – 290 + 150 – 80)	230

This is a basic cash flow statement.

CASH

Definition

Cash comprises cash in hand and deposits repayable on demand less overdrafts repayable on demand.

CASH INFLOWS AND OUTFLOWS

Cash inflows and outflows are shown under seven headings.

Operating activities

The main source of cash inflow for most businesses is its operating activities.

Returns on investments and servicing of finance

This heading covers the payments made to providers of finance, excluding dividends paid to equity shareholders which are shown separately.

It also covers receipts from third parties for whom the business provides finance.

Taxation

This heading covers payments of tax.

Capital expenditure and financial investments

Payments for the purchase of fixed assets and receipts from the sale of fixed assets are included under this heading.

Equity dividends paid

This heading covers the payments made to ordinary shareholders by way of dividend.

Management of liquid resources

Liquid resources are current asset investments which are readily disposable without causing disruption to the business. They must also be either readily convertible into known amounts of cash at or close to the carrying amount or traded in an active market.

This heading, therefore, includes payments to or withdrawals from short term deposits and payments to acquire or receipts from selling liquid investments.

Financing

This heading deals with receipts and repayments of capital and long-term loans.

Example – inflows and outflows

Limited company	**Sole trader or partnership**
Operating activities	
Profit before interest and tax, adjusted to remove accruals effect	Net profit adjusted to remove accruals effect

---

Limited company	Sole trader or partnership
Returns on investments and servicing of finance	
Preference dividends paid	Drawings
Interest paid and received	Interest paid and received
Dividends received	Dividends received
Taxation	
Corporation tax paid	For businesses, other than companies, tax is assessed on the individual owners, not the business itself
Capital expenditure and financial investments	
Purchase of fixed assets	Purchase of fixed assets
Sale of fixed assets	Sale of fixed assets
Purchase or sale of investments which are not liquid resources	Purchase or sale of investments which are not liquid resources
Equity dividends paid	
Dividends paid to ordinary shareholders	Not applicable as there are no shareholders
Management of liquid resources	
Payments into short term deposits	Payments into short term deposits
Payments to acquire liquid investments	Payments to acquire liquid investments
Withdrawals from short term deposits	Withdrawals from short term deposits
Receipts from selling liquid investments	Receipts from selling liquid investments
Financing	
Issue of shares	
Issue of debentures	Raising of long-term loans
Raising of long-term loans	Capital introduced by owners
Payment and redemption of share capital	Repayment of long-term loans
Redemption of debentures	Repayment of capital
Repayment of long-term loans	

FORMAT OF THE CASH FLOW STATEMENT

Financial Reporting Standard 1 (FRS1) (Revised 1996) deals with cash flow statements. It prescribes the following format:

Pro forma per FRS1 (Revised)

Pro forma cash flow statement for the year ended 31 March 19X2 for a single company with required supporting notes

	£	£
Net cash inflow from operating activities		A
Returns on investments and servicing of finance		
Interest received	X	
Interest paid	(X)	
Taxation		(X)
Capital expenditure		
Payments to acquire intangible fixed assets	(X)	
Payments to acquire tangible fixed assets	(X)	
Receipts from sales of tangible fixed assets	X	
		(X)
Equity dividends paid		(X)
Management of liquid resources		
Purchase of treasury bills	(X)	
Sale of treasury bills	X	
		(B)
Financing		
Issue of ordinary share capital	X	
Repurchase of debenture loan	(C)	
Expenses paid in connection with share issues	(X)	
		X
Increase in cash		D

Notes to the cash flow statement

(1) **Reconciliation of operating profit to net cash inflow from operating activities**

	£
Operating profit	X
Depreciation charges	X
Loss on sale of tangible fixed assets	X
Increase in stocks	(X)
Increase in debtors	(X)
Increase in creditors	X
Net cash inflow from operating activities	A

(2)   **Reconciliation of net cash flow to movement in net debt (note 3)**

	£	£
Increase in cash in the period	D	
Cash to repurchase debenture	C	
Cash used to increase liquid resources	B	
	—	
Change in net debt		X
Net debt at 1 April 19X1		(X)
		—
Net debt at 31 March 19X2		(X)
		—

(3)   **Analysis of changes in net debt**

	At 1 April 19X1 £	Cash flows £	Other changes £	At 31 March 19X2 £
Cash in hand, at bank	X	X		X
Overdrafts	(X)	X		–
		—		
		D		
Debt due within 1 year	(X)	C	(X)	(X)
Debt due after 1 year	(X)		X	(X)
Current asset investments	X	B		X
	—	—	—	—
Total	X	X	X	X
	—	—	—	—

Explanatory notes to the pro forma

● *Net cash inflow from operating activities*

In the pro forma, the net cashflow has been reported. However, gross cash inflows and outflows may also be shown. If this additional information is disclosed, it appears on the face of the cash flow statement.

	£	£
Operating activities		
Cash received from customers	X	
Cash payments to suppliers	(X)	
Cash paid to and on behalf of employees	(X)	
Other cash payments	(X)	
	—	
Net cash inflow from operating activities		A

This analysis appears on the face of the cash flow statement. This is sometimes known as the *direct method* of preparing a cash flow statement.

● *Reconciliation of operating profit to net cash inflow from operating activities*

This reconciliation showing separately the movements in stocks, debtors and creditors relating to operating activities and other differences between cashflows and profits (eg. depreciation) should always be given in a *note* to the cash flow statement, never on the face of the statement.

- *Reconciliation of net cash flows to movement in net debt*

Net debt comprises borrowings less cash and liquid resources.

If cash and liquid resources together exceed debt then it is classified as net funds.

The reconciliation analyses changes in net debt from b/f to c/f component amounts showing separately those arising from

- the entity's cash flows
- other non-cash changes
- recognition of changes in market value.

Exceptional and extraordinary items

Cashflows relating to exceptional items should be shown under the appropriate standard headings according to their nature.

Cashflows relating to extraordinary items should be shown separately under the appropriate standard headings. Where this is considered inappropriate, they should be shown within a separate section in the cash flow statement. (Remember, extraordinary items are very rare.)

In both cases, the nature of the cashflows should be disclosed in a note so as to explain the effect of the underlying transactions on the entity's cashflows.

Major non-cash transactions

If a company has undertaken a material transaction which has not resulted in movements of cash – for example, the inception of a finance lease or an exchange of assets – this should not appear in the cash flow statement. However, sufficient disclosure should be given so that the underlying transaction may be understood.

PREPARATION OF THE CASH FLOW STATEMENT

The practical preparation of a cash flow statement using the FRS1 pro forma is looked at below.

Example

The draft accounts of Precipitate Ltd for the year ended 30 April 19X7 are set out below:

Balance sheet at 30 April 19X7

	19X7	*19X6*
	£'000	*£'000*
Fixed assets (Note)	491	643
Current assets		
Stocks	893	688
Trade debtors	793	608
Cash at bank and in hand	7	10
	1,693	1,306
Creditors due within one year		
Trade creditors	583	563
Dividends proposed	62	28
Taxation	44	12
	(689)	(603)
Creditors due after more than one year		
Loans and debentures	(416)	(555)
	1,079	791
Share capital	820	720
Profit and loss account	259	71
	1,079	791

Note

Fixed assets

	£'000
(1) Freehold property	
At cost 30 April 19X6	455
At cost 30 April 19X7	340

Properties which originally cost £235,000 were sold during the year for £425,000.

(2)   Plant and equipment

	Cost £'000	Depreciation £'000
On 30 April 19X6	282	94
Additions at cost	53	
Disposals	(109)	(25)
Provision for the year		6
On 30 April 19X7	226	75

Profit and loss account for the year ended 30 April 19X7

		19X7 £'000	19X7 £'000	19X6 £'000	19X6 £'000
Turnover			2,930		1,563
Less:	Directors' emoluments	70		70	
	Auditors' remuneration	6		5	
	Interest on loans and debentures	39		46	
	Depreciation	6		5	
	Other operating expenses	2,724		1,431	
			(2,845)		(1,557)
Net trading profit			85		6
Profit on sale of fixed assets			205		–
			290		6
Taxation			(40)		(2)
			250		4
Proposed dividend			(62)		(28)
Retained profit for year			188		(24)
Balance brought forward			71		95
Balance carried forward			259		71

Step 1

To prepare the cash flow statement, we should start with Note 1 – *the reconciliation of operating profit to net cash inflow from operating activities.*

We are here trying to find by how much the cash balance has increased due to our operating activities.

To do this, we start with operating profit and firstly take out all items which will have no impact on cash (eg. depreciation and the increase in stocks during the year) and secondly, remove any increase in debtors and creditors during the year.

The note will appear as follows:

(1)   Reconciliation of operating profit to net cash inflow from operating activities

	£'000
Operating profit (290 + 39)	329
Depreciation charge	6
Profit on sale of fixed assets	(205)
Increase in stocks	(205)
Increase in debtors	(185)
Increase in creditors	20
	(240)

We now have the first figure to go on the face of our cash flow statement.

Step 2

Next we need to calculate the dividend paid, interest paid and tax paid. The best approach is to use a T-account to work out cash paid in the year:

Dividends

	£'000		£'000
Cash paid in year (balancing figure)	28	b/f (per balance sheet)	28
c/f (per balance sheet)	62	Proposed in year (per profit and loss account)	62

Taxation

	£'000		£'000
Tax paid	8	b/f (per balance sheet)	12
c/f (per balance sheet)	44	Charge (per profit and loss account)	40

The interest paid is £39,000 per the profit and loss account as there is no creditor at the start or end of the year.

Step 3

The fixed asset note needs to be looked at next. During the year, freehold property and plant have been disposed of. In our cash flow statement we need to determine the *cash proceeds of sale*.

	£'000
Proceeds of sale of freehold (per question)	425
Profit on sale of freehold (425 – 235)	190
∴ Profit on sale of plant (205 – 190)	15

	£'000
Proceeds of sale of plant	
NBV (109 – 25)	84
Add: Profit on sale	15
	99

Therefore total proceeds on sale of fixed assets (99 + 425) = 524

The *payments to acquire fixed assets* can be found as follows:

		£'000
Freehold property		
	Cost at 30.4.X6	455
	Disposal	(235)
	Purchases (b/f)	120
	Cost at 30.4.X7	340
Plant and equipment (per question)		53

Step 4

Finally, the financing section needs completion. It can be seen from the question that loans of £139,000 [£555,000 – £416,000] have been repaid.

We can now put the statement together and complete the notes as follows:

Precipitate Ltd
Cash flow statement for the year ended 30 April 19X7

	£'000	£'000
Net cash outflow from operating activities (Note 1)		(240)
Returns on investments and servicing of finance		
Interest paid		(39)
Taxation		(8)
Capital expenditure		
Payments to acquire tangible fixed assets (120 + 53)	(173)	
Receipts from sales of tangible fixed assets (425 + 99)	524	
		351
Equity dividends paid		(28)
Financing		
Issue of ordinary share capital	100	
Repayment of loan and debentures	(139)	
		(39)
Decrease in cash		(3)

Notes to the cash flow statement

(1)   Reconciliation of operating profit to net cash outflow from operating activities

	£'000
Operating profit	329
Depreciation charge	6
Profit on sale of fixed assets	(205)
Increase in stocks	(205)
Increase in debtors	(185)
Increase in creditors	20
Net cash outflow from operating activities	(240)

(2)   Reconciliation of net cash flow to movement in net debt (note 3)

	£'000	£'000
Decrease in cash in the period	(3)	
Repayment of loans and debentures	139	
Change in net debt		136
Net debt at 1 May 19X6		(545)
Net debt at 30 April 19X7		(409)

(3)   Analysis of changes in net debt

	At 1 May 19X6 £'000	Cash flows £'000	At 30 April 19X7 £'000
Cash at bank and in hand	10	(3)	7
Debt due after 1 year	(555)	139	(416)
Balance at 30 April 19X7	(545)	136	(409)

FURTHER POINTS

The purpose of this section is to explain how certain specific situations are treated in the cash flow statement.

Provision for doubtful debts

This is not an unusual item but its treatment in the cash flow statement warrants consideration.

You will recall that the profit and loss account charge for depreciation, loss of disposal of fixed assets etc. is added back to the profit before tax to calculate cashflow from operating activities.

The charge for increasing the provision for doubtful debts is not added back in this way. This is because the provision will reduce debtors and hence any adjustment will be effected through the movement in debtors.

Fixed asset revaluations

These need to be considered in calculating how much *cash* was spent on acquiring fixed assets.

It is permissible to revalue fixed assets. The double entry (ignoring depreciation) is:

Dr	Fixed asset		X	
	Cr	Revaluation reserve		X

The revaluation reserve does not pass through the profit and loss account but goes directly to the balance sheet.

Example

Extracts from the balance sheet of Don Ltd show:

	19X1	19X0
	£	£
Fixed assets at cost/valuation	*150*	*100*
Revaluation reserve	*20*	*–*

There were no disposals of fixed assets.

How much was spent on fixed assets?

A T-account approach is the most effective.

Fixed assets

	£		£
Balance b/f	*100*		
Revaluation	*20*		
Cash	*30*	*Balance c/f*	*150*
	150		*150*

- *Fixed assets have increased by £50.*

- *£20 of the increase is the result of a revaluation.*

- *Therefore £30 cash must have been spent on fixed assets. This is the figure that will appear in the cash flow statement.*

Advantages of producing a cash flow statement

- The cash flow statement focuses attention on *cash*. *A business has to generate cash in order to remain viable.*

- The cash flow statement gives indications of *liquidity and viability*. (It is possible for companies to fail due to lack of cash while apparently generating profits.)

- It gives indication of *financial adaptability* (eg. ability to generate cash by selling assets or raising additional capital).

- The profit and loss account and the balance sheet are prepared on *accruals basis* and are therefore to some extent *subjective*. They may be affected by an entity's choice of accounting policies. Cash flows are a matter of *fact* and difficult to manipulate.

- The note reconciling operating profit to net cash flow from operating activities highlights techniques which enhance profit performance with no cash flow advantage (eg. pre-acquisition write-downs). The cash flow statement shows how much cash has actually been generated from operating activities and therefore an entity's *ability to turn profit into cash.*

- Cash flow information has *predictive value* (cash flow is likely to have many common components from year to year).

Criticisms of the cash flow statement

- The additional disclosure of gross cash flows is *optional*. Most businesses *will not report them,* therefore depriving users of accounts (and themselves) of vital information.

- Current cash flows *may not be a reliable indicator of future cash flows* (eg. material items accrued/prepaid may result in cash flows and will not appear in the statement).

QUESTIONS

1   **Ham Ltd**

The balance sheets of Ham Ltd as on 31 December 19X1 and 19X2 were as follows:

	£	19X1 £	£	£	19X2 £	£
Fixed assets at cost			210,500			249,198
Less: Depreciation			(69,000)			(89,580)
			141,500			159,618
Investments at cost			8,967			6,658
			150,467			166,276
Current assets						
Stock		29,280			42,924	
Debtors		62,150			82,000	
Cash in hand		820			920	
Balance at bank		15,713			27,305	
		107,963			153,149	
Creditors: Amounts falling due within one year						
Creditors	48,000			59,000		
Proposed dividends	6,750			8,000		
Corporation tax	24,000			26,500		
	78,750			93,500		
			29,213			59,649
			179,680			225,925
Share capital			75,000			100,000
Share premium			–			5,000
Profit and loss account			104,680			120,925
			179,680			225,925

(1)   Fixed assets costing £11,302 (book value £9,522) were sold for £14,122 cash during the year and the profit was transferred to the profit and loss account. All additions during the year were paid for immediately with cash.

(2)   An investment which cost £5,104 was sold for £4,720 cash and the loss written off to profit and loss account.

(3)   An interim dividend of £7,500 was paid for the year. The charge for corporation tax in the accounts for the year ended 31 December 19X2 was £26,500.

(4)   No debenture interest was paid during the year.

Required

Prepare a cash flow statement for the year ended 31 December 19X2. You are required to show the reconciliation of operating profit to net cashflows from operating activities but you are not required to produce the other notes to the cash flow statement.

2 Haggis Ltd

Extracts from the draft accounts of Haggis Ltd for the year ended 31 March 19X1 are set out below:

Balance sheet at 31 March

	Notes	19X1 £'000	19X1 £'000	19X0 £'000	19X0 £'000
Fixed assets					
Intangible assets	1		63		84
Tangible assets	2		2,062		1,848
			2,125		1,932
Current assets					
Stocks		3,250		3,084	
Debtors		1,161		1,056	
Cash		721		683	
		5,132		4,823	
Creditors: Amounts falling due within one year					
Creditors		1,644		1,368	
Proposed dividend		202		190	
Taxation		257		247	
		2,103		1,805	
Net current assets			3,029		3,018
Total assets less current liabilities			5,154		4,950
Creditors: Amounts falling due after more than one year					
Debenture loans			(1,243)		(1,304)
Provisions for liabilities and charges					
Pensions and similar obligations			(355)		(331)
			3,556		3,315
Capital and reserves					
Called-up share capital					
£1 ordinary shares	3		252		216
Share premium account	4		84		–
Profit and loss account	4		3,220		3,099
			3,556		3,315

Profit and loss account for the year ended 31 March 19X1

	£'000
Turnover	46,916
Cost of sales and expenses	(45,893)
Interest	(127)
Profit before taxation	896
Taxation	(389)
Profit after taxation	507
Dividends	(386)
Retained for the year	121

Notes

(1)   Fixed assets: Intangible assets

	£'000
Development costs	
Cost at 1 April 19X0 and 31 March 19X1	210
Amortisation	
At 1 April 19X0	126
Charged to profit and loss account	21
At 31 March 19X1	147
Net book value at 31 March 19X1	63
1 April 19X0	84

(2) Fixed assets: Tangible assets

		Land & buildings £'000	Plant & equipment £'000	Total £'000
Cost				
	At 1 April 19X0	1,205	1,699	2,904
	Expenditure	154	403	557
	Disposals	(140)	(103)	(243)
		1,219	1,999	3,218
Depreciation				
	At 1 April 19X0	290	766	1,056
	Charged to profit and loss account	34	156	190
	Adjustment on disposals	(34)	(56)	(90)
At 31 March 19X1		290	866	1,156
Net book values at 31 March 19X1		929	1,133	2,062

Proceeds on disposals of land and buildings were £180,000 and of plant and equipment were £108,000.

(3) Share capital

	£'000
Ordinary shares of £1 each	
Authorised	360
Issued and fully paid at 1 April 19X0	216
Rights issue	36
At 31 March 19X1	252

(4) Reserves

	£'000
Profit and loss account	
Balance on 1 April 19X0	3,099
Retained profit for the year	121
Balance on 31 March 19X1	3,220
Share premium account	
Balance on 1 April 19X0	–
Premium on rights issue during year	84
Balance on 31 March 19X1	84
Total reserves 31 March 19X1	3,304

Required

Prepare a cash flow statement for the year ended 31 March 19X1.

3   Haversham plc

The following are extracts from the accounts of Haversham plc for the years ending 31 December 19X5 and 31 December 19X4.

Balance sheets

	19X5 £'000	19X4 £'000
Fixed assets		
Tangible assets	7,859	6,547
Investments	494	365
	8,353	6,912
Current assets		
Stocks	1,737	1,944
Debtors	393	220
Cash at bank and in hand	741	427
	2,871	2,591
Creditors: Amounts falling due within one year	(5,169)	(4,774)
Net current liabilities	(2,298)	(2,183)
Total assets less current liabilities	6,055	4,729
Creditors: Amounts falling due after more than one year		
Loans	(400)	(300)
	5,655	4,429
Capital and reserves		
Called-up share capital	1,830	947
Share premium account	75	52
Revaluation reserve	280	342
Profit and loss account	3,470	3,088
	5,655	4,429

Profit and loss account

	£'000
Operating profit	1,518
Exceptional item – loss on disposal of freehold premises	(490)
Income from other fixed asset investments	295
Interest receivable and similar income	174
Interest payable and similar charges	(386)
Profit on ordinary activities before taxation	1,111
Tax on profit on ordinary activities	(439)
Profit on ordinary activities after taxation	672
Dividends paid and proposed	(290)
Retained profit for the year	382
Retained profit at 1 January 19X5	3,088
Retained profit at 31 December 19X5	3,470

The following information is also relevant

(1) The disposal proceeds of the freehold premises were £971,000. No other tangible fixed assets were sold during the year.

(2) Creditors: amounts falling due within one year

	19X5 £'000	19X4 £'000
Taxation	399	367
Dividends proposed	180	150
Trade creditors and accruals	4,590	4,257
	5,169	4,774

(3) Fixed asset movements during the year

	Tangible assets £'000	Investments £'000
NBV at 1 January 19X5	6,547	365
Additions	3,115	215
Disposals	(1,461)	(24)
Depreciation charge	(342)	–
Revaluations	–	(62)
NBV at 31 December 19X5	7,859	494

(4) All amounts due for interest receivable and payable had been paid by the year-end. Haversham plc accounts for dividend income only when received.

Required

Prepare the cash flow statement and supporting notes for Haversham plc for the year ended 31 December 19X5.

Note: Assume the rate of ACT to be 20/80.

4   **Bark Ltd**   **(AAT Pilot CA J94)**

Data

Another of the partners in your firm has asked you to assist the accountant of Bark Ltd, a distributor of garden compost, in the production of a cash flow statement for the year ended 31 March 1994. The financial statements of Bark Ltd, produced by the company's bookkeeper for internal purposes, are set out below, along with some further information relating to the reporting year.

Bark Ltd
Profit and loss account for the year ended 31 March 1994

	1994		*1993*	
	£'000	£'000	£'000	£'000
Turnover		3,845		3,335
Opening stock	523		445	
Purchases	2,553		2,291	
Closing stock	(634)		(523)	
Cost of sales		(2,442)		(2,213)
Gross profit		1,403		1,122
Depreciation		(253)		(228)
Other expenses		(446)		(395)
Profit on sale of fixed assets		35		21
Operating profit for the year		739		520
Interest payable		(66)		(86)
Profit before tax		673		434
Taxation on profit		(235)		(152)
Profit after tax		438		282
Ordinary dividend		(85)		(65)
Retained profit		353		217

Bark Ltd
Balance sheet as at 31 March 1994

	1994 £'000	1993 £'000
Fixed assets	1,774	1,340
Current assets		
Stocks	634	523
Debtors	463	461
Cash	–	63
	1,097	1,047
Current liabilities		
Trade creditors	447	575
Dividends payable	85	65
Taxation	186	132
Bank overdraft	103	–
	821	772
Net current assets	276	275
Long-term loan	523	541
	1,527	1,074
Capital and reserves		
Called-up share capital	600	500
Profit and loss account	927	574
	1,527	1,074

Further information

(1)   Fixed assets costing £164,000 with accumulated depreciation of £98,000 were sold in the year for £101,000.

(2)   All sales and purchases were on credit. Other expenses were paid for in cash.

Assessment tasks

Task 1

Prepare a cash flow statement for Bark Ltd for the year ended 31 March 1994 using the 'indirect' method.

Task 2

Provide a reconciliation between cash flows from operating activities and operating profit.

5   Lucy Ltd

Data

You are employed in the business services department of a firm of chartered accountants. The directors of Lucy Ltd have approached your firm for assistance with the preparation of a cash flow statement.

A trainee in the firm has produced a cash flow statement for the year ended 31 March 1994 for Lucy Ltd.

Cash flow statement of Lucy Ltd for year ended 31 March 1994

	£	£
Net cash inflow from operating activities		75,000
Returns on investments and servicing of finance		
Dividends paid		(7,500)
Taxation		(35,000)
Investing activities		
Interest paid	4,500	
Payments to acquire fixed assets	9,500	
		(14,000)
Financing		
Loan repayment		5,000
Increase in cash		23,500

Further information

(1)   A fixed asset which originally cost £10,000 and was 40% depreciated was sold for £15,000 during the year. This amount has yet to be included.

(2)   An issue of shares was made on the last day of the period. The shares are £1 nominal value ordinary shares. They were issued at a 50p premium; 50% of the issue price was paid on application. The total number of shares issued (application monies received in full) was 100,000.

Assessment tasks

Task 1

Make any adjustments to the cash flow statement prepared by the trainee that you consider necessary, taking into account the further information provided.

Task 2

List FOUR advantages of cash flow accounting.

Task 3

From what would the differences between operating profit and net cash flow from operating activities normally arise?

SUMMARY

A cash flow statement shows the *cash inflows* and *cash outflows* in a business during an accounting period.

It also shows the increase or decrease in *cash* and *cash equivalents*.

Cash flows are divided into seven categories:

- operating activities

- returns on investments and servicing of finance

- taxation

- capital expenditure

- equity dividends paid

- management of liquid resources

- finance

Session 17

Interpretation of accounts

INTRODUCTION

Financial statements are prepared primarily for the members of the business, but they will inevitably be used by other interested parties.

Present and potential investors (and their advisers) will want to know whether the business is a good investment.

Lenders and suppliers will want to know if the business is a good credit risk.

The government will want to make sure that the correct amount of tax is being paid.

As part of their analysis, they will almost certainly calculate ratios, ie. they will relate one figure in the accounts to another.

Note: A ratio in itself is meaningless – we need a benchmark to judge it against.   Typical benchmarks include the performances of comparable enterprises, previous period's performance and the budget.

CALCULATIONS

To help you understand and then remember the various calculations, a set of figures is presented below. As you meet each ratio, work it out on the basis of these figures and then check your answer with ours. Don't at this stage attempt to draw any conclusions; these figures are only to give you practice in calculation.

JG Ltd
Summarised balance sheet at 31 December 19X1

	£'000	£'000
Fixed assets, at cost, less depreciation		2,600
Current assets		
Stocks	600	
Debtors	900	
Balance at bank	100	
	1,600	
Creditors: Amounts falling due within one year	800	
		800
		3,400
Creditors: Amounts falling due after		
more than one year		
Debenture stock		(1,400)
		2,000
Capital and reserves		
Ordinary share capital (£1 shares)		1,000
Preference share capital		200
Profit and loss account		800
		2,000

Summarised profit and loss account for the year ended 31 December 19X1

	£'000
Turnover	6,000
Cost of sales	(4,000)
Gross profit	2,000
Operating expenses	(1,660)
Net trading profit	340
Debenture interest	(74)
Profit before tax	266
Taxation	(106)
	160
Preference dividend	(10)
Profit available for ordinary shareholders	150

Profitability

- ### Return on capital employed (return on assets)

Capital employed is normally measured as capital and reserves plus long-term liabilities; it represents the long-term investment in the business.

Return on capital employed is frequently regarded as the best measure of profitability, indicating how successful a business is in utilising its assets. This ratio is only meaningful when the true values of assets are known and used in the formula.

Return on capital employed

$$= \frac{\text{Profit before interest and taxation}}{\text{Capital employed}} \times 100$$

$$= \frac{£}{£} \times 100 \qquad \textbf{(fill in the figures yourself)}$$

A low return on capital employed is caused by either a low profit margin or a low asset turnover or both. These two factors are measured as follows:

- ### Net profit margin (on sales)

$$\text{Margin} = \frac{\text{Net profit before interest and taxation}}{\text{Turnover}} \times 100$$

$$= \frac{£}{£} \times 100$$

A low margin indicates low selling prices or high costs or both. Comparative analysis will reveal the level of prices and costs in relation to competitors'.

- ### Asset turnover

This will show how fully a company is utilising its assets.

$$\text{Asset turnover} = \frac{\text{Turnover}}{\text{Capital employed}}$$

$$= \frac{£}{£} \times 100$$

A low turnover shows that a company is not generating a sufficient volume of business for the size of the asset investment. This may be remedied by increasing sales or by disposing of some of the assets or both.

- ### Gross profit margin

This ratio isolates the pure 'nuts and bolts' of a business, ie. ignoring indirect expenses and sundry income.

$$\text{Margin} = \frac{\text{Gross profit}}{\text{Sales}} \times 100$$

$$= \frac{£\rule{1.5cm}{0.4pt}}{£\rule{1.5cm}{0.4pt}} \times 100$$

A low margin indicates a similar position to a low net profit margin, but the causes can be traced more readily to trends in sales and cost of sales.

- **Stock turnover**

  This ratio indicates whether a business's stocks are justified in relation to its sales. If stock turnover falls, this may indicate excess stocks or sluggish sales.

  $$\text{Stock turnover} = \frac{\text{Cost of sales}}{\text{Stocks}}$$

  $$= \frac{£\rule{1.5cm}{0.4pt}}{£\rule{1.5cm}{0.4pt}}$$

Liquidity

- **Current ratio**

  This is a common method of analysing working capital (net current assets) and is generally accepted as the measure of short-term solvency. It indicates the extent to which the claims of short-term creditors are covered by assets that are expected to be converted to cash in a period roughly corresponding to the maturity of the claims.

  $$\text{Current ratio} = \frac{\text{Current assets}}{\text{Current liabilities}} = \frac{£\rule{1.5cm}{0.4pt}}{£\rule{1.5cm}{0.4pt}} =$$

- **Acid test ratio (quick ratio)**

  This is calculated in the same way as for the current ratio but stocks are excluded from current assets.

  $$\text{Acid test ratio} = \frac{\text{Current assets - stock}}{\text{Current liabilities}} = \frac{£\rule{1.5cm}{0.4pt}}{£\rule{1.5cm}{0.4pt}} =$$

  This ratio is a much better test of the immediate solvency of a business because of the length of time necessary to convert stocks into cash (via sales and debtors).

  Although increased liquid resources more usually indicate favourable trading, it could be that funds are not being used to their best advantage, (eg. a large unused cash balance).

- **Debtor days (debtors' ratio)**

  $$\text{Average collection period} = \frac{\text{Debtors}}{\text{Sales}} \times 365$$

Gearing

- *Capital*

   This measures the proportion of capital employed raised by debt (eg. debentures), as opposed to shareholders.

- Borrowing ratio $= \dfrac{\text{Loan capital}}{\text{Capital employed}} \times 100$

   $= \dfrac{\text{Loans}}{\text{Share capital} + \text{reserves} + \text{preference shares} + \text{loans}}$

   $= \dfrac{£}{£}$

ANSWERS

Before you look any further, make sure you have written down an answer for every ratio.

Return on capital employed

$$\frac{340}{2,000 + 1,400} = 10\%$$

Net profit margin

$$\frac{340}{6,000} = 5\tfrac{2}{3}\%$$

Asset turnover

$$\frac{6,000}{3,400} = 1.76 \text{ times}$$

Gross profit margin

$$\frac{2,000}{6,000} = 33\tfrac{1}{3}\%$$

Stock turnover

$$\frac{4,000}{600} = 6\tfrac{2}{3} \text{ times}$$

Current ratio

$$\frac{1,600}{800} = 2$$

Acid test

$$\frac{1,600 - 600}{800} = 1.25$$

Debtors' days

$$\frac{900}{6,000} \times 365 \cong 55 \text{ days}$$

Gearing ratio

$$\frac{1,400}{2,000 + 1,400} \cong 41\%$$

These are only some of the accounting ratios in current use but they cover the significant aspects of most businesses.

Now go back over them, making sure that you understand what each sets out to achieve.

INTERPRETATION

Introduction

- In your assessment, you may be required to comment on a set of accounts or on specific figures within a set of accounts.

- Before you start calculating ratios, read the accounts to identify any obvious points. You do not need a ratio to tell you that surplus cash should be invested, for example.

- Most of the marks will be awarded for interpretation of the ratios rather than for their calculation.

- Try to look at ratios in groups rather than in isolation; a group of ratios may provide a clearer indication of where the cause lies.

- Ratios are a key tool of analysis but other sources of information are also available:

  - Absolute comparisons can provide information without computing ratios; for example, comparing the balance sheet between the current year and the previous year may show that new shares have been issued to repay borrowings or finance new investment, which may in turn impact on gearing and ROCE.

  - Background information supplied about the nature of the business may help to explain changes or trends; for example, we may be told that the business has acquired another business or made substantial fixed asset purchases.

Return on capital employed (ROCE)

$$\frac{\text{Profit before interest and tax}}{\text{Capital employed}}$$

The aim is to see how effectively the business is using the money invested in it.

- It may be invalid to compare this ratio with, say, the interest rate offered by a building society.

  Example

  Z Ltd has ROCE of $\dfrac{5,000}{50,000}$ *= 10%*

  The Scunthorpe Building Society offers 12%.

  It would appear that the building society is a better investment.

  However, if Z Ltd's assets were worth only £30,000, the £30,000 would be better left in Z Ltd where it is earning £5,000 or 12½%.

- It may be invalid to compare this ratio with that of our rivals.

  Example

  Z Ltd's main rival is A Ltd, a long-established company. The two companies are identical except that when A Ltd started business the capital requirement was only £25,000.

  A Ltd's ROCE is therefore $\dfrac{5,000}{25,000}$ *= 20%*

  Clearly, the two different figures for ROCE do not imply that A Ltd is a better company than Z Ltd.

  Do be aware of the age structure of companies' capital before comparing them – assets bought at earlier, lower prices can appear to be more profitable.

- Often new investment does not bring immediate profits. This may be for a number of reasons. It may take time for the company's employees to learn to use the new equipment. Alternatively it may take the company time to obtain enough orders to use the new facilities to the full. (This may result in a temporary reduction in the ROCE.)

Gross and net profit margins

$$GPM = \frac{\text{Gross profit}}{\text{Sales}} \qquad\qquad NPM = \frac{\text{Net profit}}{\text{Sales}}$$

By looking at these two ratios together, we can determine whether a fall in the gross profit margin can be explained by a misclassification of cost rather than by deteriorating trade success.

Example

	19X1 £	19X0 £
Sales	100	100
Cost of sales	(85)	(80)
Gross profit	15	20
Overheads	(5)	(10)
Net profit	10	10
GPM	15%	20%
NPM	10%	10%

The fact that the net profit margin has remained constant while the gross profit margin has fallen would lead us to check that our costs had been properly classified.

This is an illustration of using more than one ratio to guide our thoughts.

Stock turnover

$$\frac{\text{Cost of sales}}{\text{Stock}}$$

This ratio provides an excellent example of the need to investigate the circumstances behind the figures.

Example

	19X1	19X0
Z Ltd's stock turnover	5	10

Interpretation one: A poor performance by Z Ltd. It is holding too much stock and some of it may be obsolete or unsaleable.

Interpretation two: Z Ltd's management has shown commendable foresight in building up its stocks to meet the extra demand that will arise from 19X2's new advertising campaign.

We cannot determine which interpretation, if either, is correct without further information. The contrasting nature of the two explanations simply illustrates the fact that the ratio provides no answers; it simply raises questions.

- Other points to consider with the stock turnover ratio are:

    - goods received on sale or return have no effect because they are never included in stock; and

    - stock turnover may be affected by the early manufacture of spare parts that will not be needed until the future. (Remember: a current asset does not have to be realisable within one year.)

Current ratio

$$\frac{\text{Current assets}}{\text{Current liabilities}}$$

The aim is to ensure that current liabilities can be met as they fall due. Sometimes textbooks suggest that if a business' current ratio is below a certain level (which is usually given as between 1.5 and 2) the business should become seriously concerned. This should not be taken to be a strict rule, because:

- current liabilities include the bank overdraft which in practice is not repayable within one year (technically, of course, repayable on demand);

- it ignores the timing of the realisation or settlement of the items,

  eg. $\dfrac{\text{Debtors}}{\text{Creditors}} = \dfrac{50,000}{10,000} = 5$

  This might appear to be an excellent situation. If the creditors are due within a month and the debtors do not pay for two months, then the situation is in fact the opposite.

Debtor days

$$\frac{\text{Debtors}}{\text{Credit sales}} \times 365$$

- Accounts do not show the split between cash and credit sales. This means that assumptions have to be made (eg. all sales on credit) that may distort the result.

- Seasonality may also distort the result. Consider the following:

  Z Ltd has a year-end of 31 December; all sales are made, on credit, in December; all customers pay at the end of February (ie. take 60 days' credit).

  Debtor days

  $$\frac{\text{Debtors}}{\text{Credit sales}} \times 365 = \frac{50,000}{50,000} \times 365 = 365 \text{ days}$$

  The ratio figure is far from reality.

Gearing ratio

$$\frac{\text{Long - term loans}}{\text{Capital employed}}$$

The greater the extent to which a business is financed by debt, the greater is the risk of investing in it.

From a lender's point of view, the more debt there is, the less likely it is that money will be recovered if the company goes into liquidation.

From a shareholder's point of view, the more debt there is the greater the variability of return.

Example

Walthamstow Ltd and Hackney Ltd are identical companies except that Hackney Ltd has £50,000 of debtor finance with interest at 10% per annum.

In 19X0 trading profits are £100,000.

In 19X1 they fall by 50% to £50,000.

In the case of Walthamstow Ltd this means that the profits available to the shareholders fall by 50% from £100,000 to £50,000.

In the case of Hackney the fall is from £95,000* to £45,000*, a fall of 53%.

The more debt there is, the riskier the investment.

* Profit available to shareholders = Trading profit minus Interest

Exactly what constitutes a long-term loan is open to discussion. Many writers argue that bank overdrafts and preference shares should be included as both have characteristics similar to long-term loans. You should either exclude these items or give a brief explanation as to why you are treating them as long-term loans.

FURTHER POINTS

Use of ratios

Ratios are a tool to assist analysis. They focus attention on trends and weaknesses and facilitate comparison over time and between companies.

Ratios are of no use in isolation. To be useful, we need a basis for comparison, such as:

- previous years
- other companies
- industry averages
- budgeted *v* actual (for management use)

Influences on ratios

Business factors

Ratios may change over time or differ between companies because of the nature of the business or management actions in running the business.

Examples of business factors influencing ratios:

- *Type of business (eg. retailer v manufacturer)*

  This affects the nature of the assets employed and the returns earned; for example, a retailer may have higher asset turnover but lower margins than a manufacturer.

- *Quality of management*

  Better managed businesses are likely to be more profitable and have better working capital management than businesses in which management is weak.

- *State of economy and market conditions*

  If the market or the economy in general is depressed, this is likely to have an adverse affect on companies and make most or all of their ratios appear worse.

- *Management actions*

  These will be reflected in changes in ratios; for example, price discounting to increase market share is likely to reduce margins but increase asset turnover; withdrawing from unprofitable market sectors is likely to reduce turnover but increase profit margins.

- *Changes in the business*

  If the business diversifies into wholly new areas, this is likely to change the resource structure and thus impact on key ratios. A new acquisition near the year-end will mean that capital employed will include all the assets acquired but profits of the new acquisition will only be included in the profit and loss account for a small part of the year, thus tending to depress ROCE.

Accounting policies

The accounting policies adopted by a business can significantly affect the view presented by the accounts and the ratios computed, without affecting the business's core ability to generate profits and cash.

Examples of accounting policies

- *Revaluations v Historic cost*

  If a business revalues its assets rather than carries them at historic cost, this will usually increase capital employed and reduce profit before tax (due to higher depreciation). Thus, ROCE, profit margins and gearing are all likely to be lower if a business revalues its assets.

- *Immediate write-off of goodwill or development costs v Capitalisation and amortisation*

  Immediate write-off has no impact on the profit and loss account for the year (contrast with amortisation) but will reduce capital employed. ROCE, profit margin and gearing are all likely to be lower if a policy of capitalisation and amortisation is adopted.

Limitations of ratios

- Ratios use historic data which may not be predictive as this ignores future actions by management and changes in the business environment.

- Ratios may be distorted by differences in accounting policies.

- Comparisons between different types of business are difficult because of differing resource structures and market characteristics.

SSAP25: SEGMENTAL REPORTING

Meaning and use of segmental reporting

Segmental reporting means analysing the reported results of an enterprise which has two or more classes of business or which operates in two or more different geographical areas.

The analysis is useful to users of financial statements because different segments may:

- earn a return on investment which is out of line with the remainder of the business; or

- be subject to different degrees of risk; or

- have experienced different rates of growth; or

- have different potentials for a future development.

Disclosure requirements of SSAP25

SSAP25 requires companies within its scope to disclose for each segment the following:

- *turnover*, distinguishing between turnover derived from external customers and turnover derived from other segments – in the geographical analysis, turnover should be shown segmentally according to *destination* of sales and *origin* of sales;

- *profit or loss*, before accounting for taxation, minority interests and extraordinary items, and normally before taking account of interest (unless all or part of the business of the entity is to earn or incur interest);

- *net assets* (defined as non-interest-bearing operating assets less non-interest-bearing operating liabilities).

The total of the amounts disclosed by segment should agree with the related total in the financial statements (with a reconciliation if necessary).

Comparative segmental figures for the preceding year should be shown.

Companies within the scope of SSAP25

SSAP25 applies to:

- all public companies or companies with a public company as subsidiary;

- banking and insurance companies;

- any entity which exceeds *ten times* the medium-sized company criteria in S248 Companies Act 1985 – that is to say, any two of the following three limits:

    - turnover > £112,000,000
    - balance sheet totals > £56,000,000
    - number of employees > 2,500

Defining segments

SSAP25 requires segmental analysis from companies within its scope which carry on two or more distinguishable classes of business or which operate in two or more different geographical areas.

It is for the directors to decide whether segmental information is necessary and SSAP25 indicates the following factors which should be taken into account in reaching a decision:

- Whether several classes of business are being carried on:

    - the nature of the products or services;
    - the nature of the production processes;
    - the markets in which the products or services are sold;
    - the distribution channels for the products;
    - the manner in which the entity's activities are organised;
    - any separate legislative framework relating to part of the business (for example, a bank or an insurance company).

- Whether a geographical analysis is required:

    Geographical variations as to:

    - expansionist or restrictive economic climates;
    - stable or unstable political regimes;
    - exchange control regulations;
    - exchange rate fluctuations.

A class of business or geographical segment should normally be regarded as significant if:

- its third party turnover is 10% or more of the total third party turnover of the entity; or

- its segment result, whether profit or loss, is 10% or more of the combined result of all segments in profit or of all segments in loss, whichever combined result is the greater; or

- its net assets are 10% or more of the total net assets of the entity.

QUESTIONS

1 Falcon Ltd

The draft accounts of Falcon Ltd for the years ended 30 June 19X3 and 30 June 19X2 are as follows:

Balance sheets

	19X3	19X3	19X2	19X2
	£	£	£	£
Freehold premises at NBV		125,000		75,000
Plant at cost	210,000		125,000	
Less: Depreciation	80,000		55,000	
		130,000		70,000
Debtors		80,000		60,000
Stock		120,000		100,000
		455,000		305,000
£1 ordinary shares		100,000		50,000
Trade creditors		45,000		30,000
7% debentures		50,000		50,000
Bank overdraft		15,000		5,000
Revenue reserves		135,000		120,000
Share premium account		90,000		35,000
Current taxation		20,000		15,000
		455,000		305,000

Profit and loss accounts

	19X3	19X3	19X2	19X2
	£	£	£	£
Sales		525,000		425,000
Trading profit		78,500		61,000
Less: Depreciation	25,000		20,000	
Debenture interest	3,500		3,500	
Corporation tax	20,000		15,000	
Dividends paid	15,000		10,000	
		(63,500)		(48,500)
Added to reserves		15,000		12,500

Required

(a)   Calculate the following ratios:

(i)   return on capital employed;
(ii)   profit margin;
(iii)   asset turnover;
(iv)   stock turnover;
(v)   current ratio;
(vi)   acid test ratio;
(vii)   debtor days;
(viii) borrowing ratio.

(b)   Write short paragraphs commenting on the profitability, liquidity and finance of Falcon Ltd as reflected in the above ratios.

2   Tiny Toys Ltd   (AAT Pilot CA D94)

Data

You have just begun work as the assistant to the financial director of Tiny Toys Ltd, a company which buys and sells toys. Your predecessor prepared an extended trial balance for the year ending 31 December 1993 prior to leaving. This includes the normal year-end adjustments. The financial director has asked you to review the trial balance in the light of some further information which may be relevant to the accounts. She has asked you to make any adjustments necessary before they are published.

The extended trial balance of Tiny Toys Ltd is set out on the following page.

Extended trial balance

Account	Trial balance Dr £	Trial balance Cr £	Adjustments Dr £	Adjustments Cr £	Profit and loss account Dr £	Profit and loss account Cr £	Balance sheet Dr £	Balance sheet Cr £
Sales		183,500				183,500		
Purchases	114,300				114,300			
Carriage outwards	3,100				3,100			
Motor expenses	6,600		150		6,750			
Rates	3,900			330	3,570			
Advertising	2,200				2,200			
Salaries and wages	75,000				75,000			
Debtors	38,900						38,900	
Creditors		17,000						17,000
Cash in hand	500						500	
Cash at bank	4,000						4,000	
Stock at 1.1.93	12,800		12,900	12,900	12,800	12,900	12,900	
Vehicles – Cost	20,000						20,000	
– Depreciation		7,500		2,500				10,000
Office equipment – Cost	4,000						4,000	
– Depreciation		1,000		500				1,500
Buildings – Cost	40,000						40,000	
– Depreciation		8,000		4,000				12,000
General expenses	500				500			
Provision for bad debts		1,800		200				2,000
Increase in provision for bad debts			200		200			
Bad debt	1,000				1,000			
Depreciation – Vehicles			2,500		2,500			
– Office			500		500			
– Buildings			4,000		4,000			
Light and heat	1,700		150		1,850			
Loss						31,870	31,870	
Prepayment (rates)			330				330	
Accrual (light and heat)				150				150
Debentures		10,000						10,000
Share capital and reserves		94,700						94,700

The following further information is provided:

(1)   An audit fee of £950 needs to be provided for.

(2)   The amount representing share capital and reserves in the extended trial balance consists of 100,000 25p shares. The first issue of 50,000 shares was at par, a subsequent issue of 50,000 shares being at a premium of 30p and this balance remains in its entirety in the shares premium account. The remainder consists of the brought forward balance on the profit and loss reserve.

(3)   A decision has been made to use half of the share premium account to make a bonus issue of ordinary 25p shares. No entries have been made in the extended trial balance to reflect this issue.

(4)   The amounts for rates and the depreciation of buildings should be split 50:50 between administrative and distribution cost classifications.

(5)   Included in the salaries are directors' emoluments of £45,000 of which £25,000 should be classed as administrative costs, the remainder being distribution costs. Also included in the salaries figure is £5,000 of the salesman's commission. The remainder of the salaries and wages should be split 60% administration and 40% distribution costs.

(6)   80% of the depreciation charge for vehicles should be classified as a distribution cost, the remainder being an administrative cost. The office equipment depreciation should be classed as an administrative expense.

(7)   Of the light and heat costs, £1,000 should be classed as administrative costs, the remainder being distribution.

(8)   £6,000 of the total motor expense are distribution costs, the remainder being administrative.

(9)   General expenses should be classed as administrative expenditure.

(10)   A building costing £35,000 (NBV £32,500) was sold for £37,500. The correct entries have been made in the buildings cost and depreciation accounts, as well as the bank account, but the profit figure does not appear to have been entered in the ETB profit and loss account.

(11)   On 1 December 1993 there was an issue of 10,000 £1 nominal 12% debentures at par. The issue has been correctly accounted for but no interest has been accrued.

(12)   The coding on the suspense account entry for £150 indicates it is an amount owing for motor expenses.

(13)   There is no tax charge for the year.

Assessment tasks

Task 1

Make any adjustments you feel necessary to the balances in the extended trial balance as a result of the matters set out in the further information. Set out your adjustments in the form of journal entries. (Ignore the effect of any adjustments on taxation.)

Task 2

Draft a profit and loss account for the year ended 31 December 1993 and a balance sheet as at that date in a form suitable for publication using Format 1 in accordance with the Companies Act as supplemented by FRS3 *Reporting financial performance*. (You are *not* required to prepare a statement of total recognised gains and losses or the reconciliation of movements in shareholders' funds required under FRS3.) You should assume that all the information relates to continuing operations.

Task 3

You have been asked to comment briefly on the following:

(a)   the constituents of the working capital of Tiny Toys Ltd;
(b)   the profitability of Tiny Toys Ltd;
(c)   the difference between cash flow and profitability.

Task 4

The Companies Act and SSAP2 require the disclosure of accounting policies in the notes to the accounts. Explain why this is useful to users of accounts, illustrating your answer with reference to:

(a)   depreciation;
(b)   research and development;
(c)   stock.

SUMMARY

Various interested parties may need to look at a business' accounts, from various standpoints. The common approach will involve comparison of figures with those of previous periods or with other companies.

Ratio analysis is one means of making such a comparison. The three main areas of comparison are:

- profitability
- liquidity
- capital gearing

Profitability:

- return on capital employed
- net profit margin
- asset turnover
- gross profit margin
- stock turnover

Liquidity:

- current ratio
- acid test (or quick) ratio
- debtor days

Gearing:

- capital gearing ratio

Sundry accounting problems

ACCOUNTING FOR PENSION COSTS

Introduction

Accounting for pension costs is an extremely complex subject in practice.

The aim of this session therefore is not to give you a detailed knowledge of the ins and outs of accounting for pension costs, but to give you an appreciation of the problems involved together with the requirements of SSAP24 *Accounting for pension costs*.

Pension arrangements

There are a large number of ways in which a company may provide pensions for its employees. The most common arrangement is that in which a separate pension fund is set up under a trust deed, into which the company and possibly the employee will pay contributions and which will pay the pensions and other benefits as and when they fall due. This is illustrated below.

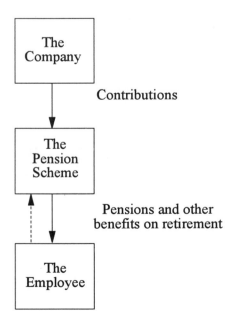

Whilst the employee works for the company, the company and possibly the employee pay contributions over to the pension scheme. When the employee retires, the pension scheme will pay him a pension.

It is the job of the actuary to tell the company what contributions should be paid over to the pension fund each year in order to build up enough assets to pay the employee's pension when he retires.

Most schemes are funded, ie. the future liabilities for benefits are provided for by the accumulation of assets held externally to the employing company's business.

Types of scheme

There are two main types of pension scheme: defined benefit and defined contribution.

- A *defined contribution scheme* (sometimes called a *money purchase scheme*) is a pension scheme in which the benefits are directly determined by the value of contributions paid in respect of each member. Normally the rate of contribution is specified in the rules of the scheme.

- A *defined benefit scheme* (sometimes called a *final salary scheme*) is a pension scheme in which the rules specify the benefits to be paid and the scheme is financed accordingly. The company cannot be certain in advance that contributions plus returns on investments will equal benefits to be paid. The actuary advises the company on the level of contributions necessary to produce the defined benefits. Formal actuarial valuations of a pension scheme take place at regular intervals, normally every three years. Contributions may be varied as a result. If there is a surplus, the actuary may recommend a contribution holiday (a period during which no contributions are made). If there is a deficit, the actuary may recommend that contributions are increased for one or more years.

The accounting problem

From the point of view of the employee, a pension may be regarded as deferred remuneration. From the point of view of the employer, it is part of the cost incurred in obtaining the employee's services. Under the accruals concept, the employer should recognise the cost of providing pensions on a systematic and rational basis over the period during which he benefits from the employee's services.

Defined contribution schemes

Defined contribution schemes present no accounting problems. Because the rate of contribution is fixed, the actual contributions payable to the pension scheme (funding) represent the cost to the company of providing pensions (accounting).

Defined benefit schemes

The amount of contributions paid to the scheme by the employer may vary from year to year in order to eliminate a surplus or a deficit. The true cost to a company of providing pensions for employees only emerges over the long term.

This means that the actual contributions payable to the pension scheme for a period may *not* represent the *actual cost* to the company of providing pensions.

SSAP24 requires that the employer should recognise the expected cost of providing pensions on a systematic and rational basis over the period during which benefit is derived from the employee's services.

The expected cost of providing pensions (given by the forecast of contributions) is spread over the average remaining service lives of the employees in the scheme. This has the effect of 'smoothing' the charge to the profit and loss account.

REPORTING THE SUBSTANCE OF TRANSACTIONS

Most transactions are reasonably straightforward and their commercial effect is the same as their strict legal form. However, in some instances this is not the case.

Example

A Ltd sells goods to B Ltd. A Ltd undertakes to repurchase the goods from B Ltd in 12 months' time.

The strict legal form of the transaction is that A has sold goods to B.

The commercial effect of the transaction is that B has made a secured loan to A.

Solution

In theory, A could record the transaction as a sale. To do so would be likely to enhance the appearance of A's financial statements. In particular, the company would appear to be less highly geared and therefore a safer investment than if A had recorded the transaction as a loan. This would, however, be very misleading.

In recent years, some companies have devised increasingly sophisticated schemes whereby it is possible for them to hold assets and liabilities which do not actually appear on the balance sheet. This practice is sometimes referred to as *off balance sheet financing*.

FRS5 *Reporting the substance of transactions* has been issued as a response to this problem. FRS5 states the following:

- An entity's financial statements should report the substance of the transactions into which it has entered.

- In order to determine the substance of a transaction, it is necessary to establish whether or not it has given rise to new assets or liabilities for the entity and whether or not it has increased or decreased the entity's existing assets and liabilities.

- Disclosure of a transaction should be sufficiently detailed to enable the user of the financial statements to understand its commercial effect.

Obviously the definition of assets and liabilities is critical. FRS5 uses the same definitions of assets and liabilities as those included in the Statement of Principles:

- *Assets* are rights or other access to future economic benefits controlled by an entity as a result of past transactions or events.

- *Liabilities* are obligations to transfer economic benefits as a result of past transactions or events.

- *Risk* is uncertainty as to amount of future benefits (gains or losses).

In addition the FRS states that:

- there is evidence that an entity has rights or other access to benefits (an asset) if it bears the *risks* inherent in the benefits.

Example

A Ltd sells goods to B Ltd under a sale and repurchase agreement (as before).

In order to determine the substance of the transaction, it is necessary to establish whether A still has rights or other access to future economic benefits associated with the goods (an asset).
Does A still have the benefits attaching to the asset?

A has a firm agreement to repurchase the goods, so it is unlikely that B has the right to sell or use them. Therefore A will eventually have the right to sell or use the goods.

Does A still bear the risks attaching to the asset?

Solution

A will eventually have the right to sell the goods. In addition, A almost certainly bears the risk that the goods will have become obsolete or otherwise fallen in value by the time that they are repurchased.

Therefore it appears that A has an asset. A also has an obligation to transfer an economic benefit (the repurchase price of the goods) to B in the future. Therefore A has a liability.

In practice, the process of determining the substance of a transaction might be very much more complicated than this. However, you are only expected to be aware of the broad principles of FRS5.

Another example of the principle of recognising the commercial substance of a transaction rather than its strict legal form is the accounting treatment of finance leases required by SSAP21.

RELATED PARTY TRANSACTIONS

The reader of the financial statements normally assumes that transactions reflected in the financial statements are made with independent parties unless told otherwise.

Readers will also normally assume that a company is owned by a number of shareholders and is not subject to control or significant influence by any one person or company unless told otherwise, eg. through the disclosure of the identity of the parent company.

Where a company does business with "related parties", for instance with shareholders or directors, these assumptions may not be valid.

For the financial statements to give a true and fair view, they must disclose the existence of any transactions with related parties and explain their effect.

SUMMARY

SSAP24

- The employer should recognise the expected cost of providing pensions on a systematic and rational basis over the period during which he derives benefit from the employees' services.

FRS5

- An entity's financial statements must report the substance of the transactions into which it has entered.

FRS8

- An entity's financial statements must disclose the existence of any related party transactions.

Group accounts – basic principles

INTRODUCTION

Until now, we have only dealt with the accounts of a single company. In this and the following sessions, we cover the major topic of group accounts.

In this session, we meet the basic principles of group accounts, which provide us with the foundation for studying the area in more detail in later sessions. In studying these sessions, you should always keep in mind these basic principles, as they are often of great value if you are having difficulty in trying to decide how to deal with something in a groups question.

This session may appear long in comparison with some others. This is because it includes several examples to illustrate the key points. If you feel that you understand the principles involved, you should treat the examples as mini-questions and work through them without looking at the solution until you have attempted the problem. As always, this is the best way to test your understanding.

GROUPS AND GROUP ACCOUNTS

Group

A group comprises a parent company and the undertakings (usually companies) under its control, which are called *subsidiaries*. The full legal definitions of a parent and subsidiaries are dealt with in Session 22 and are not important at this stage. For now, we shall assume that a parent has control of another company if it holds more than 50% of that company's ordinary shares.

Group accounts

The Companies Act 1985 requires a parent company to produce group accounts which show a true and fair view of the group to the parent's shareholders. The group accounts provide the parent's shareholders with information about the parent and the investments which it has made. Group accounts are intended for the parent's shareholders and are therefore prepared from the perspective of the parent company.

The parent's own individual balance sheet shows the investment in the subsidiary, usually at cost, and its profit and loss account shows dividend income from the subsidiary in investment income. Where the investing company has a controlling interest in another company, it is not sufficient merely to show the investment in this way as this does not reflect the substance of the relationship between a parent and its subsidiaries.

As the parent has control, it can decide how a subsidiary's assets are used to generate income in the same way that it can decide how to manage its own resources. Hence, the Companies Act requires group accounts to be in the form of consolidated accounts, which combine the results and net assets of the group members into a single set of figures.

- a consolidated balance sheet, which is presented in addition to the parent's own balance sheet as an individual company

- a consolidated profit and loss account, which is usually presented instead of the parent's own individual profit and loss account, although the parent may choose to publish its own individual profit and loss account as well

- a consolidated cash flow statement and statement of total recognised gains and losses (preparation of these for group accounts is beyond the scope of Unit 14)

- notes to the accounts, including accounting policies

The requirement to produce group accounts is subject to exemptions, which are dealt with in Session 22. Note that, although the parent does not need to publish its own profit and loss account as an individual company since it is publishing a consolidated profit and loss account instead, it must still publish its own individual balance sheet, in addition to the consolidated balance sheet.

SINGLE ENTITY CONCEPT

Group accounts *consolidate* the results and net assets of the individual group members to present the group to the parent's shareholders as a single economic entity. This contrasts with the legal form that each company is a separate legal person. This is called the *single entity concept* and is an example of reflecting economic substance in financial statements rather than strict legal form.

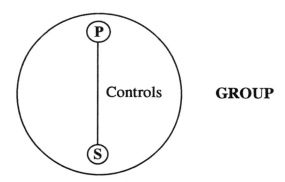

The group is viewed as a single entity.

To present the group as a single entity, the net assets and results of subsidiaries are added to those of the parent line by line to show the group's financial position and performance.

So that the group accounts do not show transactions and balances between group members, these are cancelled out on consolidation. If this were not done, the group accounts would show the effects of the group investing in and transacting with itself. In this session, we see how the parent's investment in the subsidiary is cancelled out on consolidation. We shall cover elimination of other transactions and balances between group members in later sessions. When dealing with these adjustments, you should always keep the single entity concept firmly in mind.

BASIC PRINCIPLES: CONSOLIDATED BALANCE SHEET

On the net assets side, we add together the net assets of the group members to show the resources under the parent's control. The parent's investment in the subsidiary is cancelled out and replaced by the underlying net assets of the subsidiary. We shall look at this aspect in more detail first.

Cancellation of cost of investment against net assets acquired

On consolidation we need to cancel out:

- the cost of the investment recorded in the parent company's books; against

- the net assets that the parent company has acquired as recorded in the subsidiary company's books. (This will be represented by the share capital and reserve balances on the date of the acquisition.)

Example 1

Russell Ltd has been trading for many years preparing accounts to 31 December each year. The directors of Russell Ltd decided to form a company, Bromley Ltd, which was to deal with the marketing side of their operations and in which Russell Ltd was to own the entire share capital.

Bromley Ltd was incorporated on 31 December 19X7 with an authorised share capital of 10,000 ordinary shares of £1 each, all of which were issued at par (ie. at their nominal value) to Russell Ltd in exchange for cash.

The group structure is therefore:

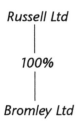

Russell Ltd

100%

Bromley Ltd

The balance sheets of the two companies at 31 December 19X7 were as follows:

		Russell Ltd		Bromley Ltd
	£	£		£
Fixed assets				
Tangible assets		30,000		
Investments: Shares in				
Bromley Ltd, at cost		10,000		
		40,000		
Current assets	130,000			10,000
Creditors: Amounts falling due				
within one year	(60,000)			
Net current assets		70,000		
Total assets less current liabilities		110,000		10,000
Capital and reserves				
Called-up share capital		50,000		10,000
Profit and loss account		60,000		–
		110,000		10,000

Bromley Ltd's balance sheet is simply made up of the newly issued shares and the cash it has received from Russell Ltd in return for those shares.

Required

Prepare the consolidated balance sheet of Russell Ltd as at 31 December 19X1.

Key principle

The cost of the investment in Russell Ltd's books will be cancelled out against the net assets acquired (represented by share capital) in Bromley's books. This applies the single entity concept.

The assets and liabilities of the two companies will be added together as they are all controlled by Russell Ltd.

Solution 1

Consolidated balance sheet at 31 December 19X7

	£	£
Fixed assets		
Tangible assets		30,000
Current assets (130,000 + 10,000)	140,000	
Creditors: Amounts falling due within one year	(60,000)	
		80,000
Total assets less current liabilities		110,000
Capital and reserves		
Called-up share capital		50,000
Profit and loss account		60,000
		110,000

This is very straightforward. However, once you understand this, much of what follows will fall into place easily.

Example 2

In this example, we will consider the purchase of the entire share capital of a company which has already been trading for a number of years.

Austin Ltd acquired the entire share capital of Reed Ltd for £15,000 cash on 31 December 19X7. The balance sheets of the two companies at that date were as follows:

	Austin Ltd		Reed Ltd	
	£	£	£	£
Fixed assets				
Tangible assets		80,000		8,000
Investments: Shares in Reed Ltd		15,000		
		95,000		
Current assets	200,000		24,000	
Creditors: Amounts falling due within one year	(165,000)		(17,000)	
Net current assets		35,000		7,000
Total assets less current liabilities		130,000		15,000
Capital and reserves				
Called-up share capital		100,000		10,000
Profit and loss account		30,000		5,000
		130,000		15,000

Required

Prepare the consolidated balance sheet of Austin Ltd as at 31 December 19X7.

Key principle

Once again, we simply need to reflect the fact that Austin Ltd now effectively owns £15,000 worth of **net assets** of Reed Ltd rather than simply £15,000 worth of shares (single entity concept).

Procedure

As previously described.

(1)   Consolidation of those net assets controlled by Austin Ltd.

						£
Fixed assets	80,000	+	8,000	=		88,000
Current assets	200,000	+	24,000	=		224,000
Creditors	(165,000)	+	(17,000)	=		(182,000)

(2)   Cancellation of cost of investment against the net assets acquired.

	£	£
Shares in Reed Ltd		15,000
Net assets acquired represented by:		
Share capital	10,000	
Profit and loss account	5,000	
		15,000
		–

(Note that as the company has already been trading, its net assets at the date of acquisition are represented not only by share capital but also by a profit and loss account balance.)

Solution 2

The consolidated balance sheet of Austin Ltd is:

	£	£
Fixed assets		
Tangible assets (80,000 + 8,000)		88,000
Current assets (200,000 + 24,000)	224,000	
Creditors: Amounts falling due within one year		
(165,000 + 17,000)	(182,000)	
Net current assets		42,000
Total assets less current liabilities		130,000
Capital and reserves		
Called-up share capital		100,000
Profit and loss account		30,000
		130,000

CONTROL AND OWNERSHIP

In the examples which we have looked at so far, the parent has owned the entire share capital of the subsidiary. However, this is not essential for the parent to have control. If the parent owns more than 50% of the subsidiary's shares, it will normally have control, assuming one vote per share. Hence the parent will be able to decide how all of the subsidiary's net assets are utilised, even though it does not own all of the subsidiary. Therefore, all of the subsidiary's net assets are added to the parent's own net assets to show the resources under the parent's control in the consolidated balance sheet.

The capital and reserves side of the consolidated balance sheet shows the ownership of the net assets controlled. The part of group net assets owned by the parent's shareholders is represented by the parent's share capital and reserves and its share of the subsidiary's reserves (covered in more detail later). The part of the subsidiary's net assets owned by the subsidiary's other shareholders (called minority interests) is shown separately under capital and reserves.

The consolidated profit and loss account, which we shall look at in detail later, is prepared using exactly the same principle. The results of the parent and subsidiary are combined in full to give the group's profit after tax, generated from the net assets controlled. This is then apportioned between the minority interests and the parent's shareholders according to ownership.

The following example illustrates how to prepare the consolidated balance sheet where there are minority interests in the subsidiary.

Example 3

Let us assume the same figures as in example 2, except that we will now assume that Austin Ltd acquired 80% of Reed Ltd's shares for £12,000 cash on 31 December 19X7 and that the current assets of Austin Ltd are £3,000 higher.

The balance sheets of the two companies at 31 December 19X7 are as follows:

| | Austin Ltd | | Reed Ltd | |
	£	£	£	£
Fixed assets				
Tangible assets		80,000		8,000
Investments: Shares in				
Reed Ltd		12,000		
		92,000		
Current assets	203,000		24,000	
Creditors: Amounts falling due				
within one year	(165,000)		(17,000)	
Net current assets		38,000		7,000
Total assets less current liabilities		130,000		15,000
Capital and reserves				
Called-up share capital		100,000		10,000
Profit and loss account		30,000		5,000
		130,000		15,000

Required

Prepare the consolidated balance sheet of Austin Ltd at 31 December 19X7.

Key principle

The distinction between control and ownership now becomes significant. As Austin Ltd has control, we need to add together the net assets of the two companies as previously, but we now need to show in the consolidated balance sheet that Austin Ltd's shareholders do not own all of those net assets. Instead, 20% of Reed Ltd's net assets are owned by the minority interests in Reed Ltd.

Procedure

We now need to add to our previous procedure. To help us identify the status of companies (eg. whether they are subsidiaries) and to enable us to deal with the various calculations, we need to identify the group structure before proceeding further.

(1)   Identify the group structure.

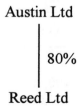

Austin Ltd

80%

Reed Ltd

The remaining 20% of Reed Ltd is held by minority interests.

(2)   Cancellation of cost of investment against net assets acquired.

Although Austin Ltd controls all of Reed Ltd's net assets, it does not own all of them. Austin Ltd has only invested in 80% of Reed Ltd's net assets, and on consolidation, Austin Ltd's investment is cancelled against its share of Reed Ltd's net assets:

	£	£
Shares in Reed Ltd		12,000
Share of net assets acquired, represented by:		
Share capital	10,000	
Profit and loss account	5,000	
	15,000	
Austin Ltd's share: 80% × 15,000		(12,000)
		–

(3)   Calculation of minority interests in Reed Ltd.

This is a new step. In the capital and reserves side of the consolidated balance sheet, we include a figure for minority interests which represents their share of Reed Ltd's net assets included in the consolidated balance sheet:

	£
Minority interests	
20% (from group structure) × £15,000 (Reed Ltd's net assets)	3,000

Solution 3

The consolidated balance sheet of Austin Ltd is as follows:

	£	£
Fixed assets		
Tangible assets (80,000 + 8,000)		88,000
Current assets (203,000 + 24,000)	227,000	
Creditors: Amounts falling due within one year		
(165,000 + 17,000)	(182,000)	
Net current assets		45,000
Total assets less current liabilities		133,000
Capital and reserves		
Called-up share capital		100,000
Profit and loss account		30,000
		130,000
Minority interests		3,000
		133,000

GOODWILL

In the above example, Austin Ltd paid £12,000 for an equal value of net assets. This situation is unlikely in practice because Reed Ltd has proved that it is already a profitable company by the existence of accumulated profits. Hence, Austin Ltd may need to pay more for Reed Ltd than simply the value of its net assets.

Example 4

Let us assume the same figures as in Example 3, except that the shares in Reed Ltd were bought by Austin Ltd for £14,000, and that the current assets of Austin Ltd are £2,000 lower.

The balance sheets of the two companies at 31 December 19X7 are as follows:

	Austin Ltd		Reed Ltd	
	£	£	£	£
Fixed assets				
Tangible assets		80,000		8,000
Investment: Shares in				
Reed Ltd (80%)		14,000		
		94,000		
Current assets	201,000		24,000	
Creditors: Amounts falling due				
within one year	(165,000)		(17,000)	
Net current assets		36,000		7,000
Total assets less current liabilities		130,000		15,000
Capital and reserves				
Called-up share capital		100,000		10,000
Profit and loss account		30,000		5,000
		130,000		15,000

Required

Prepare the consolidated balance sheet of Austin Ltd as at 31 December 19X7.

Key principle

Austin Ltd has paid £14,000 for £12,000 worth of net assets of Reed Ltd (80% × £15,000). Why has Austin paid £2,000 extra?

It must consider that Reed Ltd has *goodwill*. That is, the true value of Reed Ltd as a whole is more than that of its net assets as reflected in its balance sheet. Therefore Austin pays £12,000 for the assets in the balance sheet and £2,000 for the goodwill.

This goodwill is a value arising from the price paid of £14,000 but can only be identified and measured when we consolidate. It is therefore called *goodwill arising on consolidation*.

Procedure

Again we follow the basic two steps.

(1)   Cancellation of investment (Goodwill calculation)

	£	£
Shares in Reed Ltd		14,000
Net assets acquired represented by:		
Share capital	10,000	
Profit and loss account	5,000	
	15,000	
Austin Ltd's share (80% × £15,000)		12,000
Goodwill arising on consolidation		2,000

(2)   Consolidation of net assets controlled **together with the asset of goodwill arising on consolidation**

					£
Goodwill arising on consolidation					2,000
Tangible assets	80,000	+	8,000	=	88,000
Current assets	201,000	+	24,000	=	225,000
Creditors	(165,000)	+	(17,000)	=	(182,000)

Solution 4

The consolidated balance sheet of Austin Ltd is as follows:

	£	£
Fixed assets		
Intangible assets: Goodwill (arising on consolidation)		2,000
Tangible assets		88,000
		90,000
Current assets	225,000	
Creditors: Amounts falling due within one year	(182,000)	
Net current assets		43,000
Total assets less current liabilities		133,000
Capital and reserves		
Called-up share capital		100,000
Profit and loss account		30,000
		130,000
Minority interests (20% × £15,000)		3,000
		133,000

Note that there is no minority interest in goodwill.

The accounting treatment of goodwill on consolidation

The goodwill on consolidation arising in the previous example is one instance of purchased goodwill.

According to SSAP22, goodwill is the difference between the value of the business as a whole and the aggregate of the fair values of its separable net assets (covered in Session 11).

SSAP22 permits two possible treatments of goodwill:

- Elimination from the accounts immediately on acquisition against reserves – *immediate write-off* (Example 4A). Note that this is the treatment preferred by SSAP22.

- Elimination from the accounts by amortisation through the profit and loss account in arriving at profit or loss on ordinary activities on a systematic basis over its useful economic life – *amortisation* (Example 4B).

We shall now examine each of these methods to see the effect on our consolidated balance sheet.

Example 4A

Continue with the figures in Example 4 with the additional information that the directors have decided that the goodwill arising on the acquisition should be written off immediately to reserves.

The revised workings and consolidated balance sheet would therefore appear as follows:

Consolidation schedules

(1)   Cancellation of investment (goodwill calculation) as before:

	£
Goodwill arising on consolidation	2,000

(2)   Profit and loss account

	£
Austin Ltd per question	30,000
Less: Goodwill arising on consolidation written off	(2,000)
	28,000

Solution 4A

Austin Ltd: Consolidated balance sheet

	£	£
Fixed assets		
Tangible assets		88,000
Current assets	225,000	
Creditors: Amounts falling due within one year	(182,000)	
Net current assets		43,000
Total assets less current liabilities		131,000
Capital and reserves		
Called-up share capital		100,000
Profit and loss account		28,000
		128,000
Minority interests		3,000
		131,000

Notice the differences between this balance sheet and that in Example 4.

- There is no intangible fixed asset, as it has been written off.

- The balance on the consolidated profit and loss account is £2,000 lower, because when you write down the value of an asset the journal entry required is:

  Dr   Profit and loss account (in the schedule above)
        Cr   Asset account

  The write-off is an adjustment on consolidation as the goodwill only arises on consolidation. It will not affect the profit and loss account in the books of Austin Ltd.

Example 4B

Assuming the same figures in Example 4 once more, but in this case the directors have decided to write off goodwill arising on the acquisition through the profit and loss account over its useful economic life, which is estimated at five years. A full year's charge is to be made in the year of acquisition.

Consolidation schedules

(1)   Goodwill

	£
Goodwill arising on consolidation as previously	2,000
Less: Amortisation ($1/5 \times 2,000$)	(400)
Intangible asset: Goodwill arising on consolidation	1,600

(2)   Profit and loss account

	£
Austin Ltd per question	30,000
Less: Amortisation of goodwill arising on consolidation	(400)
	29,600

Solution 4B

Austin Ltd: Consolidated balance sheet

	£	£
Fixed assets		
Intangible assets: Goodwill arising on consolidation		
(2,000 – 400)		1,600
Tangible assets		88,000
		89,600
Current assets	225,000	
Creditors: Amounts falling due within one year	(182,000)	
Net current assets		43,000
Total assets less current liabilities		132,600
Capital and reserves		
Called-up share capital		100,000
Profit and loss account		29,600
		129,600
Minority interests		3,000
		132,600

Again the write-off is an adjustment on consolidation and will not affect the profit and loss account in the books of Austin Ltd. Next year the cumulative write-off will be £800 (ie. 2 × £400) and this amount will increase each year until it reaches £2,000 in year 5.

Negative goodwill

SSAP22 requires that negative goodwill is credited to a capital reserve in the consolidated balance sheet immediately on acquisition. No alternative treatment is allowed in this case.

Post-acquisition profits of subsidiaries

So far, we have only considered the consolidated balance sheet at the date of acquisition. We now need to consider the situation in subsequent years where the subsidiary has made profits whilst under the parent's control.

Example 5

The following balance sheets were extracted two years later from the books of Austin Ltd and Reed Ltd at 31 December 19X9:

	Austin Ltd		Reed Ltd	
	£	£	£	£
Fixed assets				
Tangible assets		85,000		11,000
Investment: Shares in				
Reed Ltd (80%)		14,000		
		99,000		
Current assets	217,000		33,000	
Creditors: Amounts falling due				
within one year	(176,000)		(25,000)	
Net current assets		41,000		8,000
Total assets less current liabilities		140,000		19,000
Capital and reserves				
Called-up share capital		100,000		10,000
Profit and loss account		40,000		9,000
		140,000		19,000

Required

Prepare the consolidated balance sheet of Austin Ltd as at 31 December 19X9, assuming that goodwill on consolidation is written off immediately to reserves.

Summary of the situation

The net assets of Reed Ltd have increased since acquisition by £4,000 to £19,000. The £19,000 of net assets must be included in the consolidated balance sheet at 31 December 19X9 and can be analysed as follows:

- **Pre-acquisition** £15,000 – This amount is financed by share capital (£10,000) and pre-acquisition profits (£5,000) 80% of which are cancelled against the cost of shares in Reed Ltd (exactly as was done on consolidating the accounts at 31 December 19X7); and

- **Post-acquisition** £4,000 – This amount is financed by post-acquisition profits (£4,000) 80% of which is credited to the consolidated profit and loss account, along with the profit and loss account of Austin Ltd. This profit was earned under Austin Ltd's control and 80% is owned by Austin Ltd's shareholders.

- The remaining 20% of Reed Ltd's net assets at 31 December 19X9 is owned by the minority shareholders in Reed Ltd and is included in the consolidated balance sheet under minority interests [£3,800 (20% × £19,000)].

It is important that you understand that the amount of goodwill arising on consolidation as calculated in 19X7 will not alter; it is calculated once and for all based on the subsidiary's net assets at acquisition.

Consolidation schedules

(1)   Goodwill

	£	£
Share in Reed Ltd		14,000
Net assets acquired represented by:		
Share capital	10,000	
Profit and loss account	5,000	
	15,000	
Austin Ltd's share (80% × £15,000)		12,000
		2,000

(2)   Profit and loss account

	£	£
Austin Ltd	40,000	
Less: Goodwill arising on consolidation	(2,000)	
		38,000
Reed Ltd per question	9,000	
Less: Pre-acquisition profits (Note)	(5,000)	
	4,000	
Austin Ltd's share (80% × 4,000)		3,200
		41,200

Note: Only post-acquisition profits are included in the group profit and loss account. These have been earned whilst under the parent's control. Pre-acquisition profits are cancelled out in the goodwill calculation.

Solution 5

Therefore the consolidated balance sheet of Austin Ltd at 31 December 19X9 is:

	£	£
Fixed assets		
Tangible assets (85,000 + 11,000)		96,000
Current assets (217,000 + 33,000)	250,000	
Creditors: Amounts falling due within one year		
(176,000 + 25,000)	(201,000)	
Net current assets		49,000
Total assets less current liabilities		145,000

Capital and reserves	£
Called-up share capital	100,000
Profit and loss account	41,200
	141,200
Minority interests (20% × £19,000)	3,800
	145,000

Make sure that you understand completely the above workings and how the figures in the consolidated balance sheet are arrived at before continuing.

The important point to grasp is that, for the first time in an example, the consolidated profit and loss account (£41,200) includes part of the accumulated profits of the subsidiary (£3,200). These are the subsidiary's profits that have accumulated post-acquisition, that is, since Reed Ltd came under the control of Austin Ltd, which are in substance owned by Austin Ltd's shareholders.

The net assets working

Our first consolidation schedule (the goodwill calculation) has so far been the cancellation of the cost of investment in the subsidiary against the net assets actually acquired for this consideration.

We have represented 'net assets' by share capital and the profit and loss account, applying the fundamental accounting equation.

From now on however the 'net assets' will be calculated in a separate working. This will ensure a methodical approach and assist us when questions become more complex.

The goodwill consolidation schedule would appear as follows:

	£
Cost of investment	14,000
Net assets acquired (80% × £15,000)	(12,000)
Goodwill	2,000

Working

	Acquisition date £
Net assets of subsidiary	
Share capital	10,000
Profit and loss account	5,000
	15,000

BASIC PRINCIPLES: CONSOLIDATED PROFIT AND LOSS ACCOUNT

Objective of the consolidated profit and loss account

The objective of the consolidated profit and loss account is to show the total results of the group as a single entity and then to show how much of that total is attributable to the members of the parent company.

This objective is achieved by aggregating the sales, expenses and profits of all companies in the group (after adjusting for intra-group transactions) and then deducting from the aggregate **profits after taxation** the profits attributable to minority interests. This will leave just the profits attributable to the members of the parent company.

Simple illustration

A simple illustration will demonstrate this approach. Suppose P Ltd has owned 80% of S Ltd for a number of years.

Profit and loss accounts for year ended 31 December 19X7

	P Ltd £		S Ltd £		Consolidated £
Profit before taxation	1,000	+	500	=	1,500
Tax	345	+	175	=	520
Profit after taxation	655	+	325	=	980
Minority interest (20% × £325)					65
Profit attributable to the members of parent company					915

In the consolidated profit and loss account, we have simply aggregated the profit before tax and the tax figures for P and S. However, P only owns 80% of S and is therefore only entitled to 80% of the profits generated by S. The remaining 20% is owned by the minority shareholders, this is reflected in the consolidated profit and loss account by deducting 20% of profit after tax of S Ltd as minority interest.

Remember that the minority interest is the minority share of S Ltd's profit after tax.

We return to the consolidated profit and loss account in more detail in Session 21.

QUESTIONS

1 Prince plc

On 1.1.19X4 Prince plc acquired 100% of the share capital of Madonna Ltd and Jackson Ltd, paying £60,000 and £40,000 respectively.

The balance sheets of the three companies are as follows at 31.12.X4:

		Prince £	*Madonna* £	*Jackson* £
Fixed assets:	Tangible	60,000	40,000	32,000
	Investments	100,000	–	–
		160,000	40,000	32,000
Current assets		90,000	86,000	52,000
Creditors: Amounts falling due within one year		(50,000)	(41,000)	(40,000)
Net current assets		40,000	45,000	12,000
Total assets less current liabilities		200,000	85,000	44,000
Creditors: Amounts falling due after more than one year		(18,000)	(30,000)	(10,000)
		182,000	55,000	34,000
Share capital		60,000	50,000	30,000
Profit and loss account		122,000	5,000	4,000
		182,000	55,000	34,000

Profit for the year:

	£
Jackson Ltd	3,000
Madonna Ltd	1,000

Required

Show how the consolidated balance sheet would look at 31 December 19X4.

2   Harvey plc

The summarised balance sheets of a group of companies at 30 June 19X8 are as follows:

	Harvey plc £	Nicholls Ltd £
Fixed tangible assets	350,000	405,000
Investment in group undertaking (shares and debentures)	198,000	–
Current account balance – due from Harvey plc	–	8,000
Net current assets	107,000	47,500
	655,000	460,500
10% debentures	(100,000)	–
8% debentures	–	(30,000)
	555,000	430,500

	Harvey plc £	Nicholls Ltd £
Capital and reserves		
Called-up share capital	50,000	100,000
Share premium	50,000	–
Profit and loss account	455,000	330,500
	555,000	430,500

Harvey plc bought 100% of the shares of Nicholls Ltd on 15 May 19X3 for £192,000 when Nicholls Ltd's reserves were £65,000. The company also owns £6,000 worth of Nicholls Ltd 8% debentures.

The following is also relevant:

(1)   Harvey plc wishes to propose a 15% dividend.

(2)   Harvey plc current account balance due to Nicholls Ltd has been included in net current assets.

(3)   The group accounting policy is to eliminate any goodwill on acquisition immediately against reserves.

Required

Prepare the draft consolidated balance sheet of the Harvey plc group at 30 June 19X8.

Note: Ignore advance corporation tax.

SUMMARY

In this session, we have met the basic principles of group accounts. Our main focus has been on the consolidated balance sheet, as this enables us to see how to apply these principles. Once you have grasped this, you should find it relatively straightforward to apply the same principles to the consolidated profit and loss account.

In the following sessions, we shall see how to deal with the consolidated balance sheet and profit and loss account in more detail. Before proceeding further, you must make sure that you understand the concept of the group as a single entity and the distinction between control and ownership. This last point is summarised in the following table:

Consolidated balance sheet	£	**Consolidated profit and loss account**	£
Net assets	X	Turnover	X
[P + S (100%) – interco items]		[P + S (100%) – interco items]	
		$\downarrow$ $\downarrow$	$\downarrow$
CONTROL	X	Profit after tax *(CONTROL)*	X
OWNERSHIP:		*OWNERSHIP:*	
Capital and reserves:		Minority interests (MI% × S's PAT)	(X)
Share capital (P only)	X		
Reserves (P + P% × S post acq)	X	Profit attributable to P's shareholders	X
Owned by P's shareholders	X	Dividends (P only)	(X)
Minority interests	X	Retained profit for the financial year	X
(MI% × S's net assets consolidated)			
	X		

Key

P = parent
S = subsidiary
P% = parent share of subsidiary
MI% = Minority interest share of subsidiary

Group accounts – consolidated balance sheet

SUMMARY OF BASIC TECHNIQUE

The basic steps for the consolidated balance sheet, which we met in the previous session, may be summarised as follows:

For the net assets side of the balance sheet, add together the net assets of the parent and subsidiary line-by-line.

For the capital and reserves side, it is best to use a series of workings:

(1)   Identify the group structure.

(2)   Identify the net assets of the subsidiary at acquisition for the goodwill computation and at the balance sheet date for minority interests. Identify the net assets by reference to the capital and reserves side of the balance sheet (ie. apply the fundamental accounting equation).

This is best done in a separate net assets working using two columns (one for the date of acquisition and one for the balance sheet date). This makes it easier to identify the subsidiary's post-acquisition profits for calculation of the consolidated profit and loss account reserve.

(3)   Cancel the cost of investment in the subsidiary, included in the parent's own balance sheet, against the share of the subsidiary's net assets acquired to give goodwill.

(4)   Calculate the minority interest share of the subsidiary's net assets (at the balance sheet date) included in the consolidated balance sheet and include this in minority interests.

(5)   Add the parent's share of the subsidiary's post-acquisition profits to the parent's own reserves and adjust for goodwill written off or amortised to calculate the group profit and loss reserve.

The workings for goodwill, minority interests and the profit and loss reserve are often called the *consolidation schedules*. These are often set out before the group structure and net assets workings.

We can now see the techniques in action in Example 1.

Example 1

The following balance sheets have been prepared at 31 December 19X8 for Dickens Ltd and its subsidiary Jones Ltd:

	Dickens Ltd		Jones Ltd	
	£	£	£	£
Fixed assets				
Tangible assets		85,000		18,000
Investment: 24,000				
shares in Jones Ltd		60,000		
		145,000		
Current assets	160,000		84,000	
Creditors: Amounts				
falling due within one year	(135,000)		(47,000)	
Net current assets		25,000		37,000
Total assets less				
current liabilities		170,000		55,000
Capital and reserves				
Called-up share capital		100,000		30,000
Profit and loss account		70,000		25,000
		170,000		55,000

Dickens Ltd acquired its holding in Jones Ltd on 31 December 19X7, when Jones Ltd's profit and loss account stood at £20,000.

Required

Prepare the consolidated balance sheet of Dickens Ltd at 31 December 19X8.

Solution

Consolidated balance sheet at 31 December 19X8

	£	£
Fixed assets		
Tangible assets (85 + 18)		103,000
Current assets (160 + 84)	244,000	
Creditors: Amounts falling due		
within one year (135 + 47)	182,000	
Net current assets		62,000
Total assets less current liabilities		165,000
Capital and reserves		
Called-up share capital		100,000
Profit and loss account (W5)		54,000
		154,000
Minority interest (W4)		11,000
		165,000

Workings

(1)   Group structure

Dickens Ltd

80%

Jones Ltd

(2)   Net assets of Jones Ltd:

	31 December 19X8	*31 December 19X7*
	£	£
Share capital	30,000	30,000
Profit and loss account	25,000	20,000
	55,000	50,000

(3)   Goodwill schedule

	£
Shares in Jones Ltd	60,000
Net assets acquired [80% (W1) × 50,000(W2)]	(40,000)
	20,000

(4)   Minority interest schedule

	£
20% × 55,000 (W2)	11,000

(5)   Profit and loss account schedule

	£
Dickens Ltd	70,000
Share of Jones Ltd post-acquisition:	
[80% (W1) × (25,000 – 20,000)(W2)]	4,000
Less: Goodwill written off (W3)	(20,000)
	54,000

Notice that the *goodwill computation* uses *reserves of Jones Ltd as at acquisition* since together with share capital, they represent the assets acquired, as such the amount of goodwill arising is fixed at the date of takeover.

When calculating the *minority interest* we refer to the *reserves at the current balance sheet date* since together with share capital, they represent the assets in which the minority interest has a share as at that date.

CANCELLATION OF INTRA-GROUP BALANCES

Introduction

As we have already discussed, when consolidating we need to cancel out items which are assets in one group company and liabilities in another.

This is an application of the single entity concept, which we met in the previous session:

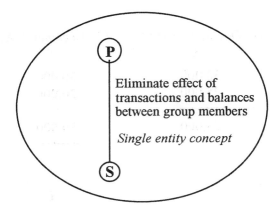

Where the group companies trade with each other, there are several ways in which balances with each other can arise. The most common of these are:

- loans and debentures
- current accounts

Loans and debentures

The cancellation process is very simple in that the credit balance of one company is offset against the debit balance of the other company, eliminating both balances from the consolidated balance sheet.

Current accounts

Current accounts are intra-group trading balances. The treatment of current accounts is the same as for loans. However, inter-company current accounts may not agree.

For example, the following balances appeared in the books of P Ltd and S Ltd in their balance sheets dated 31 December 19X0:

	Books of P Ltd £	Books of S Ltd £
S Ltd current account	10,700 Dr	
P Ltd current account		10,000 Cr

On 31 December 19X0 S Ltd had sent a cheque for £700 to P Ltd which the latter company did not record until 2 January 19X1. This is called cash-in-transit.

The necessary consolidation adjustment will be to follow the transaction to its natural conclusion by recording the receipt of the cash in P Ltd's books, thus decreasing its current account balance by £700 to £10,000, and increasing its cash balance by £700. The current account balances of £10,000 can then be cancelled out.

Example of cancellation of intra-group balances

Laura plc acquired 100% of the share capital of Ashley Ltd for £40,000 on 1 January 19X4, when the balance on the accumulated profit and loss account of Ashley Ltd stood at £8,000. The following draft balance sheets were drawn up at 31 December 19X7.

	Laura plc		Ashley Ltd	
	£	£	£	£
Fixed assets				
Tangible assets		88,000		39,000
Investments				
Shares in Ashley Ltd		40,000		–
6% debentures in				
Ashley Ltd		4,000		–
		132,000		39,000
Current assets				
Trade debtors	84,000		26,000	
Due from Laura plc	–		15,000	
Cash at bank and in hand	–		16,000	
	84,000		57,000	
Creditors: Amounts falling due				
within one year				
Trade creditors	46,000		28,000	
Due to Ashley Ltd	10,000		–	
Bank overdraft	14,000		–	
	70,000		28,000	
Net current assets		14,000		29,000
Total assets less current liabilities		146,000		68,000
Creditors: Amounts falling due after				
more than one year				
6% debentures		–		(12,000)
		146,000		56,000
Capital and reserves				
Called-up share capital		100,000		24,000
Profit and loss account		46,000		32,000
		146,000		56,000

You discover that Laura plc sent a cheque for £5,000 to Ashley Ltd on 30 December 19X7, which was not received until 3 January 19X8.

Required

Prepare the consolidated balance sheet of Laura plc as at 31 December 19X7.

Solution

Consolidated balance sheet of Laura plc at 31 December 19X7

	£	£
Fixed assets		
Tangible assets (88 + 39)		127,000
Current assets		
Trade debtors (84 + 26)	110,000	
Cash (16 + 5)	21,000	
	131,000	
Creditors: Amounts falling due within one year		
Trade creditors (46 + 28)	74,000	
Bank overdraft	14,000	
	88,000	
Net current assets		43,000
Total assets less current liabilities		170,000
Creditors: Amounts falling due after more than one year		
6% debentures (12 − 4)		(8,000)
		162,000
Capital and reserves		
Called-up share capital		100,000
Profit and loss account		62,000
		162,000

- **Current accounts**

  Adjust the receiving company's books, as if Ashley Ltd had received the cheque before the end of the year.

  Ashley Ltd's books

		£	£
Dr	Cash	5,000	
	Cr Intra-group – due from Laura		5,000

  Therefore the balance on its intra-group debtor is reduced to £10,000 and is equal to the amount shown as a creditor in Laura plc's accounts. We cancel these £10,000 balances.

- **6% debentures**

  Laura plc owns £4,000 of the debentures issued by Ashley Ltd. This asset in Laura plc's accounts must be cancelled with the liability in Ashley Ltd's books, leaving a liability due to the other debenture holders of £8,000.

- Consolidation workings

  (1)   Group structure

  Laura plc

  100%

  Ashley Ltd

  (2)   Net assets of Ashley Ltd

	Balance sheet date £	Acquisition date £
Share capital	24,000	24,000
Profit and loss account	32,000	8,000
	56,000	32,000

  (3)   Goodwill schedule

	£
Shares in Ashley Ltd	40,000
Net assets acquired (W2)	(32,000)
	8,000

  (4)   Profit and loss account schedule

	£
Laura plc	46,000
Ashley Ltd post-acquisition [32,000 – 8,000 (W2)]	24,000
Less: Goodwill (W3)	(8,000)
	62,000

DIVIDENDS

Basic approach

If a subsidiary proposes a dividend, the effects will be as follows:

- Subsidiary company books

Dr	Profit and loss	X	
	Cr Dividend creditor		X

  with the dividend payable

- Parent company books

Dr	Dividend debtor	X	
	Cr Profit and loss account		X

  with its share of the dividend receivable from the subsidiary company

- Consolidation adjustment

  The dividend debtor in the parent company's books is receivable from another group company, and should be cancelled out against all (if 100% owned) or part (if less than 100% owned) of the dividend creditor in the subsidiary company's books. Any balance on the dividend creditor of the subsidiary company represents the dividend owed to the minority shareholders of the company.

Example

The following are draft balance sheets as at 31 December 19X9 for Wells Ltd and its subsidiary, Christie Ltd:

	Wells Ltd £'000	Christie Ltd £'000
Fixed assets		
Tangible assets	300	100
Investment in Christie Ltd – 24,000 shares at cost	45	–
Current assets	300	168
Creditors: Amounts falling due within one year		
Trade creditors	(80)	(100)
Proposed dividends	(20)	–
Long-term loans	(175)	(60)
	370	108
Called up share capital – £1 ordinary shares	90	30
Profit and loss account	280	78
	370	108

Wells Ltd acquired its shares in Christie Ltd when the latter's reserves stood at £30,000. Christie Ltd wishes to propose a dividend of £8,000.

Required

Prepare the consolidated balance sheet as at 31 December 19X9.

Solution

Wells Ltd consolidated balance sheet at 31 December 19X9

	£'000	£'000
Fixed assets		
Tangible assets (300 + 100)		400.0
Current assets (300 + 168 + 6.4 – 6.4)	468.0	
Creditors: Amounts falling due within one year		
Trade creditors (80 + 100)	180.0	
Proposed dividends: Parent company	20.0	
Minority interests (20% × 8,000)	1.6	
	201.6	
Net current assets		266.4
Total assets less current liabilities		666.4
Creditors: Amounts falling due after more than one year (175 + 60)		(235.0)
		431.4
Capital and reserves		
Called-up share capital		90.0
Other reserves – capital reserve arising on consolidation		3.0
Profit and loss account		318.4
		411.4
Minority interest		20.0
		431.4

Workings

(1)   Group structure

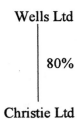

Wells Ltd

|
80%
|

Christie Ltd

(2)   Net assets of Christie:

	Balance sheet date		Acquisition date
	£'000	£'000	£'000
Share capital		30	30
Profit and loss account	78		30
Less: Proposed dividend	(8)		
		70	
		100	60

(3)   Goodwill schedule

	£'000
Shares in Christie Ltd	45
Net assets acquired [80% × 60 (W2)]	(48)
Capital reserve	(3)

(4)   Minority interest schedule

	£'000
20% × 100 (W2)	20

(5)   Profit and loss account schedule

	£'000	£'000
Wells Ltd	280	
Add: Dividend receivable (80% × 8)	6.4	
		286.4
Share of Christie Ltd		
[80% × (70 – 30)(W2)]		32
		318.4

OTHER CONSIDERATIONS

Other reserves

So far, we have only seen a profit and loss account reserve in the subsidiary's balance sheet. The pre-acquisition profit and loss reserves are cancelled out in the goodwill computation and the parent's share of the subsidiary's post-acquisition reserves is included in the group reserves calculation.

A subsidiary may have other reserves in its balance sheet, such as a revaluation reserve. On consolidation, we treat these in exactly the same way as the profit and loss reserve. Hence, the reserves at acquisition are cancelled out in the goodwill computation and the parent's share of any post-acquisition reserves is added to the parent's own reserves. However, it is important not to mix up the different categories of reserve. Therefore, if a subsidiary has a post-acquisition revaluation reserve, for example, the parent's share goes in the consolidated balance sheet under 'revaluation reserve' not 'profit and loss account'.

Accounting policies

All balances included in consolidated accounts should be based on the same accounting policies. If a subsidiary uses different accounting policies in preparing its own accounts from those adopted by the group as a whole (eg. regarding development costs), the subsidiary's accounts should be adjusted prior to consolidation for consistency. We should make any necessary adjustment to the subsidiary's profit and loss account reserve in the net assets working prior to calculating goodwill, minority interests and group reserves.

Fair values

As we saw earlier, goodwill is calculated using the *fair value* of the subsidiary's separable net assets at acquisition. Until now, we have implicitly assumed that the book value of the subsidiary's net assets at acquisition was equal to fair value. However, this will not always be the case and it may be necessary to restate the subsidiary's net assets at acquisition to fair value prior to consolidating. As with the accounting policy adjustment, we adjust for any change in net assets in the net assets working for example, by including a revaluation reserve balance.

Goodwill in a subsidiary's own books

We calculate goodwill on consolidation based on the fair value of the subsidiary's separable net assets acquired. Any goodwill recorded in the subsidiary's own balance sheet is not an asset separable from the business as a whole. Hence we need to eliminate this goodwill by adjusting the subsidiary's net assets prior to consolidating.

Note that, for uniform accounting policies, fair value adjustments and goodwill in a subsidiary's own books, we do not need to adjust in the subsidiary's own accounts as an individual company. Instead, we can make the adjustment just for the consolidated accounts.

PRO FORMA CONSOLIDATION WORKINGS

These proformas summarise the main workings for the consolidated balance sheet. Their main purpose is to illustrate how to set out and cross-reference your workings. Clear layout is absolutely crucial as you will lose marks if the assessor cannot see how you have made your calculations. These proformas do not cover every possible situation but do illustrate the main points which we have covered so far.

Workings

(1)   Group structure

<pre>
        P
        |
        | 75%
        |
        S
</pre>

(2)   S Ltd: Net assets working

		Balance sheet date	Acquisition
	£	£	£
Share capital		X	X
Share premium account		X	X
Revaluation reserve		X	X
Profit and loss account			
Per question	X		
Adjustments in S prior to consolidation:			
Proposed dividends (W6)	(X)		
Other (eg. uniform a/c policies)	X		
Final		A	C
		B	D

(3)   Goodwill schedule

		Acquisition
		£
Cost of investment in S Ltd		X
Less: Share of net assets acquired [75% × D(W2)]	X	
		X

(4)   Minority interests schedule

	Balance sheet date
	£
Their share of S's net assets at balance sheet date [25% × B(W2)]	X

(5)   Profit and loss account schedule

	Balance sheet date
	£
P's profit and loss account (draft per question)	X
Adjustments (in P's own books):	
P's dividends proposed (W6)	(X)
Dividend from S [75% × S's dividend proposed (W6)]	X
[P's own adjusted profit (can omit this line)	X]
P's share of S's post-acquisition retained profit	
[75% × (A – C) (W2)]	X
Goodwill written off (W3)	(X)
	X

(6)   Dividends [**Note:** Only post entries not already made in figures given in the question.]

   (a)   P's dividend proposed

P's books	£	£
Dr Profit and loss account (W5)	X	
Cr Creditors (consolidated balance sheet)		X

   (b)   S's dividend proposed

S's books	£	£
Dr Profit and loss account (W2 net assets)	X	
Cr Creditors (cancel 75% against P's debtor)	X	
(Remaining 25% is a creditor in the		
consolidated balance sheet due to MI)		

P's books	£	£
Dr Debtors	X	
(P's share 75% – this cancels against S's creditor)		
Cr Profit and loss account (W5)		X
(Cr Cost of investment if dividend is pre-acquisition)		

QUESTIONS

1   Roller Ltd

Balance sheets at 30 June 19X0

	Roller Ltd £	Roller Ltd £	Steam Ltd £	Steam Ltd £
Fixed assets				
Tangible assets		16,720		4,900
Investments		5,295		–
		22,015		4,900
Current assets				
Stocks	1,188		879	
Debtors	1,801		262	
Current account				
– Roller Ltd	–		300	
Cash	34		98	
	3,023		1,539	
Creditors: Amounts falling due within one year	5,614		863	
Net current (liabilities)/assets		(2,591)		676
Total assets less current liabilities		19,424		5,576
Creditors: Amounts falling due after more than one year		(5,646)		(1,382)
		13,778		4,194
Capital and reserves				
Called-up share capital (£1 ordinary shares)		2,500		1,500
Share premium account		600		500
Revaluation reserve		4,572		–
Profit and loss account		6,106		2,194
		13,778		4,194

(1)   On 1 July 19W9 Roller Ltd acquired 1,275 shares in Steam Ltd for £5,295 cash, when Steam Ltd's profit and loss account stood at £1,000 and share premium account, £500.

(2)   A cheque for £300 from Roller Ltd to Steam Ltd, sent before 30 June 19X0, was not received by the latter company until July 19X0.

Required

Prepare the consolidated balance sheet of Roller Ltd at 30 June 19X0.

2 Heavy plc

As on 31 March 19X1 the draft balance sheets of Heavy plc and its subsidiary, Side Ltd showed the following positions:

	Heavy plc £	Heavy plc £	Side Ltd £	Side Ltd £
Fixed assets (tangible)		180,000		40,000
Investment in Side Ltd		49,200		–
		229,200		40,000
Current assets				
Stock	40,000		32,000	
Inter-company account	–		10,500	
Cash at bank and in hand	–		3,000	
	40,000		45,500	
Creditors: Amounts falling due within one year				
Bank overdraft	6,000		–	
Trade creditors	41,000		17,000	
Inter-company account	8,000		–	
	55,000		17,000	
Net current (liabilities)/assets		(15,000)		28,500
Total assets less current liabilities		214,200		68,500
Creditors: Amounts falling due after more than one year				
Debenture loan		(50,000)		–
		164,200		68,500
Financed by:				
Share capital – £1 ordinary shares		100,000		10,000
Share premium account		20,000		10,000
Profit and loss account		44,200		48,500
		164,200		68,500

You are given the following additional information:

(1)   Shortly before the year-end, Heavy plc paid £2,500 to Side Ltd. At 31 March 19X1, Side Ltd had not yet received this amount.

(2)   It has been decided that Heavy plc and Side Ltd should declare dividends of 10 pence per share and 20 pence per share respectively for the year ended 31 March 19X1.

(3)   Heavy plc acquired 80% of the issued share capital of Side Ltd on 1 April 19X0. Side Ltd made a profit available for distribution for the year of £10,500.

(4)   It is group accounting policy to eliminate any goodwill on acquisition immediately against reserves.

Required

Prepare the consolidated balance sheet of Heavy plc as on 31 March 19X1, together with your consolidation schedules.

Note: Ignore advance corporation tax.

SUMMARY

In this session we have looked in depth at how to prepare a consolidated balance sheet, including how to deal with intra-group balances, dividends and adjustments to eliminate unrealised profits.

You should now be able to:

*   prepare a consolidated balance sheet together with supporting workings

*   cancel out inter-company items

*   adjust for dividends in the consolidated balance sheet

Group accounts – consolidated profit and loss account

INTRODUCTION

In this session, we switch our attention to the consolidated profit and loss account. This is prepared on the same basis as the consolidated balance sheet and thus most of the key principles will already be familiar. In particular, the single entity concept and the distinction between control and ownership are as important to the consolidated profit and loss account as they are to the consolidated balance sheet.

BASIC PRINCIPLES

The parent's own profit and loss account as an individual company will show dividend income from the subsidiary. The consolidated profit and loss account shows the incomes generated from the group's resources. Those resources are shown by the net assets in the consolidated balance sheet.

As you will recall, when we prepared the consolidated balance sheet, we added together the net assets of the parent and subsidiary line by line to show the resources under the parent's control. We apply exactly the same principle in preparing the consolidated profit and loss account by adding together the parent's and subsidiary's income and expenses line by line. This will give us the profit after tax generated from the resources under the group's control.

In the consolidated balance sheet, we showed the ownership of the group's net assets on the capital and reserves side, where we showed the minority interests separately from the capital and reserves attributable to the parent's shareholders. In the consolidated profit and loss account, we show the ownership of the profit after tax by deducting the minority interest share of the subsidiary's profit from profit after tax, leaving us with the profit owned by the parent's shareholders.

When we looked at the consolidated balance sheet, we saw how the single entity concept was applied by cancelling out intra-group items and unrealised profits, and how we apportioned unrealised profit adjustments according to ownership. As we shall see in more detail later in the session, we apply the same principles in the consolidated profit and loss account.

We shall now see in more detail how to prepare the consolidated profit and loss account.

DETAILED REQUIREMENTS

Pro forma

Work your way through the pro forma, referring to the tutorial notes which are referenced by letters in brackets.

Consolidated profit and loss account for the year ended . . . . .

		£
Turnover (a)		
Continuing operations		X
Acquisitions		X
		X
Discontinued operations		X
		X
Cost of sales (a)		(X)
Gross profit		X
Distribution costs		(X)
Administrative expenses		(X)
Other operating income		X
Operating profit		
Continuing operations	X	
Acquisitions	X	
	X	
Discontinued operations	(X)	
		X
Profit on the sale of fixed assets		X
Profit on ordinary activities before interest		X
Other interest receivable and similar income (b) (c)		X
Interest payable and similar charges (b)		(X)
Profit on ordinary activities before taxation (Note 1)		X
Tax on profit on ordinary activities		(X)
Profit on ordinary activities after taxation (d)		X
Minority interests (e)		(X)
Profit for the financial year attributable to parent's shareholders (Note 2)		X
Dividends (f)		(X)
Retained profit for the year		X

Statement of retained profits

Retained profits at beginning of year (g)	X
Retained profit for the financial year	X
Retained profits at end of year	X
Earnings per share	Xp

Notes to the accounts

(1)   Profit on ordinary activities before taxation is stated after charging the following:

	£
Depreciation of tangible fixed assets (h)	X
Auditors' remuneration and expenses (h)	X
Directors' emoluments (i)	
As directors	X
Remuneration as executives	X

(2)   The profit for the financial year of Parent Company Ltd is £X. The parent company has taken advantage of the legal exemption not to publish its own profit and loss account (j).

Tutorial notes

(a)   Intra-group sales must be eliminated from both the turnover of the selling company and the cost of sales of the buying company.

(b)   Any intra-group interest must be eliminated from interest receivable and interest payable respectively (single entity concept).

(c)   Similarly, dividends from subsidiaries must be eliminated since the whole of the profits of those subsidiaries are being consolidated and it would be double counting to include the dividends as well.

(d)   Profit on ordinary activities after taxation – Up to this point, 100% of all items for the parent company and all subsidiaries have been aggregated (subject to intra-group adjustments). It is now necessary to compute the amount of the profit after taxation that is attributable to outside (minority) shareholders.

(e)   Minority interests – This is calculated by taking the minority interest's share of the subsidiary's profit after taxation.

(f)   Dividends paid and proposed – These will be the dividends of the *parent company only* since a subsidiary's dividends are effectively intra-group items. No dividends to minority interests are included as their share of the subsidiary's profit after tax, whether or not paid out as a dividend, has already been taken out in the minority interest line.

(g)   Retained profits at beginning of year – This figure will be the retained profits brought forward of the parent company together with the parent company's share of the post-acquisition retained profits of each subsidiary, less goodwill written off. This is the figure which would appear in the opening consolidated balance sheet.

(h) Auditors' remuneration/depreciation – This disclosure will be the simple aggregation of the amounts in the parent company and each subsidiary.

(i) Directors' emoluments – This disclosure is an exception to the basic rule of aggregation. The statutory requirement is to show the total of all emoluments paid by companies within the group *to directors of the parent company only*.

(j) The amount of the profit for the financial year in the accounts of the parent company will be the profit before dividends paid and proposed in its own profit and loss account. However, if the parent's own profit and loss account does not yet include dividends due from the subsidiary, these need to be added on! This note is an extra disclosure requirement when the parent does not publish its own individual profit and loss account. (Strictly speaking, this would be a note to the *individual balance sheet* of the parent company. You are unlikely to be asked to prepare this note in the assessment.)

Example

Set out below are the draft profit and loss accounts of Smiths plc and its subsidiary company Flowers Ltd for the year ended 31 December 19X7.

On 31 December 19X5 Smiths plc purchased, ex div, 75,000 ordinary shares and £10,000 10% debentures in Flowers Ltd. At that date the profit and loss account of Flowers Ltd showed a credit balance of £3,000.

The issued share capital of Flowers Ltd is 100,000 £1 ordinary shares, and it had £30,000 10% debentures outstanding on 31 December 19X7. Flowers Ltd pays its debenture interest on 31 December each year.

	Smiths plc £	Flowers Ltd £
Turnover	600,000	300,000
Cost of sales	(427,000)	(232,000)
Gross profit	173,000	68,000
Distribution costs	(41,000)	(14,000)
Administrative expenses	(52,000)	(31,000)
Income from shares in group undertakings	7,500	–
Income from other fixed asset investments		
(dividends from UK quoted companies)	3,000	1,000
Other interest receivable – from group companies	1,000	–
Interest payable	–	(3,000)
Profit on ordinary activities before taxation (Note)	91,500	21,000
Tax on profit on ordinary activities	(38,500)	(8,000)
Profit on ordinary activities after taxation	53,000	13,000
Dividends – proposed	(30,000)	(10,000)
Retained profit for the year	23,000	3,000
Retained profits brought forward	30,000	12,000
Retained profits carried forward	53,000	15,000

Note

Profit before taxation has been arrived at after charging:

	£	£
Depreciation	*20,000*	*6,000*
Auditors' remuneration and expenses	*5,000*	*2,000*
Directors' emoluments	*10,000*	*4,000*

The following additional information is relevant:

(1)   *During the year Smiths plc sold goods to Flowers Ltd for £20,000, making a profit of £5,000. These goods were all sold by Flowers Ltd before the end of the year.*

(2)   *Included in the director's emoluments of £4,000 in Flowers Ltd's accounts is £1,000 paid to a director of Smiths plc.*

Required

Prepare for presentation to members the consolidated profit and loss account for the year ended 31 December 19X7. Smiths plc does not propose to publish its own profit and loss account.

Workings

Following through the pro forma, we will take the problems one at a time. Where you are uncertain of the treatment, refer back to the earlier tutorial notes.

Group structure

Smiths plc

75%

Flowers Ltd

Note that there are no acquisitions or discontinued operations during the year, therefore analysis of the results between continuing operations, acquisitions and discontinued operations is not required in this example.

Turnover and cost of sales

The total turnover is £900,000 but the intra-group sale has been included as part of Smiths plc's turnover. It must be eliminated, leaving £880,000.

Similarly, total cost of sales is £659,000 but the intra-group purchase has been included in cost of sales for Flowers Ltd. Therefore eliminating it leaves £639,000.

Investment income and interest payable

●   **Income from shares in group companies** represents the dividend receivable from the subsidiary (75% × £10,000). It must be excluded from the consolidated profit and loss account.

- **Interest receivable from group companies** is Smiths plc's share of the debenture interest paid by Flowers Ltd (10% × £10,000). It must be cancelled against the *interest payable* in Flowers Ltd's profit and loss account to leave the net *interest payable* to people outside the group of £2,000.

Minority interests

The minority interest is 25% of Flowers Ltd's profit after tax figure (ie. 25% × £13,000 = £3,250).

Dividends

Smiths plc's dividend only: £30,000

Retained profits brought forward

The retained profit brought forward is calculated using the profit and loss schedule which we used for the consolidated balance sheet, except that we use the figures at the *start* of the year, not the end.

Remember we only include the parent company's share of the **post-acquisition** profits of a subsidiary:

	£
Smiths plc	30,000
Flowers Ltd [75% × £(12,000 − 3,000)]	6,750
	36,750

Disclosure of directors' emoluments

Emoluments paid to directors of Smiths plc only: (£10,000 + £1,000) £11,000

Solution

Smiths plc
Consolidated profit and loss account for the year ended 31 December 19X7

	£
Turnover	880,000
Cost of sales	(639,000)
Gross profit	241,000
Distribution costs	(55,000)
Administrative expenses	(83,000)
Income from other fixed asset investments	4,000
Interest payable	(2,000)
Profit on ordinary activities before taxation (Note 1)	105,000
Tax on profit on ordinary activities	(46,500)
Profit on ordinary activities after taxation	58,500
Minority interests	(3,250)
Profit for the financial year attributable to the group (Note 2)	55,250
Dividends – proposed	(30,000)
Retained profit for the year	25,250

Statement of retained profits

	£
Retained profits brought forward	36,750
Retained profit for the year	25,250
Retained profits carried forward	62,000

Notes to the accounts

(1)   Profit before taxation has been arrived at after charging:

	£
Depreciation	26,000
Auditors' remuneration and expenses	7,000
Directors' emoluments	11,000

(2)   The profit for the financial year of Smiths plc is £53,000. The parent company has taken advantage of the legal exemption not to publish its own profit and loss account.

TREATMENT OF GOODWILL

Introduction

Remember that SSAP22 (revised) permits two treatments of goodwill:

- immediate write-off (preferred)
- amortisation

If no treatment is specified in an assessment question, you should use the preferred treatment.

We will consider the options using an illustration.

Illustration

A Ltd buys 90% of the shares of B Ltd on 1 January 19X9, the first day of its accounting period. Goodwill arising is £10,000, and has an estimated useful economic life of 10 years.

Immediate write-off

- Year 1

Statement of group reserves

	Profit and loss account £
At 1 January 19X9	X
Retained profit for the financial year	X
Goodwill written off	(10,000)
At 31 December 19X9	X

- Subsequent years

    Note that the group retained profits brought forward would be net of £10,000 goodwill written off in year 1.

Amortisation

- Years 1–10

    The group profit and loss account each year would include a charge of £1,000. This would be included under administrative expenses.

- Year 2 onwards

    Note that the group retained profits brought forward would be net of the cumulative write-off of goodwill to date:

Year 2	£1,000
Year 3	£2,000
Year 4	£3,000, etc.

LINK BETWEEN BALANCE SHEET AND PROFIT AND LOSS ACCOUNT

In studying the consolidated profit and loss account, we have seen that the statement of reserves reconciles the opening and closing balances on the profit and loss account reserve. Where there are other reserves (eg. revaluation reserve), the statement of reserves should also include these. The main components of the statement of reserves and where we can also see the figures in the balance sheet and profit and loss account, are summarised below:

Statement of reserves (in group accounts)

	Profit and loss account
	£
Brought forward (per last year's consolidated balance sheet)*	X
Retained profit for the year (from the consolidated profit and loss account)X	
Goodwill written off (on acquisitions in the year)#	(X)
Carried forward (per this year's consolidated balance sheet)*	X

* = from profit and loss schedule at relevant date
\# = from goodwill schedule

QUESTIONS

1   Courage Ltd

The following are the draft profit and loss accounts of Courage Ltd and Brains Ltd for the year ended 31 December 19X4:

	Courage Ltd £	*Brains Ltd* £
Turnover	3,000,000	900,000
Cost of sales	(1,700,000)	(600,000)
Gross profit	1,300,000	300,000
Distribution costs	(300,000)	(100,000)
Administrative expenses	(600,000)	(96,800)
Operating profit	400,000	103,200
Loss on sale of fixed asset investment	(50,000)	–
Reorganisation costs	–	(10,000)
Profit on ordinary activities before interest	350,000	93,200
Income from other fixed asset investments (dividends from UK quoted companies)	8,000	2,000
Other interest receivable – from group undertakings	1,600	–
Interest payable	–	(3,200)
Profit on ordinary activities before taxation	359,600	92,000
Tax on profit on ordinary activities	(159,600)	(40,000)
Profit on ordinary activities after taxation	200,000	52,000
Dividends: Ordinary, proposed	(20,000)	(4,000)
Retained profit for the year	180,000	48,000
Retained profits brought forward	100,000	25,000
Retained profits carried forward	280,000	73,000

You are given the following information:

(1)   Issued share capital of the two companies:

Courage Ltd	£100,000	in £1 ordinary shares
Brains Ltd	£20,000	in £1 ordinary shares

(2)   Courage Ltd bought an interest in Brains Ltd on 1 January 19X2, as follows:

12,000 ordinary shares
£20,000 (out of £40,000) 8% debentures

On 1 January 19X2 the balance of Brains Ltd's profit and loss account was £12,000.

(3)   Towards the end of the year Brains Ltd invoiced goods to Courage Ltd for £10,000.

(4) Brains Ltd has incurred exceptional reorganisation costs during the year. However, there are no discontinued operations.

(5) Courage Ltd does not account for dividends until they are received.

Required

Prepare the consolidated profit and loss account of Courage Ltd and its subsidiary Brains Ltd for the year ended 31 December 19X4.

2   Frog Ltd

The following are the draft profit and loss accounts for Frog Ltd and its subsidiary company Firkin Ltd for the year to 31 January 19X2:

	Frog Ltd		*Firkin Ltd*	
	£	£	£	£
Turnover		960,000		720,000
Cost of sales		600,000		480,000
Gross profit		360,000		240,000
Distribution costs	36,000		12,000	
Administrative expenses	190,080		99,600	
		226,080		111,600
Operating profit		133,920		128,400
Investment income				
Dividends received				
Firkin Ltd	6,720		–	
Debenture interest received (gross)				
Firkin Ltd	9,600		–	
		16,320		–
Debenture interest payable		(24,000)		(24,000)
Profit before tax		126,240		104,400
Corporation tax @ 33%		(44,200)		(36,540)
Profit after tax		82,040		67,860
Dividends: Paid	–		9,600	
Proposed	26,000		14,400	
		26,000		24,000
Retained profit		56,040		43,860
Profits brought forward		85,660		50,540
Profits carried forward		141,700		94,400

You are given the following information:

(1) Frog Ltd acquired 70% of the issued ordinary share capital of Firkin Ltd on 1 February 19X0, when the profit and loss account of Firkin Ltd was £34,800. Goodwill of £5,000 arose on this acquisition.

It is the group's accounting policy to amortise goodwill over a useful life of ten years.

Frog Ltd acquired 40% of the debentures of Firkin Ltd two years ago.

(2) Frog Ltd and Firkin Ltd trade with each other. During the year Frog Ltd sold to Firkin Ltd £96,000 of goods, making a profit of £30,000; and Firkin Ltd sold to Frog Ltd £72,000 of goods making a profit of £7,200.

(3) Provision is to be made for directors' remuneration as follows:

Frog Ltd	£20,000
Firkin Ltd	£12,000

No director of either company is a director of the other company.

(4) Frog Ltd does not account for dividends until they are received.

Required

Prepare the consolidated profit and loss account of Frog Ltd for the year ended 31 January 19X2.

SUMMARY

The key thing to remember is that the consolidated profit and loss account gives the results of the group trading with third parties.

Therefore the following adjustments are necessary:

- Eliminate the intra-group sales from turnover and cost of sales.

- Exclude dividends received from the subsidiary.

- Include minority interest, being the minority interest's share of the subsidiary company's profit after tax.

- Only include the dividends paid and proposed by the parent company.

Group accounts – legal and professional requirements

INTRODUCTION

In this final session on group accounts, we shall look at the law and Standards governing this area of financial reporting. Many of the points of principle will already be familiar; the main purpose of the session is to draw them together.

In this session, we shall look at the Companies Act 1985, as amended by the 1989 Act, FRS2 *Accounting for subsidiary undertakings* and SSAP1 *Accounting for associated companies,* as modified by the ASB Interim Statement *Consolidated Accounts.*

COMPANIES ACT 1985 REQUIREMENTS

Definition of parent and subsidiary

The full definition is given in the Act and is restated in FRS2. The key points of the definition are summarised below:

An undertaking is the parent of another (a subsidiary) if *any* of the following apply:

–   It holds a majority of voting rights.

–   It is a member and can appoint/remove directors with a majority of votes.

–   It is a member and controls a majority of votes via an agreement with other members.

–   It has a participating interest and actually exercises dominant influence or the undertakings are managed on a unified basis.

FRS2 defines *dominant influence.* In essence, the term means that the parent determines the financial and operating policies of the subsidiary, which effectively means that the parent has control.

FRS2 also defines *managed on a unified basis.* This term means that the undertakings are integrated and managed as a single unit.

Requirement to prepare group accounts

A company must prepare group accounts if it is a parent company at its year-end (ie. it has one or more subsidiaries, unless it qualifies for exemption from this requirement).

Exemptions from the requirement to prepare group accounts

Inclusion in consolidated results of a larger group

A company need not prepare group accounts if:

- its immediate parent is incorporated in the European Union (EU) and prepares accounts in accordance with (EU) requirements; and

- the company seeking the exemption does not have any securities listed on a stock exchange in the EU; and

- the company is a wholly owned subsidiary of its immediate parent; or

- the parent owns over 50% and notice requiring group accounts has not been served by:

   - holders of more than half of the remaining shares *not* held by the parent; or
   - holders of 5% of total shares.

Small and medium-sized groups

- A small or medium-sized group, not containing a public company, a banking, authorised investment or insurance company, need not prepare group accounts if it:

   - meets any two of the small/medium-size limits for two consecutive years; or
   - met size criteria and was entitled to exemption last year; or
   - meets size criteria this year and was entitled to exemption last year.

   Size limits:

	Before consolidation adjustments		After consolidation adjustments
Turnover not more than	£13,440,000	or	£11,200,000
Gross assets not more than	£6,720,000	or	£5,600,000
Average number of employees not more than		250	

- The totals before consolidation adjustments are obtained by adding together the amounts in the individual company accounts.

- The totals after consolidation adjustments are obtained from the group balance sheet (and profit and loss account).

Other Companies Act requirements for group accounts

- Group accounts must be consolidated.

- The parent and subsidiaries should have the same accounting period and year-end. If this is not practicable, the Act allows:

   - consolidation of a subsidiary's statutory accounts drawn up to date within three months prior to the parent's year-end; or

- consolidation of interim accounts for the subsidiary made up to the parent's year-end; this alternative is preferred by FRS2.

- Uniform accounting policies should be used for amounts included in the group accounts. Different accounting policies may only be used in exceptional cases. The group accounts must disclose particulars of the different policies (restated in FRS2).

- Standard formats and disclosures must be used. These are set out in the sessions on company accounts.

FRS2: ACCOUNTING FOR SUBSIDIARY UNDERTAKINGS

FRS2 deals with the preparation of group accounts, including application of the Companies Act requirements.

Objective

To require parent undertakings to provide financial information about their groups in consolidated financial statements, intended to present the parent and its subsidiaries as a single economic entity.

Key definitions

- *Consolidation* is the process of adjusting and combining financial information from individual financial statements to present information for the group as a single economic entity.

- *Control* is the ability to direct the financial and operating policies of another entity.

- *Minority interests* are the interests in a subsidiary held by or on behalf of persons other than the parent and its subsidiaries.

- *Parent and subsidiary*: see section on Companies Act 1985 provisions.

Disclosures for principal subsidiary undertakings

- The proportion of voting rights held by the parent and its subsidiaries

- An indication of the nature of the subsidiary's business

Minority interests

- The consolidated balance sheet should show separately in capital and reserves the minority interest share of the subsidiary's net assets or liabilities consolidated. Note that, if the subsidiary has net liabilities, we show this as a debit balance in capital and reserves.

- The consolidated profit and loss account should show separately the minority interest share of the subsidiary's profit or loss after tax for the period.

Intra-group transactions

- Eliminate in full any profits or losses on intra-group transactions reflected in the book value of assets included in consolidation.

- Apportion the elimination of profits or losses between the parent and minority interests in proportion to their holdings in the company recording the profit or loss in its own financial statements. Hence, when the subsidiary sells goods to the parent, the subsidiary records the profit so we apportion the elimination between the parent and minority interests.

Changes in composition of a group

- Changes in membership of a group occur on the date on which control passes.

OTHER TYPES OF INVESTMENT

We have seen that, if a company has an investment in another company, the accounting treatment of that investment depends upon whether or not that investment gives *control*. If the investment gives control, the investment is treated as a subsidiary and group accounts are prepared. If the investment does not give control, it is treated as a simple investment (see the sessions on published accounts).

In practice, there is a third possibility.

An associate is an entity (usually a company) over which the group exerts *significant influence* but *not* control. A holding of 20% to 50% usually indicates significant influence. Significant influence involves active participation in management, not simply a passive role, as would be the case with a simple trade investment.

We need to distinguish an associate from a subsidiary and from a simple trade investment because, whilst the group does not have control over the associate, it does have more than a passive interest. Hence, we need a treatment in between full consolidation and leaving the investment at cost in the group accounts.

Relationship with group

As we saw in the first session on group accounts, a group comprises a parent and its subsidiaries. As an associate is neither a parent nor a subsidiary, it is not part of the group. Instead, the group has an investment in the associate. When we identify the group structure, we include the associate, even though it is not part of the group, as this helps us to identify its status and the actual percentage interest which, as we shall see, is important. For example:

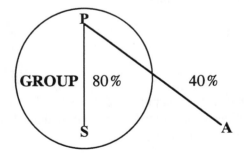

The associate is not part of the group

Treatment in investing company's own accounts

Balance sheet

We include the investment in fixed asset investments, usually at cost. In the individual company, as opposed to consolidated, balance sheet, we do not use the term *associate*. Instead, we include the investment under the sub-heading 'Participating interests'. As we shall see in more detail later, this term also includes investments other than associates. As with other investments, we may revalue this investment and must write down its value if there is a permanent diminution in value.

Profit and loss account

In the individual company profit and loss account (which, as you will recall, the parent does not need to publish if it publishes a consolidated profit and loss account), we include dividend income from the associate under the heading 'Income from participating interests'. Again, note that the term *associate* is not used in the individual company, as opposed to group, accounts.

Treatment in group accounts

In the group accounts, we use a technique called *equity accounting* for an associate. We also describe the associate as an *associated undertaking*. Note that we only use this technique in group accounts (ie. where the parent also has a subsidiary), which we consolidate as normal.

Instead of bringing in all of the associate's net assets and profits and then showing a minority interest to reflect the part not actually owned, we only include the *group share* of the associate's net assets and profits from the outset.

Balance sheet

In fixed asset investments, we replace the investment as shown in the investing company's own individual balance sheet with the *group share* of the associate's net assets at the balance sheet date, in one line, under 'Interests in associated undertakings'.

In group reserves, we include the parent's share of the associate's post-acquisition reserves (calculated in the same way as for a subsidiary).

We cancel the investment in the associate as shown in the investing company's own individual balance sheet against the group share of the associate's net assets at the date of acquisition (at fair value). The difference is a premium or discount on acquisition (in effect, goodwill).

Example

P Ltd owns 80% of S Ltd and 40% of A Ltd. Balance sheets of the three companies at 31 December 19X8 are:

	P Ltd £	S Ltd £	A Ltd £
Investment: Shares in S Ltd	800	–	–
Investment: Shares in A Ltd	600	–	–
Sundry net assets	3,600	3,800	4,400
	5,000	3,800	4,400
Share capital – £1 ordinary shares	1,000	400	800
Profit and loss account	4,000	3,400	3,600
	5,000	3,800	4,400

P Ltd acquired its shares in S Ltd when S Ltd's profit and loss reserves were £520 and P Ltd acquired its shares in A Ltd when A Ltd's profit and loss reserves were £400.

Group policy is to write off all goodwill arising on acquisition immediately against reserves.

Required

Prepare the consolidated balance sheet at 31 December 19X8.

Solution

P Ltd: Consolidated balance sheet as at 31 December 19X8

	£
Interest in associated undertakings (4,400 × 40%)	1,760
Sundry net assets (3,600 + 3,800)	7,400
	9,160
Share capital	1,000
Profit and loss account (W5)	7,400
	8,400
Minority interests (W4)	760
	9,160

Workings

(1)   Group structure

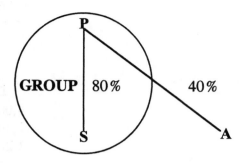

(2)   Net assets working

S Ltd

	Balance sheet date	Acquisition
	£	£
Share capital	400	400
Profit and loss account	3,400	520
	3,800	920

A Ltd

	Balance sheet date	Acquisition
	£	£
Share capital	800	800
Profit and loss account	3,600	400
	4,400	1,200

(3)   Goodwill/premium

S Ltd

	£
Cost of investment	800
Net assets acquired (80% × 920 (W2))	(736)
	64

A Ltd

	£
Cost of investment	600
Net assets acquired (40% × 1,200 (W2))	(480)
	120

(4)   Minority interests

	£
S Ltd only – (20% × 3,800)	760

(5)   Profit and loss account

	£
P Ltd – from question	4,000
Share of S Ltd [80% × (3,400 – 520)]	2,304
Share of A Ltd [40% × (3,600 – 400)]	1,280
Less: Goodwill/premium (64 + 120)	(184)
	7,400

Profit and loss account

The treatment of an associate in the consolidated profit and loss account is consistent with its treatment in the consolidated balance sheet.

We replace the dividend income from the investment in the associate, as shown in the investing company's own profit and loss account, with the *group share* of the associate's profit before tax, in one line, as 'Income from interests in associated undertakings'.

We also include the group share of the associate's tax in 'Tax on profit on ordinary activities'. The group tax and the share of the associate's tax are separately disclosed in the tax note.

Do not add in the associate's turnover or expenses line by line.

Time-apportion the results of the associate if acquired mid-year.

Example

P Ltd has owned 80% of S Ltd and 40% of A Ltd for several years. Profit and loss accounts for the year ended 31 December 19X8 are:

	P Ltd £	S Ltd £	A Ltd £
Turnover	14,000	12,000	10,000
Cost of sales	(9,000)	(4,000)	(3,000)
Gross profit	5,000	8,000	7,000
Administrative expenses	(2,000)	(6,000)	(3,000)
	3,000	2,000	4,000
Income from participating interests	400	–	–
Profit on ordinary activities before taxation	3,400	2,000	4,000
Tax on profit on ordinary activities	(1,000)	(1,200)	(2,000)
Profit on ordinary activities after taxation	2,400	800	2,000
Dividends (paid)	(1,000)	–	(1,000)
Retained profit	1,400	800	1,000

Required

Prepare the consolidated profit and loss account for the year ended 31 December 19X8.

Solution

P Ltd: Consolidated profit and loss account
for the year ending 31 December 19X8

	£	£
Turnover		26,000
Cost of sales		(13,000)
Gross profit		13,000
Administrative expenses		(8,000)
Operating profit		5,000
Income from interests in associated undertakings		1,600
Profit on ordinary activities before taxation		6,600
Tax on profit on ordinary activities		
Group	2,200	
Share of associated undertaking's tax	800	
		(3,000)
Profit on ordinary activities after taxation		3,600
Minority interests (W3)		(160)
Profit for the financial year attributable to the members of P Ltd		3,440
Dividends paid		(1,000)
Retained profit for the financial year		2,440

Workings

(1)   Group structure

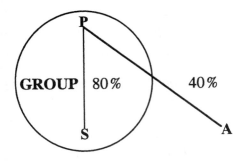

(2)   Consolidation schedule

	P Ltd	S Ltd	A Ltd (40%)	Consol
	£	£	£	£
Turnover	14,000	12,000		26,000
C of S	(9,000)	(4,000)		(13,000)
Admin	(2,000)	(6,000)		(8,000)
Income from assoc (40% × 4,000)			1,600	1,600
Tax – group	(1,000)	(1,200)		(2,200)
– assoc (40% × 2,000)			(800)	(800)
PAT		800		

(3)   Minority interest

S Ltd (20% x 800)   £160

ASSOCIATES AND THE COMPANIES ACT 1985

Participating interest

The term *participating interest* is defined in the Act and FRS2 restates the definition. A participating interest is one held on a long-term basis for the purpose of securing a contribution by the exercise of control or influence. This is presumed where the holding is 20% or more. Note that this does *not* automatically mean that there is significant influence as that term has a narrower meaning, given by SSAP1. We have already seen that the statutory formats distinguish a participating interest from smaller investments, which are classified as 'Other investments other than loans' in the balance sheet sub-headings.

Associated undertakings

- The Act defines these as undertakings, which are not subsidiaries, where the group:

    – has a participating interest
    – exercises significant influence

Significant influence is presumed, unless the contrary is shown, if the group's holding is 20% or more.

- The Act requires equity accounting for an associate in the group accounts.

SSAP1: ACCOUNTING FOR ASSOCIATED COMPANIES

This has been amended by the ASB Interim Statement *Consolidated accounts* to bring it into line with the Companies Act, pending replacement by a new FRS.

A summary of the main SSAP1 requirements, as amended by the Interim Statement follows:

Key definitions

- *Associate*

  A company which is not a subsidiary in which:

  - the group holds its interest for the long term; and

  - the group can exercise significant influence, having regard to the disposition of other share holdings. (For example, a holding of over 20% will not give rise to significant influence if another company has control.)

- *Significant influence* involves participation in the financial and operating policy decisions (including dividend policy) – for example, representation on the board of directors. Significant influence is presumed where the group's interest is 20% or more of equity voting rights.

  Note that *significant influence* is a narrower term than the Companies Act definition of a participating interest (see section on the Companies Act provisions). It is therefore possible to have a participating interest which is not an associate. No distinction is made in the individual accounts of the investing company but the statutory formats are modified for group accounts to show associated undertakings and other participating interests separately as they are accounted for differently (refer back to the sessions on the Company Accounts formats if necessary).

Accounting treatment

- In the investing company's own accounts, the associate (a *participating interest*) is treated as follows:

  - Profit and loss account: Dividends received and receivable
  - Balance sheet: Investment at cost (or valuation) less amounts written off

- Group accounts:

    - Profit and loss account: Investing group's share of profits of associated companies

    - Balance sheet:

	£
Investing group's share of net assets of associate	X
Premium/(discount) on acquisition	X/(X)
	X

OTHER METHODS OF CONSOLIDATION

You have learned to prepare consolidated accounts using the acquisition method of accounting. Acquisition accounting is the method used for the majority of business combinations. (*Business combination* is the generic term for transactions which result in one company becoming the subsidiary of another.)

The central idea behind acquisition accounting is that a parent *acquires* a subsidiary company. The assets and liabilities of the subsidiary company are taken over by the parent and absorbed into its operations. This scenario is typical of most business combinations.

However, some business combinations arise as the result of the uniting of interests of two companies so that neither company can be said to have acquired the other. This type of combination is popularly known as a *merger*. A different method of consolidation, known as the *merger method*, is used to prepare consolidated accounts in this situation.

The difference between an acquisition and a merger seems to be obvious. However, the essential distinction between the two depends on future intentions and the spirit in which the combination takes place. These are subjective, rather than matters of fact. Many business combinations involve complex transactions and arrangements and in practice it can be difficult to establish whether a particular combination is an acquisition or a merger.

The following definitions are contained in FRS6 *Acquisitions and mergers*.

- *Merger*

    A business combination which results in the creation of a new reporting entity formed from the combining parties, in which the shareholders of the combining entities come together in a *substantially equal partnership* for the *mutual sharing* of the risks and benefits of the combined entity, and in which *no party to the combination in substance obtains control over any other, or is otherwise seen to be dominant*, whether by virtue of the proportion of its shareholders rights in the combined entity, the influence of its directors or otherwise.

- *Acquisition*

    A business combination that is *not a merger*.

Note that, in practice, mergers are extremely rare.

Merger accounting method

Consolidations under acquisition accounting are based on the concept of control. This is not relevant in a merger situation where there is no control. Instead, the consolidation needs to reflect the pooling of interests of two companies.

To reflect the pooling of interests the following treatment is adopted:

(i) The parent records the investment in the subsidiary in its own balance sheet at *nominal* value of shares issued plus fair value of any other consideration, ie. the fair value of shares issued on combination is not recorded.

(ii) On consolidation, cancel the cost of the investment in the subsidiary against the nominal value of the subsidiary's shares obtained in exchange.

(iii) There is no need to adjust the net assets of the combining parties to fair value at combination for inclusion in the consolidated balance sheet.

(iv) Results and cash flows are consolidated as though the merger had always existed, ie. profits are included from the date of incorporation not the date of combination.

Example

Set out below are the summarised balance sheets of Coll plc and Tiree plc.

	Coll plc *£'000*	*Tiree plc* *£'000*
Net assets	*5,000*	*4,000*
Share capital – £1 ords	*1,000*	*1,000*
Profit and loss account	*4,000*	*3,000*
	5,000	*4,000*

Coll plc is to combine with Tiree plc by obtaining 100% of Tiree plc's shares. The consideration consists of 1,000,000 £1 ordinary shares valued at £6 each. The fair value of Tiree plc's assets is £4,600,000.

Required

Assuming that the combination is to be accounted for as a merger

(a)   prepare the balance sheet of Coll plc reflecting the issue of shares
(b)   prepare the consolidated balance sheet of the Coll group after the combination.

Solution

(a) **Balance sheet of Coll plc**

	£'000
Net assets	5,000
Investment in Tiree plc (1,000 × £1)	1,000
	6,000
Share capital (1,000 + 1,000)	2,000
Profit and loss account	4,000
	6,000

(b) **Consolidated balance sheet of Coll plc**

	£'000
Net assets (5,000 + 4,000)	9,000
Share capital	2,000
Profit and loss account (4,000 + 3,000)	7,000
	9,000

SUMMARY

The main legal and professional requirements in respect of group accounts are set out in:

- the Companies Act 1985

- FRS2 *Accounting for subsidiary undertakings*

An undertaking is the parent of another (a subsidiary) if *any* of the following apply:

- It holds a majority of voting rights.

- It is a member and can appoint/remove directors with a majority of votes.

- It is a member and controls a majority of votes via an agreement with other members.

- It has a participating interest and actually exercises dominant influence or the undertakings are managed on a unified basis.

Review of Module Two

You have now completed the second and final module of the Study Pack.

You have covered the following:

- the remaining requirements of Accounting Standards:

    - correct accounting treatments
    - disclosure requirements

- the preparation of a cash flow statement

- the interpretation of accounts

- the preparation of accounts for simple groups.

You should also have a background knowledge and appreciation of other topics which may be relevant to the preparation of final accounts (although you will not be expected to account for them). These include the following:

- long-term contracts

- leasing and hire purchase

- pension costs

- reporting the substance of transactions

- associated undertakings

- merger accounting

You should now be able to use your knowledge and understanding to:

- prepare limited company accounts which conform with the requirements of the Companies Acts and of accounting standards

- prepare a cash flow statement

- calculate simple accounting ratios

You should now attempt Practice Central Assessment 2.

Answers

SESSION 2

1   *Going concern:*   The business will continue to trade for the foreseeable future.

    Accruals: Revenue and expenditure are recognised in accounts as they are earned or incurred, rather than as they are received or paid.

    Consistency: There is consistency of accounting treatment of like items within each accounting period and from one period to another.

    Prudence: Revenue and profits are not anticipated, but are included only when realised. Liabilities and losses are provided for as soon as possible.

SESSION 3

1   VB Ltd

				Debit £	Credit £
(1)	Dr	Suspense		492	
		Cr	Sales returns account		246
		Cr	Sales		246

Being the correction of cash sales incorrectly debited to the sales returns account

(2)	Dr	Suspense		45	
		Cr	Customer's account		45

Being the correction of a transposition error on a posting to a customer's account

(3)	Dr	Bank charges		37	
		Cr	Cash		37

Being the posting of bank charges

(4)	Dr	VAT recoverable		45	
		Cr	Purchases		45

Being the correction of the posting of VAT on a supplier's invoice

(5)	Dr	Supplier's account		258	
		Cr	Customer's account		258

Being the correction of a contra entry wrongly posted

(6)	Dr	Rates		13,500	
		Cr	Creditors		13,500

Being the entering into the trial balance of a rates bill

				Debit	*Credit*
				£	£
(7)	Dr	Carriage inwards		52	
	Cr	Carriage outwards			52

Being the correction of a posting error

| (8) | Dr | Bad debts | | 40 | |
| | Cr | Customer's account | | | 40 |

Being the writing-off of a bad debt

The effect on profit for the year ended 30 April 19Y0 of each of these journals is as follows:

(1)   Increase profit by £492.
(2)   No effect
(3)   Decrease profit by £37.
(4)   Increase profit by £45.
(5)   No effect
(6)   Decrease profit by $1/6 \times £13,500 = £2,250$
(7)   No effect
(8)   Decrease profit by £40.

Answers

2 Robert Bridges

(a)

Extended trial balance at 31 December 19X8

Account	Trial balance Dr £	Cr £	Adjustments Dr £	Cr £	P & L account Dr £	Cr £	Balance sheet Dr £	Cr £
Capital		24,376						24,376
Drawings	2,015						2,015	
Fixed assets	4,900		100	400			4,600	
Depreciation (B/S)		1,250	100	863				2,013
Stock	3,180		4,567	4,567	3,180	4,567	4,567	
Debtors	4,723			7			4,716	
Provision for debts		76		34				110
Petty cash	100						100	
Creditors		1,485						1,485
Sales		36,823				36,823		
Purchases	29,467				29,467			
Discount received		518				518		
Discount allowed	581				581			
Rent	300		100		400			
Rates	750			150	600			
Electricity	224		21		245			
Casual wages	1,069		25		1,094			
Telephone	18			18				
Travel expenses	367				367			
Sundries	909		18		927			
Bank deposit a/c	15,000		1,200				16,200	
Bank current a/c	925						925	
Bad debts			41		41			
Disposal account			400	200	200			
Depreciation (P&L)			863		863			
Interest received				1,200		1,200		
Accruals				146				146
Prepayments			150				150	
					37,965			
Profit					5,143			5,143
	64,528	64,528	7,585	7,585	43,108	43,108	33,273	33,273

(b) **Trading and profit and loss account for the year ended 31 December 19X8**

		£	£
Sales			36,823
Less:	Cost of sales		
	Opening stock	3,180	
	Purchases	29,467	
		32,647	
	Closing stock	(4,567)	
			(28,080)
Gross profit			8,743
Sundry income			
	Deposit interest	1,200	
	Discount received	518	
			1,718
			10,461
Less:	Expenses		
	Casual wages	1,094	
	Sundries	927	
	Depreciation	863	
	Rates	600	
	Discount allowed	581	
	Rent	400	
	Travel expenses	367	
	Electricity	245	
	Loss on sale of assets	200	
	Bad debts	41	
			(5,318)
Net profit			5,143

(c)   **Balance sheet at 31 December 19X8**

	£	£	£
Fixed assets			
Cost			4,600
Less: Depreciation			(2,013)
			2,587
Current assets			
Stock		4,567	
Debtors	4,716		
Less: Provision	110		
	4,606		
Prepayments	150		
		4,756	
Bank deposit account	16,200		
Bank current account	925		
Petty cash	100		
		17,225	
		26,548	
Current liabilities			
Creditors	1,485		
Accruals	146		
		(1,631)	
Net current assets			24,917
Net assets			27,504

Proprietor's interest	£
Capital at 1.1.X8	24,376
Profit for the year	5,143
	29,519
Less: Drawings	(2,015)
Capital at 31.12.X8	27,504

SESSION 4

1   Brick and Stone

Trading and profit and loss account for the year ended 30 September 19Y0

	£	£
Sales (322,100 – 2,100)		320,000
Cost of sales		
Opening stock	23,000	
Purchases (208,200 – 1,000 – 6,100 + 1,700)	202,800	
	225,800	
Closing stock	(32,000)	
		(193,800)
Gross profit		126,200
Add: Discounts receivable		370
		126,570
Less: Printing, stationery and postage	3,500	
Rent and rates (10,300 – 600)	9,700	
Heat and light	8,700	
Salaries	36,100	
Telephone (2,900 + 400)	3,300	
Motor vehicle costs	5,620	
Discounts allowable	950	
Carriage outwards	2,400	
Depreciation		
Fixtures and fittings (26,000 × 10%)	2,600	
Motor vehicles (46,000 × 20%)	9,200	
Loan interest (W3)	250	
		(82,320)
Net profit		44,250

Appropriation statement

	Total £	Brick £	Stone £
Stone's salary (6/12 × 12,000)	6,000	–	6,000
Profit share 3:2	38,250	22,950	15,300
	44,250	22,950	21,300

Balance sheet as at 30 September 19Y0

	Cost £	Provision for depreciation £	NBV £
Fixed assets			
Fixtures and fittings	26,000	13,800	12,200
Motor vehicles	46,000	34,200	11,800
	72,000	48,000	24,000
Current assets			
Stock		32,000	
Trade debtors		9,000	
Prepayments		600	
Bank balance		7,700	
		49,300	
Creditors: Amounts falling due within one year			
Trade creditors	8,400		
Accruals (W3)	650		
		(9,050)	
			40,250
			64,250
Creditors: Amounts falling due after more than one year			
Loan – Brick			(10,000)
			54,250

		£	£
Represented by:			
Capital accounts (W1)			
Brick			23,000
Stone			17,000
			40,000
Current accounts (W2)			
Brick		2,550	
Stone		11,700	
		14,250	
			54,250

Workings

(1) Partners' capital accounts

	Brick £	Stone £
Balance at 1 October 19X9	33,000	17,000
Less: Transfer to Brick loan Account 1 July 19Y0	(10,000)	
	23,000	17,000

(2) Partners' current accounts

	Brick	Stone
Balance at 1 October 19X9	3,600	2,400
Salary		6,000
Profit share (from appropriation statement)	22,950	15,300
	26,550	23,700
Less: Drawings		
Goods	–	(1,000)
Cash	(24,000)	(11,000)
	2,550	11,700

(3) Accruals

	£
Telephone	400
Brick's loan interest (10,000 × 10% × 3/12)	250
	650

2 Short and Round

(a) **Trading and profit and loss account for the year ended 30 June 19X6**

	£	£
Sales		569,800
Cost of sales		
Opening stock	27,500	
Purchases (469,880 + 2,200)	472,080	
	499,580	
Closing stock	(31,200)	
		(468,380)
Gross profit		101,420
Less: Rent (27,600 – 2,800)	24,800	
Heat and light	2,300	
Telephone (1,900 + 360)	2,260	
Postage and stationery	1,750	
Wages and salaries	14,500	
Loan interest (8% × 15,000)	1,200	
Depreciation		
Fixtures and fittings (10% × 25,000)	2,500	
Motor vehicles (25% × 36,000)	9,000	
Bad debt expense ((32,500 × 5%) – 700)	925	
		(59,235)
Net profit		42,185

(b) **Appropriation statement**

	Total £	Short £	Round £
Four months to 31.10.X5			
Salary	–	–	–
Profit (70:30) (W2)	5,610	3,927	1,683
Eight months to 30.6.X6			
Salary	6,667	–	6,667
Profit (60:40)	29,908	17,945	11,963
Total (W2)	36,575	17,945	18,630

(c)

Balance sheet as at 30 June 19X6

	Cost £	Provision for depreciation £	£
Fixed assets			
Fixtures and fittings	25,000	14,700	10,300
Motor vehicles	36,000	30,000	6,000
	61,000	44,700	16,300
Current assets			
Stock		31,200	
Trade debtors (32,500 × 95%)		30,875	
Prepayments		2,800	
Cash at bank		19,400	
Cash in hand		1,200	
		85,475	
Creditors: Amounts falling due within one year			
Trade creditors	24,200		
Accruals (1,200 + 360)	1,560		
		(25,760)	
			59,715
			76,015
Creditors: Amounts falling due after more than one year			
Loan from Jones			(15,000)
			61,015

Represented by:		
	£	£
Capital accounts		
Short		22,500
Round		17,500
		40,000
Current accounts		
Short	11,662	
Round	9,353	
		21,015
		61,015

Workings

(1)   **Partners' current accounts**

	Short £	Round £		Total £	Short £	Round £
			b/f		3,790	1,040
Drawings	14,000	12,000	Appropriations			
			4 months	5,610	3,927	1,683
c/f	11,662	9,353	8 months	36,575	17,945	18,630
	25,662	21,353			25,662	21,353

(2)   Profit allocation

	Total £	4 months to 31.10.X5 £	8 months to 30.6.X6 £
Gross profit (1:3)	101,420	25,355	76,065
Expenses (4:8)	(59,235)	(19,745)	(39,490)
Profit for period	42,185	5,610	36,575

3   Metro, Goldwyn and Mayer

(a)   **Trading and profit and loss account for the year ended 31 March 19X8**

	£	£
Sales		40,000
Less: Cost of goods sold		
Opening stock	3,800	
Purchases	21,500	
	25,300	
Less: Closing stock	4,100	
		(21,200)
Gross profit		18,800

		3 months to 30.6.X7			9 months to 31.3.X8	
	£	£	£	£	£
Gross profit (£18,800 apportioned in ratio of sales 8:32)			3,760		15,040
Expenses (apportioned on a time basis 3:9)					
Shop wages	3,320				
Salaries (7,200 – 1,200 – 720 – 500)	4,780				
Rent etc. (1,400 – 200)	1,200				
Professional charge (360 – 160)	200				
Amortisation of lease (W)	408				
Depreciation					
Motor vehicles (W)	400				
Shop fittings (W)	160				
	10,468	2,617		7,851	
General expenses (2,800 + 120)	2,920	910		2,010	
Doubtful debts (279 – 240)/(298 – 279)		39		19	
			(3,566)		(9,880)
			194		
Add: Profit on disposal			100		
Net profit			294		5,160

Appropriation statement

	Total £	Metro £	Goldwyn £	Mayer £
Period to 30 June 19X7				
Interest on capital	105	60	45	
Balance 2:1	189	126	63	
	294	186	108	
Period to 31 March 19X8				
Interest on capital	405	180	135	90
Salary	225			225
Balance 2:2:1	4,530	1,812	1,812	906
	5,160	1,992	1,947	1,221

(b) **Balance sheet at 31 March 19X8**

	Cost £	Dep'n £	£
Fixed assets (W)			
Leasehold premises including legal costs	8,160	408	7,752
Motor vehicles	2,000	1,100	900
Shop fittings	1,600	760	840
	11,760	2,268	9,492
Current assets			
Stock		4,100	
Debtors less provision		1,202	
Prepayment		200	
Cash		3,060	
		8,562	
Creditors: Amounts falling due within one year			
Creditors and accrued expenses (2,800 + 120)		(2,920)	
Net current assets			5,642
Total net assets			15,134

Partners' accounts	Metro £	Goldwyn £	Mayer £	Total £
Capital	4,000	3,000	2,000	9,000
Current	6,178	1,235	(1,279)	6,134
	10,178	4,235	721	15,134

(c) **Partners' current accounts**

	Metro £	Goldwyn £	Mayer £		Metro £	Goldwyn £	Mayer £
Goodwill (new ratio 2:2:1)	6,000	6,000	3,000	Balances b/f	1,200	900	
Drawings	1,200	720	500	Introduced			1,000
Balances c/f	6,178	1,235	–	Goodwill (old ratio 2:1)	10,000	5,000	
				Appropriation statement – division of profits:			
				30.6.X7	186	108	
				31.3.X8	1,992	1,947	1,221
				Balances c/f			1,279
	13,378	7,955	3,500		13,378	7,955	3,500

Workings

	Lease Cost £	Amortisation £	Vehicles Cost £	Dep'n £	Fittings Cost £	Dep'n £
Cost	8,000					
Professional charges	160					
Brought forward			2,600	1,400	1,600	600
Cash transferred to disposals account			400			
			3,000			
Sales			1,000	700		
			2,000	700		
Profit and loss account		408		400		160
Balance sheet totals	8,160	408	2,000	1,100	1,600	760

4   Jack, Hugh and Clive

(a)

Revaluation account

	£	£		£
Freehold premises – book value		8,000	Freehold premises at valuation	15,000
Plant – book value		4,200	Plant at valuation	3,500
Motor car – book value		450	Motor car taken over	400
Doubtful debts – new value		600	Doubtful debts – book value	400
Provision for repainting – new value		2,000	Provision for repainting – book value	1,400
Stock – book value		3,600	Stock – revalued value	3,200
Creditors – revalued value		4,350	Creditors – book value	4,600
Profit on revaluation				
Jack	2,650			
Hugh	1,590			
Clive	1,060			
		5,300		
		28,500		28,500

(b)

Partners' capital accounts

	Jack £	Hugh £	Clive £		Jack £	Hugh £	Clive £
Motor vehicle	400			Balances b/f	12,000	6,000	4,000
Goodwill		4,200	2,800	Profit on revaluation	2,650	1,590	1,060
Loan account	17,750						
Balances c/f		5,490	3,660	Goodwill (W)	3,500	2,100	1,400
	18,150	9,690	6,460		18,150	9,690	6,460

(c)   **Jack's account**

	£		£
Cash	3,000	Loan account	3,000
Cash (10% × 17,750)	1,775	Capital account	17,750
Balance c/f	15,975		
	17,750		17,750

(d)   **Hugh and Clive**

Balance sheet at 1 July 19X3

	£	£	£
Fixed assets at revaluation			
Freehold premises			15,000
Plant and equipment			3,500
Motor vehicles (2,100 – 450)			1,650
			20,150
Current assets			
Stock		3,200	
Debtors	5,200		
Less: Provision for doubtful debts	600		
		4,600	
Balance at bank (8,300 – 1,775 – 3,000)		3,525	
		11,325	
Less: Current liabilities			
Provision for repainting of premises	2,000		
Creditors	4,350		
		(6,350)	
Net current assets			4,975
			25,125
Loan account – Jack			(15,975)
			9,150
Representing			
Partners' capital accounts			
Hugh		5,490	
Clive		3,660	
			9,150

5   Vigor, Twist and Slater

(a)

Realisation account

	£	£			£
Fixed assets		7,000	Vigor – car taken over		800
Stock		3,400	Twist – car taken over		460
Debtors – bad debts/			Cash proceeds –		
discounts allowed		300	fixed assets		15,000
Partners' capital a/cs –			Creditors – discount received		200
profit on realisation:					
Vigor (1/2)	2,880				
Twist (1/3)	1,920				
Slater (1/6)	960				
		5,760			
		16,460			16,460

(b)

Cash account

	£		£	£
Balance b/f	6,100	Loan account		2,000
Debtors	4,200	Creditors		3,300
Proceeds – fixed assets	15,000	Balance, due to partners		
		Vigor	9,480	
		Twist	6,260	
		Slater	4,260	
				20,000
	25,300			25,300

(c)

Current accounts

	Vigor	Twist	Slater		Vigor	Twist	Slater
	£	£	£		£	£	£
Transfer to capital a/cs	2,400	1,800	1,300	Balances b/f	2,400	1,800	1,300

Capital accounts

	Vigor £	Twist £	Slater £		Vigor £	Twist £	Slater £
Realisation a/c – cars taken over	800	460		Balances b/f	5,000	3,000	2,000
				Transfer from current a/cs	2,400	1,800	1,300
				Realisation a/c – profit	2,880	1,920	960
Bank – balance due	9,480	6,260	4,260				
	10,280	6,720	4,260		10,280	6,720	4,260

6 Barrow, Mark, Williams and James

Task 1

Profit appropriation account for Barrow, Mark, Williams and James for the year ended 30 June 1994

	£	£
Profit		40,000
Add: Salaries		13,000
Interest on loan		300
		53,300
Less: Interest on loan		300
Profit available for appropriation		53,000
Less: Salaries		
Mark	7,000	
James	6,000	
		13,000
Less: Interest on capital		
Barrow	1,250	
Mark	750	
Williams	150	
James	500	
		2,650
		37,350
Balance of profit shared in PSR:		
Barrow	11,205	
Mark	14,940	
Williams	7,470	
James	3,735	
		37,350

Task 2

Capital accounts

	Barrow £	Mark £		Barrow £	Mark £
			b/f	15,000	15,000
c/f	25,000	15,000	1.1.94 Bank	10,000	
	25,000	15,000		25,000	15,000

Capital accounts

	Williams £	James £		Williams £	James £
			b/f	3,000	5,000
c/f	3,000	10,000	1.2.94 Bank		5,000
	3,000	10,000		3,000	10,000

Capital accounts

	Barrow £	Mark £		Barrow £	Mark £
Drawings	17,000	20,000	b/f	2,500	1,800
c/f		4,490	Loan interest	300	
			Salary		7,000
			Capital interest	1,250	750
			Profit	11,205	14,940
			c/f	1,745	
	17,000	24,490		17,000	24,490

Capital accounts

	Williams £	James £		Williams £	James £
b/f	1,000		b/f		2,000
Drawings	5,000	13,000	Salary		6,000
c/f	1,620		Capital interest	150	500
			Profit	7,470	3,735
			c/f		765
	7,620	13,000		7,620	13,000

Task 3

In the absence of either an express or implied partnership agreement, the Partnership Act 1890 will apply. The following provisions are contained in the Act:

- Profits to be shared equally

- No salaries to be paid

- No interest on capital to be paid

- Interest of 5% payable on loans

- Interest of 5% payable to retiring partner on any retained capital in partnership

- On dissolution, assets should be used to pay outside creditors, the partners' loans then partners' capital, remainder to be shared in PSR

- All existing partners must consent to admission of a new partner

Task 4

An appropriation is an allocation of net profit which is credited to the owner of a business. In a partnership, appropriations may be in the form of salaries, interest on capital or profit shares. In a limited company, dividends payable are appropriations, also scrip dividends, transfers to reserves and payments of tax.

An expense is business expenditure undertaken by an enterprise; for example, loan interest is a tax-deductible business expense and as such is an element in determining the net profit.

Task 5

Additional capital
More skills/specialisms
More ideas
Partners may cover for each other
Economies of scale (eg. premises, admin. costs)

SESSION 5

1   Regis Ltd

Profit and loss account for the period ended 30 April 19X1

	£	£
Turnover (799,701 – 414 + 89,371)		888,658
Cost of sales		
Purchases (564,532 – 36,371)	528,161	
Closing stock	(77,971)	
		(450,190)
Gross profit		438,468
Expenses		
Bank charges	571	
Debenture interest (300,000 × 10% × 15/12)	37,500	
Wages	43,271	
Rent and rates	97,000	
Light and heat	35,382	
Interest	1,225	
Commission	43,125	
Postage	4,112	
Depreciation (W1)	24,688	
Bad debt expenses (W4)	90,325	
Loss on disposal (W2)	1,125	
		378,324
Profit before tax		60,144
Tax		(23,712)
Profit after tax		36,432
Dividends proposed (200,000 × 10p)		(20,000)
Retained profit		16,432

Balance sheet as at 30 April 19X1

	Cost £	Dep'n £	NBV £
Fixed assets			
Land and buildings	500,000	5,000	495,000
Motor vehicles	45,000	14,063	30,937
Office equipment	15,000	3,750	11,250
	560,000	22,813	537,187
Current assets			
Stock		77,971	
Debtors (293,428 – 18,085)		275,343	
Bank (23,572 – 571)		23,001	
Cash		150	
		376,465	
Creditors due within one year			
Trade creditors (332,379 -- 36,371)	296,008		
Tax creditor	23,712		
Dividend creditor	20,000		
Debenture interest	37,500		
		377,220	
Net current liabilities			(755)
Total assets less current liabilities			536,432
Creditors due after one year			
10% debenture 19X5			(300,000)
			236,432
Share capital			200,000
Share premium			20,000
Profit and loss account			16,432
			236,432

Workings

(1)   **Depreciation**

   (a)   Buildings

	£
Cost (196,000 × 100/98)	200,000
NBV	196,000
Therefore depreciation charged	4,000
Correct depreciation (200,000 × 2% × 15/12)	5,000
Therefore additional charge	1,000

   (b)   Motor vehicles

	£
Cost (45,000 × 100/75)	60,000
NBV	45,000
Therefore depreciation charged	15,000
Correct depreciation	
Vehicle sold (15,000 × 25% × 6/12)	1,875
Vehicles remaining (45,000 × 25% × 15/12)	14,063
Therefore additional charge	938

   (c)   Office equipment

	£
Cost (13,500 × 100/90)	15,000
Correct depreciation (15,000 × 20% × 15/12)	3,750
Already charged (£15,000 – £13,500)	1,500
Therefore additional depreciation	2,250

Total depreciation

	£
Per trial balance	20,500
Extra depreciation	
Buildings	1,000
Vehicles	938
Equipment	2,250
	24,688

(2) Disposal of vehicle

	£		£
Cost	15,000	Proceeds	12,000
		Depreciation (W6)	1,875
		Loss	1,125
	———		———
	15,000		15,000
	———		———

(3) Debtors ledger control account

	£		£
Balance b/f (253,211 + 16,431)	269,642	Returns	414
SDB	89,371	Contra	1,500
		BDE Speedie	47,000
		Burrows	16,671
		Balance c/f	293,428
	———		———
	359,013		359,013
	———		———

(4) Bad debts expense

	£		£
Per trial balance	25,000	Profit and loss account	90,325
DLCA Speedie	47,000		
Burrows	16,671		
Provisions for DD	1,654		
	———		———
	90,325		90,325
	———		———

(5) Provision for doubtful debts

	£		£
Balance c/f	18,085	Balance b/f	16,431
		Bad debts expense	1,654
	———		———
	18,085		18,085
	———		———
		Balance b/f	
		Drinkell (50% × 12,450)	6,225
		Edwards (80% × 8,000)	6,400
		General [2% (293,428 –	
		12,450 – 8,000)]	5,460
			———
			18,085
			———

(6)   **Suspense account**

	£		£
Share premium	40,000	Balance b/f per TB	53,500
Disposal proceeds	12,000		
Contra	1,500		
	53,500		53,500

2   Withers Ltd

Profit and loss account for the year ended 30 September 19X6

	£
Turnover	290,000
Cost of sales	(217,500)
Gross profit	72,500
Net operating expenses (W1)	(58,450)
Operating profit	14,050
Interest payable and similar charges	(1,500)
Profit before taxation	12,550
Taxation	(6,860)
Profit after taxation	5,690
Proposed dividends (W3)	(4,100)
Retained profit for the year	1,590
Retained profit brought forward	18,500
Retained profit carried forward	20,090

Balance sheet at 30 September 19X6

	£	£
Fixed assets		
Plant (71,500 – 31,800)		39,700
Investments		13,000
		52,700
Current assets		
Stock	28,650	
Debtors	52,430	
Bank	3,215	
	84,295	
Creditors: Amounts falling due within one year (W2)	(46,905)	
Net current assets		37,390
Total assets less current liabilities		90,090
Creditors: Amounts falling due after more than one year		
Bank loan		(15,000)
		75,090

Capital and reserves		£
Called-up share capital		
Preference shares of £1 each fully paid		30,000
Ordinary shares of 25p each fully paid		25,000
		55,000
Profit and loss account		20,090
		75,090

Workings

(1)   Net operating expenses

	£	£
Per question		36,475
Add: Audit fee		975
Directors' remuneration		
Salaries	18,500	
Fees	1,500	
Widow's pension	1,000	
		21,000
		58,450

(2)   Creditors: Amounts falling due within one year

		£
Trade creditors		27,920
Add:	Audit fee	975
	Directors' fees	1,500
	Widow's pension	1,000
		31,395
	Proposed dividend (W5)	4,100
	Corporation tax (6,860 + 4,550)	11,410
		46,905

(3)   Proposed dividends

	£
Preference (30,000 × 7p)	2,100
Ordinary (100,000 × 2p)	2,000
	4,100

3   Billesley Ltd

(a)   **Profit and loss account for the year ended 30 June 19X2**

	£	£
Turnover		500,000
Cost of sales (46 + 280 − 52)		274,000
Gross profit		226,000
Distribution costs	65,000	
Administrative expenses	110,000	
		175,000
Profit on ordinary activities before taxation		51,000
Tax on profit on ordinary activities		12,000
Profit for the financial year		39,000
Dividends (10 + 6 + 8 + 6)		30,000
		9,000
Transfer to general reserve		5,000
		4,000
Profit and loss account brought forward		135,000
Profit and loss account carried forward		139,000

Balance sheet as at 30 June 19X2

	£	£	£
Fixed assets			
Land and buildings	500,000	80,000	420,000
Plant	180,000	105,000	75,000
Vehicles	150,000	90,000	60,000
	830,000	275,000	555,000
Current assets			
Stocks		52,000	
Debtors (116 – 12)		104,000	
Investment		75,000	
Cash at bank and in hand		63,000	
		294,000	
Creditors: Amounts falling due within one year			
Creditors and accruals	74,000		
Corporation tax	12,000		
Proposed dividends (8 + 6)	14,000		
		100,000	
Net current assets			194,000
Total assets less current liabilities			749,000
Creditors: Amounts falling due after more than one year			
12% debentures			150,000
			599,000
Capital and reserves			
Called-up share capital			400,000
Share premium account			25,000
Capital redemption reserve			20,000
General reserve (10 + 5)			15,000
Profit and loss account			139,000
			599,000

(b) (1) The nominal value of Billesley Ltd's ordinary share capital is £200,000. This is made up of 400,000 50 pence ordinary shares.

(2) The share premium account is a statutory reserve that must be set up if the company issues shares at a price that is greater than their nominal value. Therefore at some time in the past Billesley Ltd must have issued some shares at a price that was £25,000 more than the nominal value of those shares.

(3) Most companies will produce both management accounts and financial accounts. Management accounts are produced for the internal use of the

management of the company. The financial accounts (as produced in part (a)) are produced for the shareholders or owners of the company. The managers and the shareholders will have different information needs and the management accounts and financial accounts will reflect these different needs.

SESSION 6

1   Punch

Manufacturing account for the year ended 31 March 19X1

	£	£
Raw materials consumed		
Opening stock	12,725	
Purchases	82,550	
	95,275	
Less: Closing stock	(9,650)	
		85,625
Factory wages		64,750
Prime cost		150,375
Factory overheads		
Rent (W4) (70%)	20,038	
Repairs to buildings (80%)	4,400	
Depreciation – Plant and machinery (W1)	3,650	
– Buildings (80%)	720	
Electricity and power (W2)	12,373	
		41,181
Opening WIP	18,000	
Closing WIP	(21,000)	
		(3,000)
Factory cost of goods produced		188,556

Trading and profit and loss account for the year ended 31 March 19X1

		£	£
Sales			362,720
Less:	Cost of goods sold		
	Opening stock	20,500	
	Transfers from factory	188,556	
		209,056	
Closing stock		(24,500)	
			184,556
Gross profit			178,164
Less:	Selling and distribution expenses		
	Wages	26,920	
	Selling expenses (22,000 + 60% × 240)	22,144	
	Bad and doubtful debts (700 + 354) (W3)	1,054	
	Depreciation of motor vans	4,950	
	Sales manager's commission (W5)	20,516	
			(75,584)
Less:	Administration expenses		
	Wages	24,360	
	Electricity and power (W2)	6,187	
	Rent (30%) (W4)	8,587	
	Repairs to buildings (20%)	1,100	
	Depreciation buildings (20%)	180	
	Sundry (850 + 5,900 + 40% × 240)	6,846	
			(47,260)
Net profit			55,320

Balance sheet as at 31 March 19X1

	Cost £	Depreciation £	£
Fixed assets			
Freehold land and buildings	45,000	3,600	41,400
Plant and machinery	36,500	8,150	28,350
Motor vans	19,800	8,650	11,150
	101,300	20,400	80,900
Current assets			
Stocks – Raw materials		9,650	
– WIP		21,000	
– Finished goods		24,500	
Debtors (W3) (38,270 – 1,914)		36,356	
Cash in hand		45	
		91,551	
Current liabilities			
Bank overdraft		6,320	
Creditors		42,230	
Accruals			
[960 + 240 + 850 + 6,625 (W4) + 20,516 (W5)]			29,191
		77,741	
			13,810
Net current assets			94,710

Represented by:	£
Capital @ 1.4.X0	39,390
Profit for the year	55,320
	94,710

Workings

(1) Depreciation – Land and buildings = $2\% \times 45{,}000 = 900$
                       – Plant and machinery = $10\% \times 36{,}500 = 3{,}650$
                       – Motor vehicles = $25\% \times 19{,}800 = 4{,}950$

(2) Electricity and power

	£
Per question	17,600
Accruals	960
	18,560
Factory (2/3)	12,373
Admin. (1/3)	6,187

(3) Debtors

	£
Per question	38,970
Less: Bad debt provision	(700)
	38,270

	£
Provision: $5\% \times 38{,}270$	1,914
Opening provision	1,560
Increase	354

(4) Rent

Charge for the year = $22{,}000 + 3/12 \times 26{,}500$
                      = $22{,}000 + 6{,}625$
                      = 28,625

Factory (70%) = 20,038
Admin. (30%) = 8,587

(5) Sales manager's commission

	£
Gross profit	178,164
Less: Expenses (26,920 + 22,144 + 1,054 + 4,950)	(55,068)
	123,096 (120%)
Commission (20%)	(20,516)
	102,580

2   Gnome Ltd

(a)   **Manufacturing account for the year ended 31 May 19X5**

	£	£
Opening stock of raw materials	108,400	
Purchases	750,600	
	859,000	
Less: Closing stock of raw materials	(112,600)	
	746,400	
Carriage inwards	10,500	
Direct materials		756,900
Direct labour		250,000
Prime cost		1,006,900
Overhead expenses	125,000	
Depreciation of plant and machinery (8% × 150,000)	12,000	
		137,000
Add: Opening work in progress	32,750	
Less: Closing work in progress	(37,800)	
		(5,050)
Factory cost of goods produced		1,138,850
Add: Opening stock of finished goods	184,500	
Less: Closing stock of finished goods	(275,350)	
		(90,850)
Cost of sales		1,048,000

Trading and profit and loss account for the year ended 31 May 19X5

	£	£	£
Turnover			1,347,300
Cost of sales			(1,048,000)
Gross profit			299,300
Administration expenses		158,100	
Amortisation of leasehold premises (£75,000/50)		1,500	
Selling and distribution expenses		116,800	
Financial, legal and professional expenses		54,100	
Debenture interest (10% × £100,000)		10,000	
Depreciation: Fixtures and fittings			
(10% × 50,000)	5,000		
Motor vehicles [20% × (75,000 – 25,000)]	10,000		
		15,000	
			355,500
Net loss for the year			(56,200)
Profit and loss account at 1 June 19X4			359,350
Profit and loss account at 31 May 19X5			303,150

(b)   **Balance sheet at 31 May 19X5**

	£	£	£
Fixed assets			
Intangible assets: Goodwill	165,500	–	165,500
Tangible assets			
Freehold land and buildings	300,000	–	300,000
Leasehold property	75,000	16,500	58,500
Plant and machinery	150,000	80,500	69,500
Fixtures and fittings	50,000	20,750	29,250
Motor vehicles	75,000	35,000	40,000
	815,500	152,750	662,750
Current assets			
Stocks		425,750	
Debtors (less provision for doubtful debts)		171,880	
Cash at bank and in hand		1,520	
		599,150	
Creditors: Amounts falling due within one year			
Bank loans and overdrafts	51,250		
Trade creditors	97,500		
Accruals and deferred income (debenture interest payable)	10,000		
		(158,750)	
Net current assets			440,400
Total assets less current liabilities			1,102,150
Creditors: Amounts falling due after more than one year			
10% debentures			(100,000)
			1,003,150

Capital and reserves	
	£
Called-up share capital	
100,000 12% cumulative preference shares of £1 each fully paid	100,000
300,000 ordinary shares of £1 each fully paid	300,000
	400,000
Share premium account	100,000
Capital redemption reserve	50,000
General reserve	150,000
Profit and loss account	303,150
	1,003,150

SESSION 7

1   Austen plc

Balance sheet as at 31 December 19X2

	Note	£'000	£'000
Fixed assets			
Intangible assets	1	25	
Tangible assets	2	300	
Investments	3	30	
		——	
			355
Current assets			
Stocks	4	70	
Debtors	5	65	
Cash at bank and in hand		10	
		——	
		145	
Creditors: Amounts falling due within one year	6	(130)	
		——	
Net current assets			15
			——
Total assets less current liabilities			370
Creditors: Amounts falling due after more than			
one year	7		(100)
			——
			270
			——
Capital and reserves			
Called-up share capital	8		250
Profit and loss account			20
			——
			270
			——

. . . . Director

These accounts were approved by the board of directors on . . . .

Notes to the accounts

(1)   Fixed assets – Intangible assets

	£'000
Goodwill	
Cost 1.1.X2 and 31.12.X2	60
	—
Amortisation 1.1.X2	30
Charge for year	5
	—
Amortisation 31.12.X2	35
	—

	£'000
Net book value 31.12.X2	25
Net book value 1.1.X2	30

(2) Fixed assets – tangible assets

	Land and buildings £'000	Plant and machinery £'000	Fixtures, fittings, tools and equipment £'000	Total £'000
Cost 1.1.X2	200	280	100	580
Additions during year	–	20	10	30
Disposals during year	–	(10)	–	(10)
Cost 31.12.X2	200	290	110	600
Depreciation 1.1.X2	46	142	44	232
Disposals during year	–	(5)	–	(5)
Charge for year	4	58	11	73
Depreciation 31.12.X2	50	195	55	300
Net book value 31.12.X2	150	95	55	300
Net book value 1.1.X2	154	138	56	348

(3) Fixed assets – investments

The investments are listed on the Stock Exchange. Their market value at 31.12.X2 amounted to £45,000.

(4) Stocks

Stocks are valued at the lower of cost and net realisable value and are made up as follows:

	£'000
Raw materials	20
Work in progress	25
Finished goods	25
	70

(5) Debtors

	£'000
Trade debtors	60
Prepayments and accrued income	5
	65

(6) Creditors: Amounts falling due within one year

These are made up as follows:

	£'000	£'000
Bank loans and overdrafts		35
Trade creditors		50
Other creditors including taxation and social security		
Value added tax	22	
Mainstream corporation tax	20	
		42
Accruals and deferred income		3
		130

(7) Creditors: Amounts falling due after more than one year

	£'000
Debentures	100

The debentures, secured by a floating charge on the company's assets, are repayable in 19X8 at par. Interest accrues at 12% per annum.

(8) Share capital

Authorised share capital:

	£'000
200,000 8% preference shares £1 each	200
400,000 ordinary shares £1 each	400
	600

Issued, allotted and fully paid:

	£'000
50,000 8% preference shares £1 each	50
200,000 ordinary shares £1 each	200
	250

(9) Reserves

	£'000
Profit and loss account at 1.1.X2	X
Profit for current year	X
Profit and loss account at 31.12.X2	20

2 Radical Ltd

Balance sheet as at 30 September 19X2

	Note	£	£
Fixed assets			
Tangible assets	1		336,265
Investments	2		22,632
			358,897
Current assets			
Stocks		192,734	
Debtors	3	161,238	
Cash at bank and in hand		45,166	
		399,138	
Creditors: Amounts falling due within one year	4	116,450	
Net current assets			282,688
Total assets less current liabilities			641,585
Creditors: Amounts falling due after more than one year	5		150,000
			491,585

	Note	£	£
Capital and reserves			
Called-up share capital	6		350,000
Share premium account			52,400
Profit and loss account			89,185
			491,585

. . . . Director

These accounts were approved by the board of directors on . . . .

Notes to the balance sheet

(1)   Tangible fixed assets

	Freehold property £	Motor vehicles £	Total £
Cost			
At 1 October 19X1	105,000	366,345	471,345
Additions	26,000	40,450	66,450
At 30 September 19X2	131,000	406,795	537,795
Accumulated depreciation			
At 1 October 19X1	2,500	112,530	115,030
Charge for year	2,500	84,000	86,500
At 30 September 19X2	5,000	196,530	201,530
Net book value – At 30 September 19X2	126,000	210,265	336,265
– At 1 October 19X1	102,500	253,815	356,315

(2)   Fixed asset investments

All investments are listed on the Stock Exchange.

(3)   Debtors

	£
Trade debtors (172,062 – 13,420)	158,642
Prepayments and accrued income	2,596
	161,238

(4)   Creditors: Amounts falling due within one year

	£
Trade creditors	64,700
Other creditors including taxation and social security	
Corporation tax	26,750
Proposed dividend	25,000
	116,450

(5)   Creditors: Amounts falling due after more than one year

	£
Debenture loans	
9½ % Loan Stock, repayable 1 October 19Y9	150,000

(6)   Called-up share capital

		£
Authorised, issued and fully paid		
1,000,000 ordinary shares of 25p each		250,000
200,000 8% cumulative preference shares of 50p each		100,000
		350,000

SESSION 8

1   Bronte plc

Profit and loss account for the year ended 31 December 19X2

	Notes	£'000	£'000
Turnover			1,515
Cost of sales (W)			(900)
Gross profit			615
Distribution costs (W)			(100)
Administrative expenses (W)			(90)
Operating profit	1		425
Income from other fixed asset investments			20
Other interest receivable and similar income			10
Interest payable and similar charges	2		(65)
Profit on ordinary activities before taxation			390
Tax on profit on ordinary activities	3		(141)
Profit on ordinary activities after taxation			249
Dividends paid and proposed	4		(60)
Retained profit for the year			189
Profit and loss account at 1.1.X2			1,190
Profit and loss account at 31.12.X2			1,379

Notes

(1)   Operating profit

Operating profit is after charging:

	£'000
Audit fee	3
Depreciation of tangible fixed assets	55
Directors' emoluments	71
Hire charges on plant	1

(2)   Interest payable

All interest payable is in respect of loans repayable in more than five years.

(3)   Tax on profit on ordinary activities

	£'000
UK corporation tax	141

(4)   Dividends paid and proposed

	£'000
Interim dividend paid – 10p per share	20
Final dividend proposed – 20p per share	40
	60

(5)   Directors and employees

     (a)   Individual directors' emoluments

Chairman's emoluments	£12,000
Highest paid director	£34,000
Other directors' emoluments fall within the following band £20,001 – £25,000	1

     (b)   Staff numbers

Staff totalled 17 which may be analysed as to:

	Number of employees
Distribution	7
Administration	10
	17

Working

	Cost of sales £'000	Distribution costs £'000	Administration expenses £'000
Stock 1 January 19X2	109		
Salaries		55	60
Expenses		31	17
Purchases	884		
Depreciation			
Office equipment			5
Motor vehicles		10	
Property	28	4	8
Stock 31 December 19X2	(121)		
Total to profit and loss account	900	100	90

2   Church's Ltd

Profit and loss account for the year ended 31 December 19X0

	Notes	£
Turnover		595,932
Cost of sales		349,996
Gross profit		245,936
Distribution costs (W1)		164,017
Administrative expenses (W1)		43,498
Operating profit	1	38,421
Income from fixed asset investments	4	1,326
Interest payable and similar charges	5	800
Profit on ordinary activities before taxation		38,947
Tax on profit on ordinary activities	6	12,410
Profit on ordinary activities after taxation		26,537
Dividends	7	16,900
Retained profit for the financial year		9,637

Notes to the accounts

(1)   Operating profit

Operating profit is stated after charging

	£
Directors' emoluments (13,500 + 13,000 + 858 + 7,500 + 750)	35,608
Auditors' fees	700
Depreciation of tangible fixed assets (5,290 + 520 + 1,000)	6,810

(2)   Staff

    (a)   Aggregate payroll costs (amounts include those in respect of executive directors)

	£
Wages and salaries (62,917 + 7,500)	70,417
Social security costs	4,250
Other pension costs	750
	75,417

    (b)   The average number of employees working for the company in the financial year was 10.

Tutorial note: There is no need for notes concerning the emoluments of the chairman and highest paid director, or the banding of directors' emoluments, as the aggregate director's emoluments is less than £60,000.

(3)   Income from fixed asset investments

		£
Listed		780
Unlisted		546
		1,326

(4)   Interest payable and similar charges

On debenture loan repayable after more than five years   £800

(5)   Tax on profit on ordinary activities

UK corporation tax   £12,410

(6)   Dividends

		£
Preference:	6½ % paid	6,500
Ordinary:	5.2p per share proposed	10,400
		16,900

Workings

(1)

	Distribution costs £	*Administrative expenses* £
Motor expenses	79,842	–
Depreciation	5,290	1,520
Other	39,420	5,746
Wages and salaries	34,715	28,202
Pension to former director's widow	–	750
Superannuation scheme	2,250	2,000
Audit	–	700
Provision for directors' fees	2,500	5,000
Discounts received	–	(420)
	164,017	43,498

(2)   Staff costs

	Distribution costs £	Administrative expenses £	£
Wages + salaries			
Per question	34,715	28,202	
Provision for directors' fees	2,500	5,000	
	37,215	33,202	70,417
Social security costs			
Superannuation scheme	2,250	2,000	4,250
Other pension costs			
Director's widow	–	750	750

SESSION 9

1   Collins plc

(a)   **Profit and loss account for the year ended 31 March 19X2**

	Notes	£'000
Turnover		5,125
Cost of sales (W)		(4,081)
Gross profit		1,044
Distribution costs		(200)
Administrative expenses (610 + 5)		(615)
Operating profit	1	229
Profit on the sale of fixed assets	2	30
Profit on ordinary activities before interest		259
Income from other fixed asset investments	3	8
Interest payable and similar charges	4	(42)
Profit on ordinary activities before taxation		225
Tax on profit on ordinary activities	5	(36)
Profit for the financial year		189

Notes to the profit and loss account

(1)   Operating profit

	£'000
Operating profit is stated after charging	
Auditors' fees	5.0
Depreciation of tangible fixed assets	65.0
Directors' emoluments	
Fees	7.5
Other	123.0
Amortisation of intangible fixed assets	7.5

(2)   Profit on the sale of fixed assets

Profit on the sale of fixed assets relates to the disposal of a fixed asset investment. As a result of this disposal the taxation charge for the year has been increased by £9,000.

(3)   Income from other fixed asset investments

This item is wholly in respect of listed investments.

(4)   Interest payable and similar charges

	£'000
On bank loans, overdrafts and other loans repayable ithin five years	12
On other loans	30
	42

(5)   Tax on profit on ordinary activities

	£'000
UK corporation tax	
Current year (25 + 9)	34
Prior year	2
	36

(6)   Staff

The average number of persons employed by the company (including directors) was as follows:

Manufacturing	120
Distribution	10
Administrative	35
Total	165

The aggregate payroll costs of these persons were as follows:

	£'000
Wages and salaries	1,489
Other pension costs	276
	1,765

(7)   Directors' emoluments

The emoluments of the chairman were	£36,500
The emoluments of the highest paid director were	£42,500
The emoluments of the other directors working wholly or substantially in the UK fell within the following ranges:	
Up to £5,000	1
£20,001 to £25,000	1

Working

Cost of sales

	£
Purchases and factory wages	4,100
Opening stock (50 + 75 + 150)	275
	4,375
Closing stock (45 + 79 + 170)	(294)
	4,081

(b)   **Balance sheet as at 31 March 19X2**

	Notes	£'000	£'000
Fixed assets			
Intangible asset: Goodwill	8		140
Tangible assets	9		2,310
Investments	10		30
			2,480
Current assets			
Stocks	11	294	
Debtors	12	304	
Cash at bank and in hand		2	
		600	
Creditors: Amounts falling due within one year	13	293	
Net current assets			307
Total assets less current liabilities			2,787
Creditors: Amounts falling due after more than one year	14		375
			2,412

	Notes	£'000	£'000
Capital and reserves			
Called-up share capital			500
Share premium account	15		150
Other reserves			
Capital redemption reserve	15		50
Profit and loss account			1,712
			2,412

. . . . Director

These accounts were approved by the board of directors on . . . .

Notes to the balance sheet

(8) Intangible fixed assets: Goodwill

	£'000
Cost	
At 31 March 19X2 and 1 April 19X1	150.0
Accumulated amortisation	
At 1 April 19X1	2.5
Charge for the year	7.5
At 31 March 19X2	10.0
Net book value	
At 31 March 19X2	140.0
At 1 April 19X1	147.5

(9) Tangible fixed assets

	Freehold land and buildings £'000	*Plant and machinery* £'000	*Motor vehicles* £'000	*Total* £'000
Cost				
At 1 April 19X1	1,010	480	120	1,610
Additions	1,000	20	–	1,020
At 31 March 19X2	2,010	500	120	2,630
Accumulated depreciation				
At 1 April 19X1	50	175	30	255
Charge for the year	10	35	20	65
At 31 March 19X2	60	210	50	320
Net book value				
At 31 March 19X2	1,950	290	70	2,310
At 1 April 19X1	960	305	90	1,355

Tutorial note: Separate disclosure of motor vehicles within the fixed assets note is not required. However, it is common practice to do so.

(10) Investments: Listed investments

Cost	£'000
At 1 April 19X1	30
Additions	42
Disposals	(42)
At 31 March 19X2	30

(11) Stocks

	£'000
Raw materials and consumables	45
Work in progress	79
Finished goods and goods for resale	170
	294

(12) Debtors

	£'000
Trade debtors	300
Prepayments and accrued income	4
	304

(13) Creditors: Amounts falling due within one year

	£'000
Bank loans and overdrafts	41
Trade creditors	210
Other creditors including taxation and social security	
Mainstream corporation tax (25 + 9)	34
Accruals and deferred income (6 + 2)	8
	293

(14) Creditors: Amounts falling due after more than one year

	£'000
Debenture loans: 10% loan stock, redeemable 19X9 (secured by floating charge)	300
Bank loans and overdrafts	75
	375

(15) Called-up share capital – ordinary £1 shares

	£'000
At 1 April 19X1	350
Issued during year	150
	500

During the year, shares of a nominal value of £150,000 were issued for £300,000 in order to part fund the acquisition of freehold land and buildings.

(16) Movements on reserves

	Share premium £'000	*Capital redemption* £'000	*Profit and loss* £'000
At 1 April 19X1	–	50	1,523
On issue of shares	150	–	–
Profit for year	–	–	189
At 31 March 19X2	150	50	1,712

(c) Accounting policies

(1) Basis of accounting

The accounts have been prepared under the historical cost convention.

(2) Depreciation

Depreciation has been provided on all fixed assets with a limited useful life to write off their cost over their estimated useful economic lives.

These lives are:

Goodwill	20 years
Buildings	50 years
Plant and machinery	20 years
Motor vehicles	5 years

(3) Stocks

Stocks have been valued at the lower of cost and net realisable value. Cost includes overheads attributable to their stage of manufacture and is computed on the first in, first out method of valuation.

(4) Turnover

Turnover comprises the amount received and receivable for goods manufactured during the year, excluding value added tax.

2   Claret Ltd

Statement of total recognised gains and losses for the year ended 31 December 19X8

	£'000
Profit for the financial year (1,825 + 250 − 62 + 55)	2,068
Unrealised surplus on revaluation (W1)	40
	2,108
Prior period adjustment (note 1)	(55)
Total gains and losses recognised since last annual report	2,053

Notes to the accounts

(1)   **Reconciliation of opening and closing totals of shareholders' funds**

	£'000
Balance 1 January 19X8 (W2)	21,741
Prior period adjustment (note 3)	(55)
As restated	21,686
Profits for the financial year (W4)	2,068
Dividends	(250)
Surplus on revaluation	40
Goodwill written off (W3)	(120)
Shares issued (160 × £2.10)	336
Balance 31 December 19X8	23,760

(2)   **Prior period adjustment**

The prior period adjustment is in respect of a fundamental error in the valuation of stock. Closing stock and, hence, reserves at 31 December 19X7 were overstated by £55,000.

Workings

(1)   Unrealised surplus on revaluation

	£'000	£'000
Revalued amount		430
Original cost	650	
Accumulated depreciation to 31 December 19X8 $(650 \times {}^{8}\!/_{20})$	(260)	
Net book value at revaluation		(390)
		40

(2)   Opening total shareholders' funds

	£'000
Share capital (2,000 × 50p)	1,000
Profit and loss account	20,658
Revaluation reserve	83
	21,741

(3)   Goodwill written off

	£'000	£'000
Purchase consideration		370
Business net assets	260	
Doubtful debts adjustment	(10)	
		(250)
		120

(4)   Profit for financial year

	£'000	£'000
Retained profit		1,825
Add back: Dividend		250
Profit for financial year		2,075
Less: Overstatement of stock		
Opening stock	55	
Less: Closing stock	(62)	
		(7)
		2,068

SESSION 10

1   Ford plc

Accounting policy note

(1)   Tangible fixed assets

Interests in buildings are stated at a valuation.

Other tangible fixed assets are stated at cost, together with any incidental expenses of acquisition.

Depreciation is calculated so as to write off the net cost or valuation of tangible fixed assets over their expected useful economic lives. A full year's charge is provided in the year of acquisition. The rates and bases used are as follows:

Buildings	2% pa
Plant and machinery	10% pa
Office equipment and fixtures – on the straight-line basis	20% pa
Motor vehicles – on the reducing-balance method	30% pa

(2)   Operating profit

Operating profit is stated after charging:

	£'000
Depreciation of tangible fixed assets	562

(3)   Tangible fixed assets

	Freehold land and buildings £'000	Plant and machinery £'000	Motor vehicles £'000	Fixtures, fittings, tools and equipment £'000	Total £'000
Cost or valuation					
At 1 January 19X7	1,440	1,968	449	888	4,745
Additions	500	75	35	22	632
Revaluations	760	–	–	–	760
At 31 December 19X7	2,700	2,043	484	910	6,137
Depreciation					
At 1 January 19X7	144	257	194	583	1,178
Revaluation adjustment	(144)				(144)
Charge for year	60	233	87	182	562
At 31 December 19X7	60	490	281	765	1,596
Net book value					
At 31 December 19X7	2,640	1,553	203	145	4,541
At 1 January 19X7	1,296	1,711	255	305	3,567

(a) Buildings were valued for the purposes of the 19X7 accounts at open market valuation with existing use. This valuation was made by a firm of independent chartered surveyors. The historical cost of the factory is £1,940,000 and the related depreciation is £183,000 (W).

(b) The company's depreciation policy on motor vehicles has been changed from a rate of 25% pa on cost to a rate of 30% pa on reducing balance in order to give a fairer presentation of the results and of the financial position. The effect of this change is to reduce the depreciation charge for the year by £34,000.

Working

Historical cost depreciation of factory

	£'000
Factory $6/50 \times 1,440$	173
Extension $1/50 \times 500$	10
	183

2   Cribbage plc

(a) The properties will be included in the balance sheet at their valuation:

	19X1 £'000	19X2 £'000	19X3 £'000
Fixed assets			
Investments			
Other investments other than loans			
Investment properties	1,310	1,260	1,180

(b) The profit and loss account would include no depreciation charge but, as this is a departure from the Companies Act requirement to depreciate all fixed assets having a limited useful economic life, the notes to the accounts would have to disclose particulars of the departure, the reason for it and its effect.

(c) The company should set up an 'investment revaluation reserve' which should be displayed under 'Other reserves' in the financial statements. The movement on the investment revaluation reserve would be:

	19X1 £'000	19X2 £'000	19X3 £'000
Other reserves			
Investment revaluation reserve			
Balance brought forward	–	110	60
Revaluation surplus (deficit) for the year	110	(50)	(60) (see note)
Balance carried forward	110	60	–

Note: If the total of the investment revaluation reserve is insufficient to cover a deficit, the amount by which the deficit exceeds the balance on the investment revaluation reserve should be charged in the profit and loss account.

(d) There would be no effect on the profit and loss account except in the year ended 31 December 19X3 when a deficit of £20,000 will be charged to the profit and loss account. This £20,000 is calculated as follows:

	£
Deficit for year	(80,000)
Balance in investment revaluation reserve	60,000
Deficit to be charged to profit and loss account	(20,000)

Note: Cribbage plc would also have to prepare a statement of recognised gains and losses and a note of historical cost profits and losses. These are required by FRS3 *Reporting financial performance*, which is covered in Session 9.

(e) The statement of total recognised gains and losses should appear as follows:

	19X1 £'000	*19X2* £'000	*19X3* £'000
Profit for the financial year	X	X	X
Unrealised surplus/(deficit) on revaluation of properties	110	(50)	(80)
Total recognised gains and losses relating to the year	X	X	X

(f) There would be no effect on the note of historical cost profits and losses as the property revaluation gains remain unrealised and the properties are not depreciated.

SESSION 11

1 Newprods Ltd

(a) (i) Pure research expenditure is expenditure incurred on experimental or theoretical work undertaken in order to gain new scientific or technical knowledge for its own sake. Pure research is not primarily directed towards any specific practical aim or application.

(ii) Applied research expenditure is expenditure incurred on an original or critical investigation which has been undertaken in order to gain new scientific or technical knowledge which is directed towards a specific practical aim or objective.

(iii) Development expenditure is expenditure incurred in using scientific or technical knowledge in order to produce new or substantially improved materials, devices, products or services, to install new processes or systems prior to the commencement of commercial applications, or substantially to improve those already produced or installed.

(b)   Expenditure on pure and applied research should be written off in the year of expenditure. However, the cost of fixed assets acquired or constructed in order to provide facilities for research and development activities over a number of years should be capitalised and written off over their useful life.

Expenditure on development should be written off in the year of expenditure except in the following circumstances when it may be carried forward:

(i)   there is a clearly defined project;

(ii)   the related expenditure is separately identifiable;

(iii)   the outcome of such a project was assessed with reasonable certainty as to:

–   its technical feasibility; and

–   its ultimate commercial viability considered in the light of factors such as likely market conditions (including competing products), public opinion, consumer and environmental legislation;

(iv)   the aggregate of the deferred development costs, further development costs and related production, selling and administration costs is reasonably expected to be exceeded by related future sales or other revenues; and

(v)   adequate resources exist, or are reasonably expected to be available, to enable the project to be completed and to provide any consequential increases in working capital.

The principle behind the above rules is that development expenditure should only be carried forward if the recovery of that expenditure can reasonably be regarded as assured.

(c)   *Project 3*

Project 3 may be regarded as development (as defined in SSAP 13) and therefore it may be correct to carry forward a certain amount of the expenditure. However, the cost of producing the new compound is comparable to that of the existing raw material and therefore unless selling prices are increased the expenditure which has been incurred in developing the new compound will not be recovered in future periods.

Assuming that selling prices cannot be increased the expenditure should be shown as follows.

Balance sheet

	£
Fixed assets	
Tangible assets (at cost less depreciation)	9,000

Profit and loss account

	£
Development expenditure written off	11,000
Depreciation	1,000

Project 4

This is also development expenditure. As the yield of the operation is being greatly improved the material costs will obviously decrease and greater profits will be made. Thus the expenditure incurred in development may be recovered in future years. To determine how much of the expenditure may be carried forward it is necessary to calculate whether the aggregate of costs already incurred and future costs will be covered by the saving of material costs which is predicted.

The saving of material costs per annum is £30,000 and the life of the plant is ten years. Therefore, assuming no increases in the costs of the materials the new process will produce a saving of £30,000 per annum for some years. As the costs to date are only £22,000 plus fixed assets cost of £20,000 it seems highly probable that the expenditure will be recovered in future years. It is necessary to assume that the market for the product and its selling price will remain unchanged.

The treatment of the expenditure on Project 4 will therefore be as follows.

Balance sheet

	£
Fixed assets	
Intangible asset: development costs (22,000 + 2,000)	24,000
Tangible assets (20,000 – 2,000)	18,000

A note to the balance sheet should state:

(i)   the reasons for capitalising the expenditure; and
(ii)   the period over which the costs are being written off.

Note: No charge for development expenditure has been made this year as the commercial production has not yet commenced. The development costs should be amortised over a period coincident with the commercial use of the process.

Project 5

This project should be regarded as development work which is being carried out on behalf of a third party. If there is a firm contract which states that the expenditure is to be fully reimbursed then any such expenditure which has not been reimbursed at the balance sheet date should be included in work in progress.

The treatment would therefore be as follows.

Balance sheet

	£
Fixed assets	
Tangible assets	4,500
Current assets	
Stocks: Work in progress	44,500

2   Gill Wood Ltd

(a)   Goodwill is the difference between the value of a business as a whole and the aggregate of the fair values of its separable net assets.

Purchased goodwill is goodwill which is established as a result of the purchase of a business accounted for as an acquisition. Goodwill arising on consolidation is one form of purchased goodwill.

(b)   The amount of goodwill arising in the books of Gill Wood Ltd in 19X7 is as follows:

		£
Cost of acquisition		
Cash		40,000
Shares 60,000 × 2.40		144,000
		184,000
Less:	Fair value of separable net assets	168,590
		15,410

This will be dealt with as follows.

(i)   It should not be carried as a permanent item in the balance sheet of the company.

(ii)   It should normally be eliminated from the accounts immediately on acquisition against reserves.

(iii)   As an alternative to (ii) it may be eliminated from the accounts by amortisation through the profit and loss account in arriving at profit or loss on ordinary activities on a systematic basis over its useful economic life.

3   Woodpecker Ltd

Task 1

			£'000	£'000
(1)	Dr	Ordinary share capital	400	
	Cr	Share premium		400

Being correction of error in crediting proceeds of share issue to ordinary share capital (800,000 shares @ 50p premium each = £400,000)

			£'000	£'000
(2)	Dr	Share premium	100	
	Cr	Ordinary share capital		100

Representing bonus share issue (2,400,000 ordinary shares in issue at the year-end; 1 for 6 issue, ie. 400,000 ordinary shares of 25p each; reserves used in order: capital redemption reserve, share premium, other reserves)

			£'000	£'000
(3)	Dr	Preference share dividend	15	
	Cr	Preference share dividend payable		15

Being final preference dividend (10% × £300,000 shares = £30,000 less interim dividend paid £15,000)

(4)	Dr	Interest charge	36	
	Cr	Accruals		36

Being interest on debentures payable (8% debentures of £450,000 = £36,000)

(5)	Dr	Investment revaluation reserve	150	
	Dr	Amounts written off investments (profit and loss a/c)	50	
	Cr	Investment property		200

Being write-down of investment property to valuation (as there is an insufficient balance in the investment revaluation reserve, the remaining £50,000 is written off to the profit and loss account)

(6)	Dr	Audit fees	25	
	Cr	Accruals		25

Being accrual for audit fees

(7)	Dr	Taxation charge	275	
	Cr	Taxation payable		275

Being taxation charge for the year

(8)	Dr	Amortisation of goodwill	5	
	Cr	Goodwill		5

Being amortisation of goodwill for the year (£50,000 divided by ten years = £5,000)

Task 2

(a)   **Financial statements for publication**

Woodpecker Ltd
Profit and loss account for the year ended 31 March 1994

	£'000
Turnover	
Continuing operations	8,086
Cost of sales	(4,829)
Gross profit	3,257
Distribution costs	1,751
Administrative expenses	631
Operating profit	
Continuing operations	875
Amounts written off investments	50
Amortisation of goodwill	5
Interest payable and similar charges	36
Profit (or loss) on ordinary activities before taxation	784
Tax on profit (or loss) on ordinary activities	275
Profit (or loss) on ordinary activities after taxation	509
Dividends	30
Retained profit for the financial year	479

Woodpecker Ltd
Balance sheet as at 31 March 1994

	£'000	£'000
Fixed assets		
Intangible assets	15	
Tangible assets	1,963	
Investments property	600	
		2,578
Current assets		
Stocks	937	
Debtors	842	
Cash at bank and in hand	3	
	1,782	
Creditors: Amounts falling due within one year	(1,103)	
Net current assets (liabilities)		679
Total assets less current liabilities		3,257
Creditors: Amount falling due after more than one year		(450)
		2,807
Capital and reserves		
Called-up share capital		1,000
Share premium		550
Profit and loss account		1,257
		2,807

Workings

(1)   Calculation of turnover

	£'000
Sales	8,270
Less: Returns inwards	184
Turnover	8,086

(2)   Calculation of cost of sales

	£'000	£'000
Opening stock	731	
Purchases	5,051	
Add: Carriage inwards	25	
Less: Returns outwards	(41)	
	5,766	
Less: Closing stock	(937)	
Cost of sales		4,829

(3)   Allocation of expenses

	Distribution costs £'000	Administrative expenses £'000
Advertising	56	–
Salaries and wages (75/25)	1,004	335
Increase in provision for doubtful debts	–	17
Discounts allowed	23	–
Motor expense	47	31
Salesmen's commission	83	–
Rates	15	5
Light and heat	20	6
Insurance	14	4
Audit	–	25
General expenses	186	48
Directors' remuneration	49	102
Depreciation motor vehicles	151	38
Depreciation fixtures and fittings	65	–
Depreciation office equipment	22	15
Depreciation buildings	16	5
	1,751	631

(4)   Dividend

	£'000
Interim preference dividend	15
Final preference dividend proposed	15
	30

(5)   Fixed assets

	Cost £'000	Accumulated depreciation £'000	Net book value £'000
Land and buildings	1,267	138	1,129
Fixtures and fittings	632	241	391
Motor vehicles	745	408	337
Office equipment	194	88	106
	2,838	875	1,963

(6)   Debtors

Debtors are made up as follows:

	£'000	£'000
Trade debtors	840	
Less: Provision for doubtful debts	37	
		803
Prepayment		39
		842

(7)   Creditors: Amounts falling due within one year

This is made up of:

	£'000
Bank overdraft	139
Trade creditors	568
Corporation tax payable	275
Dividends payable	15
Accruals	106
	1,103

(8)   Called-up share capital

Issued, allotted and fully paid is:

	£'000
2,800,000 ordinary shares of 25p	700
300,000 10% preference shares of £1	300
	1,000

(9)   Profit and loss account

	£'000
At 1 April 1994	778
Retained profit for the year	479
At 31 March 1994	1,257

(b)   **Notes to the accounts**

(1)   Share capital

Authorised share capital is:

	£
4,000,000 ordinary shares of 25p	1,000,000
500,000 10% preference shares of £1	500,000
	1,500,000

Issued, allotted and fully paid is:

	£
2,800,000 ordinary shares of 25p	700,000
300,000 10% preference shares of £1	300,000
	1,000,000

(2)   Directors' remuneration

The amounts paid to directors were:

	£
Fee as directors	7,000
Other emoluments (including pension contributions)	144,000

Emoluments of the chairman (excluding pension contributions) amounted to £33,000. The emoluments of the highest paid director amounted to £59,000 (excluding pension contributions). Other directors' emoluments were within the following range:

£40,000 – £45,000   1

Task 3

Goodwill, as defined by SSAP22, is the difference between the value of a business as a whole and the aggregate of the fair values of its separable assets. The alternative to amortisation of goodwill is to write off goodwill from the accounts of a company immediately on acquisition against reserves.

SESSION 12

1   Jackson Ltd

(a)   In inflationary conditions, the LIFO method will lead to lower closing stock valuations as items in stock will be valued at earlier, lower prices. The effect of this is that the cost of sales will be at the latest prices, thus leading to a lower profit figure. This situation approximates to **current cost profit**.

The FIFO method leads to the reverse situation; closing stocks are valued at the latest price and consequently cost of sales will be at a lower historical cost. This leads to higher closing stock values and higher profit figures.

(b)   (i)   Cost is defined in relation to the different categories of stocks and work in progress as being that expenditure which has been incurred in the normal course of business in bringing the product or service to its present location and condition. This expenditure should include, in addition to cost of purchase (which include import duties, transport and handling costs less trade discounts, rebates and subsidies), such costs of conversion, including production and other attributable overheads, as are appropriate to that location and condition.

(ii)   Net realisable value is defined as the actual or estimated selling price (net of trade but before settlement discounts) less:

–   all further costs to completion; and
–   all costs to be incurred in marketing, selling and distribution.

(c)   The principal situations in which net realisable value is likely to be less than cost are where there has been:

(i)   an increase in costs or a fall in selling price;

(ii)   physical deterioration of stocks;

(iii)   obsolescence of products;

(iv)   a decision as part of a company's marketing strategy to manufacture and sell products at a loss; and

(v)   errors in production or purchasing.

Furthermore, when stocks are held which are unlikely to be sold within the normal turnover period in that company (ie. excess stocks), the impending delay in realisation increases the risk that the situations outlined in (i) to (iii) above may occur before the stocks are sold and needs to be taken into account in assessing net realisable value.

SSAP9 states that the comparison of cost and net realisable value needs to be made in respect of each item of stock separately.

(d)   SSAP9 states the following:

(i)   Stocks should be valued at the lower of cost and net realisable value.

(ii)   Cost is that expenditure which has been incurred in bringing the product to its present location and condition.

(iii)   Cost includes an appropriate proportion of overheads based on the normal level of activity.

Statement 1

This statement is erroneous in that it suggests the inclusion of all costs in the stock valuation. The costs of the sales department and the administration costs have not been incurred in bringing the product to its present location and condition and therefore should be excluded.

Statement 2

This statement suggests spreading the costs over the 4,000 units actually produced but SSAP9 requires that the apportionment of overheads should be on the basis of normal activity levels, (ie. 5,000). Any amount of overheads not absorbed should be written off during the year. The valuation suggested also includes the administrative costs which, as costs of general management are not directly related to current production, should be excluded.

Statement 3

This statement suggests the exclusion of all overheads which is against SSAP9 which specifically states that all production overheads including those accruing on a time basis should be included in the valuation of stock.

Recommended valuation

	£
Raw material	10.00
Import duties	1.00
Direct labour	15.00
	26.00
Share of overheads $£\dfrac{3,000 + 2,000 + 7,000}{5,000}$	2.40
	28.40

Note: It should be checked that this is lower than the net realisable value as calculated:

	£
Selling price	50.00
Further costs to completion $\dfrac{£8,000}{5,000}$	(1.60)
	48.40

SESSION 14

1   Times Ltd

Profit and loss account (extract) for year ended 30 June 19X4

	£	£
Income from fixed asset investments (£4,320 × 100/80)		5,400
Tax on ordinary activities		
Corporation tax on ordinary activities at 33%	75,000	
Underprovision for previous year (£52,500 – £50,000)	2,500	
Tax credit on UK dividends received (£5,400 – £4,320)	1,080	
		78,580
Dividends		
Paid	8,100	
Proposed	16,200	
		24,300

Balance sheet (extract) at 30 June 19X4

	£	£
Debtors – ACT recoverable after more than one year		
(£16,200 × 20/80 on the proposed dividend)		4,050
Creditors: Amounts falling due within one year		
Other creditors including taxation and social security		
Mainstream corporation tax (75,000 – 945 (W))	74,055	
Other taxation and social security (16,200 × 20/80)	4,050	
Proposed dividend	16,200	
		94,305

Working

ACT paid in year to 30 June 19X4

	£
ACT on the dividends paid (20/80 × £8,100)	2,025
ACT on dividends received (20/80 × £4,320)	(1,080)
	945

2   Fairbrother Ltd

Balance sheet at 30 June 19X6

	Note	£
Fixed assets		
Tangible assets	1	555,000
Investments	2	59,000
		614,000
Current assets		
Stocks		97,862
Debtors	3	142,637
Cash at bank and in hand		11,220
		251,719
Creditors: Amounts falling due within one year	4	(263,339)
Net current liabilities		(11,620)
Total assets less current liabilities		602,380
Creditors: Amounts falling due after more than one year	5	(100,000)
		502,380
Capital and reserves		
Called-up share capital	6	250,000
Profit and loss account (W3)		252,380
		502,380

. . . .   Director

The accounts were approved by the board of directors on . . . .

(1)   Tangible fixed assets

	Land and buildings £	Plant and machinery £	Motor vehicles £	Total £
Cost				
At 1 July 19X5	370,000	270,000	60,000	700,000
Additions	–	70,000	20,000	90,000
At 30 June 19X6	370,000	340,000	80,000	790,000
Depreciation				
At 1 July 19X5	25,000	127,500	28,000	180,500
Charges for year	5,000	42,500	7,000	54,500
At 30 June 19X6	30,000	170,000	35,000	235,000

	£	£	£	£
Net book value at 30 June 19X6	340,000	170,000	45,000	555,000
Net book value at 1 July 19X5	345,000	142,500	32,000	519,500

(2)   Investments

These comprise listed investments (market value £73,000)

(3)   Debtors

	£
Trade debtors	130,000
Prepayments	6,387
ACT recoverable (W2)	6,250
	142,637

The ACT is recoverable after more than one year from the balance sheet date.

(4)   Creditors: Amounts falling due within one year

	£
Bank loans and overdrafts	53,500
Trade creditors	97,000
Other creditors including taxation and social security	
Corporation tax (W1)	58,650
Other taxation and social security [6,250 (W2) + 1,107]	7,357
Proposed dividend	25,000
Other creditors (directors' fees)	12,000
Accruals and deferred income	9,832
	263,339

(5)   Creditors: Amounts falling due after more than one year

	£
Debenture loan	100,000

The debenture loan carries interest at 8% per annum, is redeemable at par in 19Y9 and is secured on the company's land and buildings.

(6)   Share capital

	£
Authorised, issued and fully paid 250,000 shares of £1 each	250,000

Workings

(1) Corporation tax liability

	£
Provision for year	59,000
Less: ACT paid [$^{20}/_{80}$ × (10,000 – 8,600)]	(350)
	58,650

(2) ACT payable and recoverable

On proposed dividend (250,000 × 10% × $^{20}/_{80}$)	£6,250

(3) Profit and loss account

	£
Per trial balance	348,380
Less: Corporation tax provision	(59,000)
Directors' fees	(12,000)
Proposed dividend	(25,000)
	252,380

SESSION 15

1   Trunfair Ltd

(1)   **Faulty products**

Although the major design fault was not found until after the year-end, it related to a condition existing at the year-end and, therefore, any loss arising to the extent that it relates to the situation at the year-end should be reflected in the financial statements in accordance with SSAP17 *Accounting for post balance sheet events*.

If the company had committed itself irrevocably during the year to advertising expenditure on the new product of £300,000, then this loss to the extent that it is not considered likely to be recoverable from the manufacturers should be fully accrued in the financial statements for the year ended 31 July 19X3. It may be possible, however, under the terms of the advertising agreement to switch the advertising to a different product, in which case the loss which should be recognised would be £150,000, plus the cost of any advertising in respect of the faulty product that had taken place after the year-end but before the switch in advertising could be effected.

Any advertising expenditure so written off may require separate disclosure as an exceptional item in accordance with FRS3.

Consideration must be given to the position relating to the stocks purchased by Trunfair Ltd and subsequently returned to the supplier for a full refund. If it is probable that the supplier will give a full refund and that no loss will crystallise, then the financial statements should include the cost of those goods as closing stock. If it is probable that a loss will occur it should be recognised in the financial statements

---

by reducing the value of the stocks, since the condition of the major design fault existed at the year-end.

Consideration should also be given to any contingent liability which may arise in respect of faulty goods sold by Trunfair Ltd which may be returned to them by customers for a full refund, although it is likely that Trunfair Ltd would make a counterclaim against the manufacturer. SSAP18 *Accounting for contingencies* requires that if any net loss is probable, after taking into account the probable outcome of the counterclaim, then that loss should be accrued in the financial statements. The likelihood of success and the probable amounts of the claim and the counterclaim should be separately assessed and separately disclosed where appropriate. If it is not probable that a net loss will crystallise, disclosure of the loss is required except where the possibility of the loss is remote. If a contingency is disclosed, the following would need to be disclosed in respect of it:

(a)   the nature of the contingency;

(b)   the uncertainties which are expected to affect the ultimate outcome; and

(c)   a prudent estimate of the financial effect, made at the date on which the financial statements are approved by the board of directors, or a statement that it is not practicable to make such an estimate.

(2)   **Uninsured stock loss**

The uninsured stock loss totalling £200,000 arising from flood damage occurred after the year-end, and therefore since the condition did not exist at the year-end, the loss would be a non-adjusting event within the definition given in SSAP17. It should be disclosed if it is considered to be of such materiality that its non-disclosure would affect the ability of the users of the financial statements to reach proper understanding of the financial position. The disclosure that would be required would be:

(a)   the nature of the event; and

(b)   an estimate of the financial effect before taking account of taxation and the taxation implications should be explained where necessary for a proper understanding of the financial position.

(3)   **Insolvency of a debtor**

This is a post balance sheet event within the definition given in SSAP17 *Accounting for post balance sheet events* and would be an adjusting event since it provides additional evidence of a condition existing at the balance sheet date.

The £120,000 should therefore be either provided for as a doubtful debt or, alternatively, written off as a bad debt. (The treatment would depend on the likelihood of any of the debt being recovered.) It may also be necessary to disclose the provision or write-off as an exceptional item in the notes to the accounts.

2   Vacs Ltd

MEMORANDUM

To: The directors of Vacs Ltd
From: G Force, Chief Accountant
Subject: Year-end accounts – 30 September 19X3
Date: 14 November 19X3

Set out below are the implications for the financial statements for the year ended 30 September 19X3 of the items mentioned at our recent meeting.

(1)   **Overdraft guarantee**

The company has guaranteed to pay an overdraft if another company cannot repay it.

This item is dependent upon the occurrence or non-occurrence of a contingency. The treatment and disclosure of contingent losses depends upon the likelihood that the loss will crystallise in the future and this can be summarised as follows:

Likelihood		*Accounting*
(a)	Probable	Loss accrued in the financial statements.
(b)	Possible	Loss disclosed by way of a note to the financial statements.
(c)	Remote	No disclosure required by SSAP18, although Companies Act 1985 appears to suggest disclosure of any contingent liabilities not provided for.

The financial circumstances of the other company need to be established. Assuming that the losses are not probable, generally accepted accounting practice, following the Companies Act 1985, is to disclose the losses by way of note. The note will state the nature of the item (unlimited guarantee of overdraft) and the financial effects (the overdraft).

(2)   **Claim by former director**

As we have just noted, SSAP18 requires that a material contingent loss should be accrued in the financial statements where it is probable that a future event will confirm a loss which can be estimated with reasonable accuracy at the date on which the financial statements are approved by the board of directors.

With respect to the claim by the former director, it would appear that it is not probable that any claim will succeed. If this is the case, then no provision need be made.

It is not clear on what basis the existing provision of £50,000 has been made. Since the company's legal advisers do not think that *any* claim will succeed, it would be reasonable to write back the provision. If, on the other hand, the provision has been made on the basis of a probable settlement, then it should remain.

Assuming that the provision is written back, the treatment in the financial statements in accordance with SSAP18 should be to disclose by way of note the nature of the contingency, the uncertainties which are expected to affect the outcome and a prudent estimate of the financial effect (which would be £100,000 since the claim has already been reduced from the initial amount of £150,000).

The financial statements should include an accrual for all legal fees incurred to the balance sheet date.

(3)   **Realisable value of stock**

The post balance sheet reduction in the net realisable value of stock is the result of the competitors' product development, a condition which did exist at the balance sheet date. This is an adjusting event per SSAP17.

The net realisable value of stock at the balance sheet date should be adjusted downwards to £373,750. The Companies Act 1985 requires stock to be stated at the lower of cost and net realisable value. The stock should thus be written down by £201,250, from its cost of £575,000 to its net realisable value of £373,750.

By virtue of its size, the write-down should be treated as an exceptional item and disclosed by way of note to the profit and loss account, giving a description of the item and the amount.

Appendix – Working

	£
Cost of stock	575,000
Normal selling price (130% × 575,000)	747,500
New selling price (50% × 747,500)	373,750

SESSION 16

1   Ham Ltd

Cash flow statement for the year ended 31 December 19X2

	£	£
Net cash inflow from operating activities (note)		53,895
Taxation (W7)		(24,000)
Capital expenditure and financial investments		
Payments to acquire fixed assets (W8)	(50,000)	
Payments to acquire investments (W9)	(2,795)	
Receipts from sales of fixed assets	14,122	
Receipts from sale of investments	4,720	
		(33,953)
Equity dividends paid (W6)		(14,250)
Financing		
Issue of ordinary share capital (W5)		30,000
Increase in cash		11,692

Note: Reconciliation of operating profit to net cash inflow from operating activities

	£
Operating profit (profit before tax) (W1)	53,645
Depreciation charges (W2)	22,360
Loss on sale of investments (W4)	384
Increase in stocks	(13,644)
Increase in debtors	(19,850)
Increase in creditors	11,000
Net cash inflow from operating activities	53,895

Workings

		£	£
(1)	Profit and loss account balance 31 December 19X2		120,925
	Profit and loss account balance 31 December 19X1		(104,680)
	Increase		16,245
	Add: Dividends		
	Interim	7,500	
	Final	8,000	
	Interest		15,500
	Taxation		26,500
	Less: Profit on disposal of fixed assets (W3)		(4,600)
	Profit before taxation		53,645

(2)

Provision for depreciation

	£		£
Depreciation on disposals		Balance b/f	69,000
(11,302 – 9,522)	1,780	Depreciation charge	
Balance c/f	89,580	(balancing figure)	22,360
			91,360
	91,360		

(3)

Disposal of fixed assets

	£		£
Fixed assets	11,302	Depreciation	1,780
Profit on disposal		Cash proceeds	14,122
(balancing figure)	4,600		
	15,902		15,902

or Profit = £14,122 – £9,522 = £4,600

(4)   Loss on sale of investment = 4,720 – 5,104 = £(384)

(5)   Issue of shares

		£
Nominal value		25,000
Share premium		5,000
Cash proceeds		30,000

(6)   Dividends paid

Proposed dividends

	£		£
Dividends paid (balancing figure)	14,250	Balance b/f	6,750
Balance c/f	8,000	Dividends for year	15,500
	22,250		22,250
		Balance b/f	8,000

(7)   Tax paid

Tax liability

	£		£
Tax paid (balancing figure)	24,000	Balance b/f	24,000
Balance c/f	26,500	Charge for year	26,500
	50,500		50,500
		Balance b/f	26,500

(8)   **Fixed assets (cost)**

	£		£
Balances b/f	210,500	Disposals	11,302
Additions (balancing figure)	50,000	Balance c/f	249,198
	260,500		260,500
Balance b/f	249,198		

(9)   **Investments (cost)**

	£		£
Balances b/f	8,967	Disposal	5,104
Additions (balancing figure)	2,795	Balance c/f	6,658
	11,762		11,762
Balance b/f	6,658		

2   Haggis Ltd

Cash flow statement for the year ended 31 March 19X1

	£'000	£'000
Net cash flow from operating activities (note 1)		1,128
Returns on investments and servicing of finance		
Interest paid		(127)
Taxation (W2)		(379)
Capital expenditure		
Payments to acquire land and buildings	(154)	
Payments to acquire plant and equipment	(403)	
Receipts from sale of fixed assets	288	
		(269)
Equity dividends paid		(374)
Financing		
Receipts from rights issue (W3)	120	
Repayments of long term borrowings	(61)	
		59
Increase in cash		38

Notes to the cash flow statement

(1)   Reconciliation of operating profit to net cash inflow from operating activities

	£'000
Operating profits [896 + 127 – 135 (W4)]	888
Depreciation	190
Amortisation of intangible fixed assets	21
Provision for unfunded pensions	24
Increase in stocks	(166)
Increase in debtors	(105)
Increase in creditors	276
Net cash inflow from operating activities	1,128

(2)   Reconciliation of net cash flow to movement in net debt (note 3)

	£'000	£'000
Increase in cash in the period	38	
Cash to repurchase debentures	61	
Change in net debt		99
Net debt at 1 April 19X0		(621)
Net debt at 31 March 19X1		(522)

(3)   Analysis of changes in net debt

	At 1 April 19X0 £'000	Cash flows £'000	At 31 March 19X1 £'000
Cash at bank and in hand	683	38	721
Debt due after 1 year	(1,304)	61	(1,243)
Total	(621)	99	(522)

Workings

(1)   Dividends paid

	£'000
b/f at 1.4.X0	190
Charge for year	386
c/f at 31.3.X1	(202)
Paid in year	374

(2)   Corporation tax paid

	£'000
b/f at 1.4.X0	247
Charge for year	389
c/f at 31.3.X1	(257)
	379

(3)   Receipts from rights issue

	£'000
Increase in share capital	36
Increase in share premium	84
	120

(4)   Profit on disposal of fixed assets

	Land and buildings £'000	Plant and machinery £'000	Total £'000
Cost	140	103	243
Depreciation	(34)	(56)	(90)
Net book value	106	47	153
Proceeds	(180)	(108)	(288)
Profit	(74)	(61)	(135)

3 Haversham plc

Cash flow statement for the year ended 31 December 19X5

	£'000	£'000
Net cash inflow from operating activities (Note 1)		2,227
Returns on investments and servicing of finance		
Interest received	174	
Interest paid	(386)	
Dividends received (295 × $^{80}/_{100}$)	236	
		24
Taxation (W2)		(348)
Capital expenditure and financial investments		
Purchase of tangible fixed assets	(3,115)	
Purchase of fixed asset investments	(215)	
Sale of tangible fixed assets	971	
Sale of fixed asset investments (Tutorial note below)	24	
		(2,335)
Equity dividends paid		(260)
Financing		
Issue of shares	906	
New loans	100	
		1,006
Increase in cash		314

Notes to the cash flow statement

(1) *Reconciliation of operating profit to net cash inflow from operating activities*

	£'000
Operating profit	1,518
Depreciation	342
Decrease in stocks	207
Increase in debtors	(173)
Increase in creditors	333
Net cash inflow from operating activities	2,227

Tutorial note: In the absence of further information, it is assumed that the investments were sold at their book value (£24,000) and thus there was no profit or loss arising.

(2)   *Reconciliation of net cash flow to movement in net debt (note 3)*

	£'000	£'000
Increase in cash in the period	314	
Cash from new loans	(100)	
Change in net debt		214
Net debt at 1 January 19X5		127
Net debt at 31 December 19X5		341

(3)   *Analysis of changes in net debt*

	At 1 January 19X5 £'000	Cash flows £'000	At 31 December 19X5 £'000
Cash at bank and in hand	427	314	741
Debt due after 1 year	(300)	(100)	(400)
Total	127	214	341

Workings

(1)

Dividends payable			
	£'000		£'000
Dividends paid (balancing figure)	260	Balance b/f	150
Balance c/f	180	Charge for the year	290
	440		440

(2)

Taxation			
	£'000		£'000
Tax paid (balancing figure)	348	Balance b/f	367
Balance c/f	399	P&L (439 – 59 tax on FII)	380
	747		747

4   Bark Ltd

Task 1

Cash flow statement of Bark Ltd for year ended 31 March 1994

	£'000
Net cash inflow from operating activities	716
Returns on investments and servicing of finance	
Interest paid	(66)
Taxation	(181)
Investing activities	
Payments to acquire tangible fixed assets	(753)
Sale of asset	101
Equity dividends paid	(65)
Financing	
Repayment of loan	(18)
Issue of ordinary share capital	100
Decrease in cash	(166)

Task 2

Reconciliation between the cash flows from operating activities and the operating profit

	£'000
Operating profit	739
Depreciation charges	253
Profit on sale of tangible fixed assets	(35)
Increase in stock	(111)
Increase in debtors	(2)
Decrease in creditors	(128)
Net cash inflow from operating activities	716

Tutorial note: According to FRS3, profits or losses on disposal of fixed assets should normally be disclosed on the face of the profit and loss account, below operating profit (meaning that it is unnecessary to adjust for them in the reconciliation between cash flows from operating activities and operating profit). This approach has been taken in Questions 1–3 above. However, profits or losses on disposal may be included in operating profit if they are immaterial. This is the approach taken in questions 4 (above) and 5.

Workings

(1)   Cash paid to the tax authorities

<table>
<tr><th colspan="5" align="center">Taxation</th></tr>
<tr><td></td><td>£'000</td><td></td><td>£'000</td></tr>
<tr><td>Cash</td><td>181</td><td>Opening balance</td><td>132</td></tr>
<tr><td>Closing balance</td><td>186</td><td>Profit and loss</td><td>235</td></tr>
<tr><td></td><td>367</td><td></td><td>367</td></tr>
</table>

(2)   Purchase of fixed assets

	£'000
Difference between opening and closing balances on fixed assets	434
Net book value of assets sold	66
Depreciation	253
Assets purchased	**753**

ie. £1,340 + 753 – 253 – 66 = £1,774

The cash outflow from purchase of fixed assets is thus £753.

5   Lucy Ltd

Task 1

Cash flow statement for Lucy Ltd for the year ended 31 March 1994

	£'000	£'000
Net cash inflow from operating activities		66,000*
Returns on investments and servicing of finance		
Interest paid		(4,500)
Taxation		(35,000)
Capital expenditure		
Payments to acquire fixed assets	(9,500)	
Sale of fixed assets	15,000	
		5,500
Equity dividends paid		(7,500)
Financing activities		
Issue of shares	75,000	
Repayment of loan	(5,000)	
		70,000
Net increase in cash		94,500

* Full credit was also given to students who made the assumption that the net cash flow from operating activities had already been adjusted for the profit on sale of fixed assets. If this were the case, the net increase in cash and cash equivalents would be £103,500.

Task 2

Advantages of cash flow accounting

(a)   Cash is an easier concept for users to understand than profit.

(b)   Survival in business is dependent upon the ability to generate cash and cash flow accounting focuses on this.

(c)   Cash flow is less dependent upon accounting policies and this makes inter-company comparison more useful.

(d)   Creditors are interested in a company's ability to pay, shareholders may be interested in dividend payments, employees in the ability to pay (and increase) wages, so cash flow accounting is very relevant to the needs of many users of accounts.

Task 3

Differences attributable to:

- Depreciation
- Profit on sale of fixed assets
- Loss on sale of fixed assets
- Changes in stock
- Changes in debtors
- Changes in creditors
- Net cash flows in respect of discontinued activities
- Reorganisation costs

SESSION 17

1   Falcon Ltd

As a first step, you should have redrafted accounts into a presentable form to throw out the figures you need:

Balance sheets

	19X3 £	19X3 £	19X2 £	19X2 £
Fixed assets				
Premises		125,000		75,000
Plant		130,000		70,000
		255,000		145,000
Current assets				
Stock	120,000		100,000	
Debtors	80,000		60,000	
	200,000		160,000	
Creditors: Amounts falling due within one year				
Creditors	45,000		30,000	
Overdraft	15,000		5,000	
Taxation	20,000		15,000	
	80,000		50,000	
		120,000		110,000
		375,000		255,000
Creditors: Amounts falling due after more than one year				
7% Debentures		(50,000)		(50,000)
		325,000		205,000
Capital and reserves				
£1 ordinary shares		100,000		50,000
Share premium account		90,000		35,000
Profit and loss account		135,000		120,000
		325,000		205,000

Profit and loss accounts

	19X3 £	19X2 £
Turnover	525,000	425,000
Operating profit (trading profit less depreciation)	53,500	41,000
Debenture interest	(3,500)	(3,500)
Profit before tax	50,000	37,500
Tax	(20,000)	(15,000)
Profit after tax	30,000	2,500
Dividends	(15,000)	(10,000)
Retained profit	15,000	12,500

(a)   (i)   **Return on capital employed**

19X3

$$\frac{53,500}{375,000} \times 100 = 14.27\%$$

19X2

$$\frac{41,000}{255,000} \times 100 = 16.08\%$$

(ii)   **Profit margin**

19X3

$$\frac{53,500}{525,000} \times 100 = 10.19\%$$

19X2

$$\frac{41,000}{425,000} \times 100 = 9.65\%$$

(iii)   **Asset turnover**

19X3

$$\frac{525,000}{375,000} = 1.4$$

19X2

$$\frac{425,000}{255,000} = 1.67$$

(iv)   **Stock turnover**

19X3

$$\frac{525,000}{120,000} = 4.37$$

19X2

$$\frac{425,000}{100,000} = 4.25$$

(v)   **Current ratio**

19X3

$$\frac{200,000}{80,000} = 2.5$$

19X2

$$\frac{160,000}{50,000} = 3.2$$

(vi)   **Acid test ratio**

19X3	19X2

$$\frac{80,000}{80,000} = 1.0 \qquad\qquad \frac{60,000}{50,000} = 1.2$$

(vii)   **Debtor days**

19X3	19X2

Average daily sales $\dfrac{525,000}{365} = £1,438 \qquad \dfrac{425,000}{365} = £1,164$

$$\frac{80,000}{1,438} = 56 \text{ days} \qquad\qquad \frac{60,000}{1,164} = 52 \text{ days}$$

(viii)   **Borrowing ratio**

19X3	19X2

$$\frac{50,000}{375,000} \times 100 = 13.33\% \qquad\qquad \frac{50,000}{255,000} \times 100 = 19.6\%$$

(b)   **Comments**

Profitability: The return on capital employed has worsened and this is as a result of less efficient use of assets; the asset turnover has deteriorated, whereas the profit margin has improved. If we look at the assets individually, the stock turnover and the debtors' turnover should not have caused any overall reduction of the asset turnover; the major change appears to have occurred in the fixed assets where, at some point during the year, extra capital has been raised for a major investment in fixed assets. If these assets were purchased towards the end of the year, then this would have made the figure for assets at the year-end unrepresentative of the assets used throughout the year. If we take the average of the beginning and year-end assets, the return on capital employed is 16.98%, ie. $\dfrac{53.5}{\frac{1}{2}(255+375)}$. Therefore, before we can draw any firm conclusions about the performance of the company, we need further information about the purchase of the fixed assets.

Liquidity: The ratios used to measure liquidity have also worsened during the year. This is mostly due to a large increase in the overdraft perhaps to part-finance the purchase of the fixed assets. Once again, it is necessary to establish whether the year-end picture is really representative of the year as a whole before coming to any firm conclusions.

Finance: The borrowing ratio has been reduced over the year due entirely to the large amount of share capital raised to finance the purchase of the fixed assets.

2 Tiny Toys Ltd

Task 1

			£	£
(1)	Dr	Audit fees	950	
	Cr	Accruals		950

Being provision for audit fees

(2)	Dr	Share premium account	7,500	
	Cr	Ordinary share capital		7,500

Being a bonus issue of ordinary shares

(3)	Dr	Suspense account	150	
	Cr	Accruals (motor expenses)		150

Being correction of a misposting for motor expenses
not yet billed

(4)	Dr	Suspense account	5,000	
	Cr	Profit and loss account		5,000

Being the profit made on the sale of a building, incorrectly
posted to the suspense account

(5)	Dr	Interest payable	100	
	Cr	Creditors		100

Being the accrual of one month's interest on the 12% debentures

Task 2

Financial statements for publication

Tiny Toys Ltd
Profit and loss account for the year ended 31 December 1993

	£	£
Turnover		
Continuing operations		183,500
Cost of sales		114,200
Gross profit		69,300
Less: Administrative costs	49,185	
Distribution costs	52,935	
		102,120
Operating loss – Continuing operations		32,820
Profit on sale of fixed asset		5,000
Loss on ordinary activities before interest		27,820
Interest payable and similar charges		100
Loss on ordinary activities for the financial year		27,920

Tiny Toys Ltd
Balance sheet as at 31 December 1993

	£	£
Fixed assets		
Tangible assets		40,500
Current assets		
Stocks	12,900	
Debtors	37,230	
Cash in hand and at bank	4,500	
	54,630	
Current liabilities		
Creditors: Amounts falling due within one year	18,350	
Net current assets		36,280
Total assets less current liabilities		76,780
Creditors: Amount falling due after more than one year		
Debentures		10,000
		66,780

Represented by:

	£	£
Capital and reserves		
Called-up share capital	32,500	
Share premium	7,500	
Profit and loss account	26,780	
		66,780

Workings

(1)   Cost of sales

	£
Opening stock	12,800
Purchases	114,300
Closing stock	(12,900)
	114,200

(2)   Profit on sale of fixed assets

Net book value £32,500, proceeds £37,500, therefore profit £5,000

(3)   Costs

	Administrative £	Distribution £
Audit fee	950	
Rates (3,900 – 330 = 3,570)	1,785	1,785
Bad debt	1,000	
Provision for bad debts	200	
Light and heat	1,000	850
Carriage outwards		3,100
Motor expenses	750	6,000
Advertising		2,200
Directors' salaries	25,000	20,000
Saleman's commission		5,000
Salaries (£75,000 – £45,000 – £5,000)	15,000	10,000
Vehicles depreciation	500	2,000
Buildings depreciation	2,000	2,000
Office equipment depreciation	500	
General expenses	500	
Total	49,185	52,935

(4)   Tangible assets

	Cost £	Accumulated depreciation £	Net book value £
Premises	40,000	12,000	28,000
Equipment	4,000	1,500	2,500
Vehicles	20,000	10,000	10,000
	64,000	23,500	40,500

(5)

	£
Debtors	38,900
Less: Provision	2,000
Add: Prepayments	330
	37,230

(6)

	£	£
Creditors		17,000
Accruals		
Audit fee	950	
Light and heat	150	
Motor expenses	150	
Interest	100	
		1,350
Total		18,350

(7)   Called-up share capital and reserves

	£	£
OSC (25,000 + 7,500)		32,500
Share premium account (15,000 – 7,500)		7,500
Profit and loss account		
b/f	54,700	
In year	(27,920)	
c/f		26,780
Total		66,780

Task 3

The following solution gives an example of an approach to this question. Where interpretation is required, credit is given for all relevant points made. The inclusion of ratios is not necessary; candidates may score equally well from discussion made without ratios.

Working capital

Working capital is the total current assets less current liabilities (ie. net current assets). The control of working capital is vital to the business being able to continue; for example, if debtor control is weak, payment may be late (if at all) and the company will not have the resources to pay its own suppliers.

Liquidity may be measured by the use of ratio analysis.

The acid test compares current assets (less stock) with current liabilities.

Tiny Toy's acid test = £54,630 – 12,900/18,350 = 2.3 times

This seems reasonable, although without comparative figures (previous years, industry averages), it is difficult to comment. It is important to break down the analysis of working capital into its components.

Stock turnover is 8.9 times (114,200/12,850)

Debtor days are 77 days (38,900/182,500 × 365)

Creditor days are 54 days (17,000/114,200 × 365)

Stock turnover appears high. Although keeping a tight control on stocks is good working capital management, sufficient stock must be held to avoid loss of sales due to items being out of stock. Stock levels are relatively low and this should be investigated.

Debtor days also seems quite high, especially compared with creditor days. The former should be more tightly controlled, whilst the latter should be extended, although not at the expense of lost 'prompt payment discounts'.

Since Tiny Toys have sold an asset for cash for £37,500 during the year and just made a debenture issue for £10,000, the balance of cash appears small. The actual amount is reasonable for the size of company but it is worrying that it has achieved this balance through a fixed asset sale and debenture issue, rather than operating activities. The company cannot continue to sell its assets (assuming they are saleable) without adversely affecting its operating performance and cash balance. For example, if the space supplied by the building which has just been sold is still needed, a similar amount of space will need to be rented; rent will require cash payments and will also appear as an expense in the profit and loss account.

With respect to the balance currently held at the bank, interest-bearing accounts should be investigated.

Profitability

Tiny Tots has made a very large net loss, reducing its brought forward balance of reserves by approximately half. Again trends need to be considered (within the company, the industry and the economy). However, the gross profit margin is 38%. Since this becomes a loss after expenses, further investigation is obviously critical.

Sales levels and mix and sales prices should be compared with previous years and industry averages. The costs of the company also need to be investigated. For example, are all staff being fully employed, could premises be rented rather than owned, are all vehicles required for business purposes? The size of directors' emoluments relative to the results of the company should also be considered. The size of the loss makes the questions extremely urgent and finding solutions may well be critical to the survival of the company.

Profit and cash

The profit and loss account and the balance sheet are prepared on the accruals concept. The accruals concept is defined in SSAP2 as the matching of costs against those revenues they help to produce, and the matching of income and changes to the financial period in which they occur (as opposed to when they are received/paid).

The profit figure is therefore based on the accruals concept. However, it is also important to consider cash. A high profit figure does not necessarily mean large cash receipts; for example, a company may have a poor credit control system whereby debtors delay payment for considerable periods. A company needs cash to pay suppliers to produce its products or provide a service; if cash is not received it will be unable to pay for supplies and therefore unable to continue to supply its own products/service. It is therefore vital to understand the difference between profit and cash and ensure sufficient cash is available to be able to generate profit.

Task 4

Disclosure of accounting policies

SSAP2 defines an accounting policy as the specific accounting bases selected and consistently followed by a business enterprise as being, in the opinion of its management, appropriate to its circumstances and best suited to present fairly its results and financial position.

An accounting base is a method developed for expressing or applying fundamental accounting concepts (ie. going concern, consistency, prudence, accruals) to financial transactions. More than one recognised accounting base may exist for dealing with particular items.

As there may be a range of accounting bases available to a company, users need to know the base used in order to be able to understand the figures presented in the financial statements. For this reason, the accounting policy note to the accounts is extremely important.

Depreciation (required by SSAP12 *Accounting for depreciation*) spreads the net cost of a fixed asset over its useful economic life, in line with the accruals concept. However, there are many bases on which this may be done, such as straight line or reducing balance. The base selected will affect the annual depreciation charge and therefore the profit figure and balance sheet total.

Development costs, which satisfy certain criteria, may be carried forward under SSAP13 *Accounting for research and development* or written of in the year incurred. The accounting policy may vary between companies and, where significant amounts are involved, inter-company comparison would be meaningless without policy disclosure.

Stock must be valued at the lower of cost and net realisable value in accordance with SSAP9 *Stocks and long-term contracts*. The determination of cost will depend upon company policy (for example, FIFO, LIFO, average cost). Stock is generally a significant figure in the financial statements so it is important for users to understand how it has been determined.

SESSION 19

1   Prince plc

Consolidated balance sheet at 31 December 19X4

	£	£
Fixed assets		
Tangible assets		132,000
Current assets	228,000	
Creditors: Amounts falling due within one year	(131,000)	
Net current assets		97,000
Total assets less current liabilities		229,000
Creditors: Amounts falling due after more than one year		(58,000)
		171,000
Capital and reserves		
Called-up share capital		60,000
Profit and loss account (W4)		111,000
		171,000

Workings

(1)   Group structure

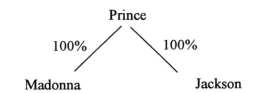

(2)   Net assets at acquisition

	Madonna	Jackson
	£	£
Share capital	50,000	30,000
Profit and loss account	4,000	1,000
	54,000	31,000

(3)   Goodwill schedule

	Madonna	Jackson
	£	£
Cost of investment	60,000	40,000
Net assets acquired	(54,000)	(31,000)
Goodwill	6,000	9,000

(4)   Profit and loss account schedule

	£
P	122,000
M's post-acquisition profit	1,000
J's post-acquisition profit	3,000
	126,000
Less: Goodwill (W3)	(15,000)
	111,000

2   Harvey plc

Consolidated balance sheet at 30 June 19X8

	£	£
Fixed assets – tangible assets		755,000
Net current assets (W7)		155,000
Total assets less current liabilities		910,000
Creditors: Amounts falling due after more than one year		
8% debentures (W6)	24,000	
10% debentures	100,000	
		(124,000)
		786,000
Capital and reserves		
Called-up share capital		50,000
Share premium account		50,000
Profit and loss account (W4)		686,000
		786,000

Workings

(1)   Group structure

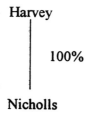

Harvey

100%

Nicholls

(2)   Net assets of Nicholls Ltd

	Acquisition date £
Share capital	100,000
Profit and loss account	65,000
	165,000

(3)   Goodwill schedule

	£
Shares in Nicholls Ltd (198,000 – 6,000)	192,000
Net assets acquired (W2)	(165,000)
	27,000

(4)   Profit and loss account schedule

	£	£
Harvey plc	455,000	
Less: Goodwill arising on consolidation (W3)	(27,000)	
Proposed dividend (W5)	(7,500)	
		420,500
Nicholls Ltd	330,500	
Less: Pre-acquisition profits	(65,000)	
		265,500
		686,000

(5)   Proposed dividend

	£
Dr Profit and loss account (£50,000 × 15%)	7,500
Cr Creditors – proposed dividend	7,500

(6)   Cancellation

Debentures – Included in Harvey plc's balance sheet under the heading 'Investment in Nicholls Ltd' is £6,000 8% debentures due from Nicholls Ltd. Cancelling these leaves £24,000 payable to debenture-holders outside the group.

(7)   Net current assets

	£
Harvey plc	107,000
Less: Proposed dividend	(7,500)
Add: Current account – due to Nicholls Ltd	8,000
	107,500
Nicholls Ltd	47,500
	155,000

SESSION 20

1   Roller Ltd

Consolidated balance sheet at 30 June 19X0

	£	£
Fixed assets		
Tangible assets (16,720 + 4,900)		21,620
Current assets		
Stocks (1,188 + 879)	2,067	
Debtors (1,801 + 262)	2,063	
Cash at bank and in hand (34 + 98 + 300)	432	
	4,562	
Creditors: Amounts falling due within one year (5,614 + 863)	6,477	
Net current liabilities		(1,915)
Total assets less current liabilities		19,705
Creditors: Amounts falling due after more than one year (5,646 + 1,382)		(7,028)
		12,677
Capital and reserves		
Called-up share capital		2,500
Share premium account		600
Revaluation reserve		4,572
Profit and loss account (W5)		4,376
		12,048
Minority interests (W4)		629
		12,677

Workings

(1)   Group structure

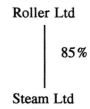

Roller Ltd

|
85%
|

Steam Ltd

(2)   Net assets of Steam Ltd

	At balance sheet date	*At acquisition*
	£	£
Share capital	1,500	1,500
Share premium account	500	500
Profit and loss account	2,194	1,000
	4,194	3,000

(3)   Goodwill schedule

	£
Cost of the investment in Steam Ltd	5,295
Net assets acquired [85% × 3,000 (W2)]	(2,550)
	2,745

(4)   Minority interest schedule

15% × 4,194 (W2)	£629

(5)   Profit and loss account schedule

	£
Roller Ltd	6,106
Steam Ltd [85% × (2,194 – 1,000) (W2)]	1,015
Less: Goodwill (W3)	(2,745)
	4,376

(6)   Cash in transit

In Steam Ltd's books

Dr	Cash		300	
	Cr	Current account		300

2   Heavy plc

Consolidated balance sheet as on 31 March 19X1

	£	£
Fixed assets: Tangible assets (180 + 40)		220,000
Current assets		
Stocks (40 + 32)	72,000	
Cash at bank and in hand (3 + 2.5) (W6)	5,500	
	77,500	
Creditors: Amounts falling due within one year		
Bank loans and overdrafts	6,000	
Trade creditors (41 + 17)	58,000	
Proposed dividends – parent company	10,000	
– minority interests	400	
	74,400	
Net current assets		3,100
Total assets less current liabilities		223,100
Creditors: Amounts falling due after more than one year		
Debenture loans		(50,000)
		173,100
Capital and reserves		
Called-up share capital – £1 ordinary shares		100,000
Share premium account		20,000
Profit and loss account (W5)		39,800
		159,800
Minority interests (W4)		13,300
		173,100

Workings

(1)   Group structure

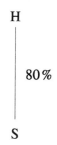

H

80%

S

(2) Net assets of Side Ltd

		Balance sheet date	Acquisition
	£	£	£
Share capital		10,000	10,000
Share premium		10,000	10,000
Profit and loss			
Per question	48,500		
Dividend proposed	(2,000)		
		46,500	38,000
		66,500	58,000

Reserves at acquisition = £48,500 – £10,500

(3) Goodwill

	£
Cost of acquisition	49,200
Share of net assets acquired	
80% × 58,000 (W2)	(46,400)
	2,800

(4) Minority interest

20% × 66,500 (W2)	13,300

(5) Profit and loss

	£
Heavy plc	44,200
Dividend proposed	(10,000)
Dividend receivable (80% × 2,000)	1,600
Side Ltd post-acquisition	6,800
[80% × (46,500 – 38,000) (W2)]	
Goodwill (W3)	(2,800)
	39,800

(6) Cash in transit

		£	£
Dr	Cash at bank	2,500	
	Cr Inter-company account		2,500

SESSION 21

1   Courage Ltd

Consolidated profit and loss account for the year ended 31 December 19X4

	£
Turnover (3,000 + 900 – 10)	3,890,000
Cost of sales (1,700 + 600 – 10)	(2,290,000)
Gross profit	1,600,000
Distribution costs	(400,000)
Administrative expenses	(696,800)
Operating profit	503,200
Loss on sale of fixed asset investment	(50,000)
Reorganisation costs	(10,000)
Profit on ordinary activities before interest	443,200
Income from other fixed asset investments	10,000
Interest payable and similar charges (3.2 – 1.6)	(1,600)
Profit on ordinary activities before taxation	451,600
Tax on profit on ordinary activities	(199,600)
Profit on ordinary activities after taxation	252,000
Minority interests (W2)	(20,800)
Profit for the financial year attributable to members of Courage Ltd	231,200
Dividends – proposed	(20,000)
Retained profit for the financial year	211,200
Retained profits brought forward (W3)	107,800
Retained profits carried forward	319,000

Workings

(1)   Group structure

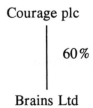

Courage plc

60%

Brains Ltd

(2)   Minority interest

	£	*Minority share* £
Profit on ordinary activities after taxation	52,000 x 40%	20,800

(3)   Retained profits brought forward

	£
Courage Ltd	100,000
Brains Ltd [60% × (25,000 − 12,000)]	7,800
	107,800

2   Frog Ltd

Consolidated profit and loss account for the year ended 31 January 19X2

	£
Turnover (960,000 + 720,000 − 168,000)	1,512,000
Cost of sales (600,000 + 480,000 − 168,000)	912,000
Gross profit	600,000
Distribution costs	48,000
Administrative expenses (W2)	322,180
Operating profit	229,820
Interest payable and similar charges (24,000 + 24,000 − 9,600)	38,400
Profit on ordinary activities before taxation	191,420
Tax on profit on ordinary activities	80,740
Profit on ordinary activities after taxation	110,680
Minority interests (W3)	16,758
Profit for the financial year attributable to the members of Frog Ltd	93,922
Dividends	26,000
Retained profit for the financial year	67,922
Profit and loss account brought forward (W4)	96,178
Profit and loss account carried forward	164,100

Answers

Workings

(1)   Group structure

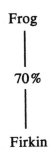

Frog

|

70%

|

Firkin

(2)   Administrative expenses

			£
Frog Ltd			
	– per question		190,080
	– directors' remuneration		20,000
Firkin Ltd	– per question		99,600
	– directors' remuneration		12,000
Goodwill amortised (£5,000 ÷ 10)			500
			322,180

(3)   Minority interests

	£
Firkin Ltd profit after tax per question	67,860
Less: Directors' remuneration	12,000
	55,860
Minority interest (30%)	16,758

(4)   Profit brought forward

	£
Frog Ltd	85,660
Firkin Ltd – group share of post-acquisition retained profits [70% × (50,540 – 34,800)]	11,018
Less: Goodwill amortised in 19X1	(500)
	96,178

Unit 10: Practice Central Assessment 1

Time allowed: 2¹/₂ hours

This practice assessment is in two parts.

You are advised to spend 1¹/₂ hours on Part 1 and 1 hour on Part 2.

Complete all tasks in both parts.

PART 1

Introduction

You have just joined the firm of Ramsay & Partners, a manufacturing business, as accountant.

The business is owned by Geoffrey Ramsay and Richard Tansley, who have been in partnership for many years. Although both Ramsay and Tansley have considerable business acumen, neither of them is qualified as an accountant.

An extended trial balance has been extracted from the books as at 31 March 19X0 (see pp 466–467).

You are supplied with the following additional information.

(1)   The partnership agreement includes the following clauses:

– Ramsay is to be paid a salary of £20,000 per annum.

– The partners are allowed interest of 10% per annum on capital. The amount is to be calculated on the balances on their capital accounts on 1 April each year.

– The balance of profits and losses is shared in the ratio Tansley two thirds, Ramsay one third.

– Specific loans made to the partnership by the partners carry interest at 20% per annum.

– Separate partnership capital and current accounts are to be maintained in the books of account.

– Goodwill is not to be retained in the books of account.

Ramsay & Partners

Extended trial balance at 31 March 19X0

Account	Trial balance at 31.3.X0 Dr £'000	Cr £'000	Adjustments Dr £'000	Cr £'000	P & L account Dr £'000	Cr £'000	Balance sheet Dr £'000	Cr £'000
Capital accounts at 1.4.W9								
Tansley		100						100
Ramsay		40						40
Cash at bank	20						20	
Current accounts at 1.4.W9								
Tansley		5						5
Ramsay	3						3	
Tansley: loan account		30						30
Drawings (year to 31.3.X0)								
Tansley	35						35	
Ramsay	25						25	
Fixed assets at cost at 31.3.X0								
Plant and equipment	50						50	
Fixtures and fittings	30						30	
Motor vehicles	20						20	
Fixed assets depreciation at 1.4.W9								
Plant and equipment		20		10				30
Fixtures and fittings		20		3				23
Motor vehicles		8		4				12
Sales		430				430		
Purchases (raw materials)	250				250			
Wages and salaries								
Factory	40				40			
Office	20				20			
Ramsay	10						10	
c/f	503	653		17	310	430	193	240

Continued . . . .

Account	Trial balance at 31.3.X0 Dr £'000	Trial balance at 31.3.X0 Cr £'000	Adjustments Dr £'000	Adjustments Cr £'000	P & L account Dr £'000	P & L account Cr £'000	Balance sheet Dr £'000	Balance sheet Cr £'000
b/f	503	653		17	310	430	193	240
Rent and rates								
Factory	30		4		34			
Office	10		1		11			
Heat and light								
Factory	10		2		12			
Office	5		1		6			
Insurance								
Factory	5			1	4			
Office	5			1	4			
Motor vehicle expenses	18				18			
Office expenses	24				24			
Stocks at 1.4.W9								
Raw materials	10		7	7	10	7	7	7
WIP	5		3	3	5	3	3	3
Finished goods	12		6	6	12	6	6	6
Provision for unrealised profit on stock at 1.4.W9		2	1					1
Trade debtors	65						65	
Trade creditors		47						47
Depreciation								
Plant & equipment			10		10			
Fixtures & fittings			3		3			
Motor vehicles			4		4			
Loan interest			6		6			
Unrealised profit on stock				1		1		
Accruals				14				14
Prepayments			2				2	
					473	447		
Loss						26	26	
	702	702	50	50	473	473	302	302

Financial Training

435

(2)   On 1 April 19X0, Tansley retired from the partnership. The following arrangements were made:

–   Plant and equipment was revalued at £22,000, fixtures and fittings at £14,000 and motor vehicles at £14,000.

–   Goodwill was estimated to be worth £60,000.

–   Tansley agreed to loan a new partnership half the total amount owing to him on the dissolution of the old partnership, the other half being paid to him in cash on 1 April 19X0.

(3)   On 1 April 19X0, Charles Briscoe joined Geoffrey Ramsay in a new partnership. The following arrangements were made:

–   Briscoe paid £40,000 in cash into the new partnership.
–   It was agreed that goodwill would not be retained in the books of the new partnership.
–   Profits and losses were to be shared equally.

Complete all the following tasks

Task 1

Draft a manufacturing, trading and profit and loss appropriation account for Ramsay and Partners for the year ended 31 March 19X0.

Task 2

Prepare current accounts for Tansley and Ramsay at 31 March 19X0 in columnar form.

Task 3

Draft journal entries to reflect the adjustments to the partners' capital accounts on the retirement of Tansley and the admission of Briscoe.

Task 4

Transfer the balances on Tansley and Ramsay's current accounts to their capital accounts and prepare capital accounts for Tansley, Ramsay and Briscoe at 1 April 19X0. The capital accounts should be presented in columnar form.

Task 5

Draft the balance sheet of Ramsay and Briscoe at 1 April 19X0.

Task 6

Following your production of the financial statements for the year ended 31 March 19X0, you have received the memo below.

Draft a suitable memo in reply.

MEMORANDUM

To: Alex Jones

From: Geoffrey Ramsay

Date: 2 June 19X0

Subject: Draft financial statements for the year ended 31 March 19X0

I have now had an opportunity to look through the financial statements which you have prepared.

I remember that Richard and I were asked to come up with an estimated figure for goodwill. However, I notice that goodwill does not appear in the balance sheet.

Although I am not particularly familiar with these matters, I understand that goodwill is rather controversial. Therefore I assume that you are being prudent in omitting it from the balance sheet. As I know you are well aware, we now have a bank overdraft and I shall have to show these accounts to our bank manager. We have always had a good relationship with the bank but, nevertheless, I should like to be able to show him a positive picture of our financial position.

Can you explain why we cannot include goodwill in our balance sheet?

Task 7

You have received a letter from Charles Briscoe, who has recently joined the partnership.

Draft a suitable letter in reply.

---

21 Lighthouse Mews
Woolton
WL5 6XX

4 June 19X0

A Jones
Financial Accountant
Ramsay and Partners
Seaview Industrial Estate
Woolton
WL6 7JT

Dear Alex

As you probably know, when I agreed to join Geoffrey in partnership the terms were set out in a letter. The details were very straightforward. I introduced capital of £40,000 and Geoffrey and I are to share profits and losses equally.

We have not yet drawn up a formal partnership deed. I would feel more comfortable if this were done, but legal fees can be extortionate.

Geoffrey says that there is a Partnership Act which provides for situations in which no formal agreement exists. What would be the effect if those provisions applied?

Yours sincerely

Charles Briscoe

PART 2

Davenport Ltd, a retail business, has an authorised share capital of 400,000 £1 ordinary shares and 500,000 8% £1 redeemable preference shares. You have recently joined the company as accountant.

You have been asked to assist in preparing draft final accounts for the year ended 31 December 19X5.

The balances of the company as at 31 December 19X5 (after preparing the trading and profit and loss account) were as follows:

	£
Provision for depreciation	
Fittings	150,000
Vehicles	374,000
Goodwill	120,000
Issued share capital	
200,000 £1 ordinary shares	200,000
500,000 8% £1 redeemable preference shares	500,000
Share premium account	40,000
Trade debtors	170,800
Land and buildings at valuation (cost £440,000)	540,000
Capital redemption reserve fund	300,000
Fittings at cost	350,000
Motor vehicles at cost	794,000
10% Debentures	160,000
Trade creditors	96,000
Short term investments (market value £86,000)	78,000
Stock at 31 December 19X5	296,000
Bank overdraft	54,000
Net profit for the year before taxation	144,000
Undistributed profit at 1 January 19X5	146,000
General reserve	110,000
Provision for doubtful debts	4,800
Interim dividends paid	
Ordinary	10,000
Preference	20,000
Revaluation reserve	100,000

The directors wish to:

(i)   transfer £50,000 to general reserve;
(ii)   provide for a final ordinary dividend of 5% and the final preference dividend;
(iii)   write £40,000 off the goodwill account;
(iv)   provide for £40,000 for corporation tax.

Task 1

Draft a balance sheet for Davenport Ltd as at 31 December 19X5 in a form suitable for publication using Format 1 in accordance with the Companies Act. (You are provided with a Companies Act balance sheet pro forma.)

Task 2

Answer the following questions about the year-end accounts.

(a)   What is the difference between fixed assets and current assets?

(b)   What are debentures?

(c)   Are reserves the same as profits?

Pro forma balance sheet (Format 1)

	£	£
Fixed assets		
Intangible assets		
Tangible assets		
Investments		
	———	
Current assets		
Stocks		
Debtors		
Investments		
Cash at bank and in hand		
	———	
Creditors: Amounts falling due within one year		
Net current assets (liabilities)		———
		———
Total assets less current liabilities		
Creditors: Amounts falling due after more than one year		
Provisions for liabilities and charges		
		———
		———
Capital and reserves		

Unit 10: Practice Central Assessment 2

Time allowed: 3 hours

This assessment is in three parts

Complete all tasks in each part

PART 1

Introduction

The tasks in this part are based on the accounts of Wild Rose Ltd, a small company which manufactures cosmetics from natural ingredients.

The financial controller is Mr Stephens and you are employed as his assistant.

Wild Rose Ltd draws up accounts to 30 June each year and the accounts for the year ended 30 June 19X1 are currently being prepared.

Unfortunately Mr Stephens has been rushed to hospital for an emergency operation and is unlikely to be back at work for several weeks. In the meantime the accounts must be prepared for a board meeting and for publication.

Before he was taken ill, Mr Stephens had extracted the extended trial balance, which is attached. You also have a working paper file which contains information which you will need in order to carry out the tasks listed below.

You are provided with a pro forma profit and loss account and balance sheet based on the Companies Act Format 1.

Wild Rose Ltd

Extended trial balance at 30 June 19X1

Account	Trial balance Dr £	Trial balance Cr £	Adjustments Dr £	Adjustments Cr £	P & L account Dr £	P & L account Cr £	Balance sheet Dr £	Balance sheet Cr £
Ordinary shares, fully paid		500,000						500,000
Share premium		200,000						200,000
Leasehold land & buildings at cost at 30.6.X1	655,000						655,000	
Plant & machinery at cost at 30.6.X1	544,000						544,000	
Motor vehicles at cost at 30.6.X1	206,500						206,500	
Leasehold land & buildings depreciation at 1.7.X0		327,500		32,750				360,250
Plant & machinery depreciation at 1.7.X0		302,900		68,000				370,900
Motor vehicles depreciation at 1.7.X0		64,200		41,300				105,500
Stock on hand at 1.7.X0								
Raw materials	42,560		45,800	45,800	42,560	45,800	45,800	
Work in progress	31,920		34,350	34,350	31,920	34,350	34,350	
Finished goods	31,920		34,350	34,350	31,920	34,350	34,350	
Trade debtors	567,500						567,500	
Provision for doubtful debts 1.7.X0		10,300		1,050				11,350
Cash at bank								
Current account		105,320						105,320
Deposit account	1,079,320						1,079,320	
Cash in hand	10,600						10,600	
Trade creditors		400,000						400,000
8% debentures 19Z5		400,000						400,000
Sales		2,805,200				2,805,200		
Purchases	1,095,180				1,095,180			
Direct labour	730,120				730,120			
c/f	4,994,620	5,115,420	114,500	257,600	1,931,700	2,919,700	3,177,420	2,453,320

Continued . . . .

Account	Trial balance Dr £	Trial balance Cr £	Adjustments Dr £	Adjustments Cr £	P & L account Dr £	P & L account Cr £	Balance sheet Dr £	Balance sheet Cr £
b/f	4,994,620	5,115,420	114,500	257,600	1,931,700	2,919,700	3,177,420	2,453,320
Salaries	186,480				186,480			
Sales								
Administration	116,830				116,830			
Directors	76,000				76,000			
Depreciation								
Leasehold land and buildings			32,750		32,750			
Plant and machinery			68,000		68,000			
Motor vehicles			41,300		41,300			
Postage and packaging	46,620				46,620			
Rent and rates	56,400		14,100		70,500			
Light and heat	11,650		8,500		20,150			
Audit and accountancy			3,160		3,160			
Travel and entertainment	10,160				10,160			
Sundry expenses	8,180				8,180			
Telephone	6,440		1,400		7,840			
Doubtful debts			1,050		1,050			
Debenture interest	32,000				32,000			
Bank overdraft interest	8,000				8,000			
Interim dividend paid	24,500				24,500			
ACT	6,125						6,125	
Corporation tax		10,000				10,000		
P & L a/c at 1.7.X0		458,585						458,585
Accruals				27,160				27,160
Profit					244,480			244,480
	5,584,005	5,584,005	284,760	284,760	2,929,700	2,929,700	3,183,545	3,183,545

Extracts from working paper file

(1)   Depreciation has been provided as follows:

Leasehold land and buildings	5% (straight line)
Plant and machinery	12.5% (straight line)
Motor vehicles	20% (straight line)

Depreciation is charged as follows:

Leasehold land and buildings	Administrative expenses
Plant and machinery	Cost of sales
Motor vehicles	Distribution costs

(2)   Fixed asset additions were as follows:

	£
Motor vehicles	34,910
Plant and machinery	122,600

There were no fixed asset disposals during the year.

(3)   Stocks are valued at the lower of cost and net realisable value.

(4)   Directors' remuneration was as follows:

	Salary £	Benefits in kind £	Pension £	Total £
A (Chairman)	34,000		4,000	38,000
B	32,500	1,000	3,500	37,000
C	1,000			1,000
D	1,000			1,000

(5)   The average number of people employed by the company (including directors) during the year were as follows:

Production	175
Distribution	50
Administration	25
	250

Employer's National Insurance contributions payable for the year ended 30 June 19X1 totalled £115,935. This figure has been included in salaries in the extended trial balance.

(6)   The corporation tax charge for the year ended 30 June 19X1 has been estimated at £86,000, based on a rate of 33%. The balance in the extended trial balance is in respect of an over-provision for the year ended 30 June 19X0. The tax is payable nine months after the year-end.

(7)   The directors wish to propose a final dividend of 7p per share.

(8)   The company has an authorised share capital of £750,000 made up of ordinary shares of £1 each.

(9)   The rate of ACT is 20/80.

(10) The debentures are secured by a floating charge over the assets of the company.

(11) The bank overdraft is repayable on demand.

(12) Legal proceedings have been brought against the company by a customer who claimed that she suffered an adverse reaction from using Dandelion Enriching Cream. The case is pending. The company's solicitors have advised that the chances of the claim succeeding are approximately 40%. The amount of the liability is not quantifiable.

Pro forma balance sheet (Format 1)

	£	£
Fixed assets		
Intangible assets		
Tangible assets		
Investments		
	―――	
Current assets		
Stocks		
Debtors		
Investments		
Cash at bank and in hand		
	―――	
Creditors: Amounts falling due within one year		
Net current assets (liabilities)		―――
		―――
Total assets less current liabilities		
Creditors: Amounts falling due after more than one year		
Provisions for liabilities and charges		
		―――
		―――
Capital and reserves		
		―――

Pro forma profit and loss account

(Format 1 as supplemented by FRS3)

	£	£
Turnover		
Continuing operations		
Acquisitions		
	———	
Discontinued operations		
	———	
Cost of sales		———
Gross profit (or loss)		
Distribution costs		
Administrative expenses		
Operating profit (or loss)		
Continuing operations		
Acquisitions		
	———	
Discontinued operations		
	———	
Profit (or loss) on disposal of discontinued operations		———
Other operating income		
Income from shares in group undertakings		
Income from participating interests		
Income from other fixed asset investments		
Other interest receivable and similar income		
Amounts written off investments		
Profit (or loss) on ordinary activities before interest		———
Interest payable and similar charges		
Profit (or loss) on ordinary activities before taxation		———
Tax on profit (or loss) on ordinary activities		
Profit (or loss) on ordinary activities after taxation		———
Extraordinary items		
Profit (or loss) for the financial year		———
Dividends		
Retained profit for the financial year		———

Complete all the following tasks

Task 1

Adjust the accounts in order to provide for:

(a)   taxation
(b)   proposed dividends

Set out your adjustments in the form of journal entries.

Task 2

Draft a profit and loss account for the year ended 30 June 19X1 and a balance sheet at that date in a form suitable for publication using Format 1 in accordance with the Companies Act as supplemented by FRS3 *Reporting financial performance*. (You are *not* required to prepare a statement of total recognised gains and losses or the reconciliation of movements in shareholders' funds required under FRS3.) You should assume that all the information relates to continuing operations.

Task 3

Provide suitable notes to the financial statements, in so far as the information given permits.

PART 2

Introduction

You are employed by Walmer & Partners, a firm of accountants. Your clients include Pargeter Ltd, a small trading company.

The accountant at Pargeter Ltd, Mrs Brewer, trained some years ago. She has prepared the balance sheet and profit and loss account for the year ended 30 June 19X3 but has asked your firm for help in preparing the cash flow statement.

You are provided with the following:

(1)   Balance sheets of Pargeter Ltd at 30 June 19X2 and at 30 June 19X3

(2)   Profit and loss account of Pargeter Ltd for the year ended 30 June 19X3

(3)   Extracts from the notes to the above accounts

(4)   A pro forma cash flow statement as prescribed by FRS1 (Revised)

Task 1

Prepare a cash flow statement for Pargeter Ltd for the year ended 30 June 19X3, using the information above.

Task 2

Prepare a reconciliation of operating profit to net cash inflow from operating activities. (**Note:** You are not required to prepare the other notes to the cash flow statement.)

Pargeter Ltd

The accounts of Pargeter Ltd for the year ended 30 June 19X3 show the following:

Balance sheet as at 30 June 19X3

	Note	19X3 £'000	19X3 £'000	19X2 £'000	19X2 £'000
Fixed assets					
Tangible assets	1		1,987		1,315
Investments			240		–
			2,227		1,315
Current assets					
Stocks	2	197		125	
Debtors	3	1,046		679	
Cash at bank and in hand		29		415	
		1,272		1,219	
Creditors: Amounts falling due within one year	4	1,241		1,202	
Net current assets			31		17
Total assets less current liabilities			2,258		1,332
Creditors: Amounts falling due after more than one year	5		(144)		(312)
			2,114		1,020
Capital and reserves	6				
Called-up share capital			720		480
Share premium			360		192
Revaluation reserve			475		216
Profit and loss account			559		132
			2,114		1,020

Profit and loss account for the year ended 30 June 19X3

	£'000
Turnover	9,121
Cost of sales	(4,320)
Gross profit	4,801
Distribution costs	(2,385)
Administrative expenses	(782)
Operating profit	1,634
Income from other fixed asset investments	120
Profit on disposal of fixed assets	38
Profit on ordinary activities before interest	1,792
Interest payable and similar charges	(326)
Profit on ordinary activities before taxation	1,466
Tax on profit on ordinary activities	(487)
Profit on ordinary activities after taxation	979
Dividends paid and proposed	(552)
Retained profit for the year	427

Notes to the accounts include the following:

(1)   Tangible fixed assets

	Investment properties (at valuation) £'000	Motor vehicles £'000	Plant and machinery £'000	Total £'000
Cost or valuation at 1.7.X2	832	743	505	2,080
Additions	–	271	395	666
Revaluations	259	–	–	259
Disposals	–	(158)	(66)	(224)
Cost or valuation at 30.6.X3	1,091	856	834	2,781
Accumulated depreciation at 1.7.X2	–	306	459	765
Charge for the year	–	35	23	58
Eliminated on disposal	–	(20)	(9)	(29)
Accumulated depreciation at 30.6.X3	–	321	473	794
Net book value at 30.6.X3	1,091	535	361	1,987
Net book value at 30.6.X2	832	437	46	1,315

(2)   Stocks

	19X3 £'000	*19X2* £'000
Raw materials and consumables	115	84
Long-term contract balances	82	41
	197	125

(3)   Debtors

	19X3 £'000	*19X2* £'000
Trade debtors	806	535
Other debtors	91	38
Amounts recoverable under long-term contracts	149	106
	1,046	679

(4)   Creditors: Amounts falling due within one year

	19X3 £'000	*19X2* £'000
Bank overdraft	190	-
Trade creditors	168	415
Accruals	12	26
Proposed dividends	360	300
Payments on account on long-term contracts	24	-
Corporation tax	487	461
	1,241	1,202

(5)   Creditors: Amounts falling due after more than one year

	19X3 £'000	*19X2* £'000
6% debentures	144	312

(6)   Reserves

	Share premium £'000	*Revaluation reserve* £'000	*Profit and loss account* £'000	*Total* £'000
At 1 July 19X2	192	216	132	540
Revaluation in the year		259		259
Issue during the year	168			168
Retained profit			427	427
At 30 June 19X3	360	475	559	1,394

Additional information

(1) Disposal proceeds from disposal of tangible fixed assets were £233,000.
(2) Other debtors solely comprise accrued income in respect of interest receivable.
(3) Accruals solely comprise interest payable.

Pro forma cash flow statement

XYZ Group plc
Cash flow statement for the year ended 31 March 19XX

	£'000	£'000
Net cash inflows from operating activities		X
Returns on investments and servicing of finance		
Interest received	X	
Interest paid	(X)	
Dividends received	X	
	—	
		X
Taxation		(X)
Capital expenditure and financial investments		
Payments to acquire investments	(X)	
Payments to acquire tangible fixed assets	(X)	
Receipts from sales of investments	X	
Receipts from sales of tangible fixed assets	X	
	—	
		(X)
Equity dividends paid		(X)
Financing		
Issue of ordinary share capital	X	
Issues of debenture loan	X	
Repurchase of debenture loan	(X)	
	—	
		X
		—
Increase in cash		X

PART 3   (AAT CA PILOT J94)

Data

You have been asked by Middlemarch & Co, a partnership, to attend a meeting of the partners at which they will agree the year-end accounts. The partnership has a bookkeeper who has kept the books and produced a profit and account for the partnership but he requires some assistance to produce the final financial statements for the year ended 31 March 1994. You have had a preliminary meeting with the bookkeeper and have made notes of the information given as follows:

(1)   The original partners of Middlemarch & Co were Brooke, Featherstone and Lydgate. They shared profits and losses in the following proportions: Brooke $5/10$, Featherstone $3/10$ and Lydgate $2/10$.

(2)   On 1 April 1993, Mary Garth was admitted to the partnership. She agreed to introduce £8,000 in cash into the business. It was agreed that the new profit-sharing ratios were to be as follows:

Brooke	$4/10$
Featherstone	$3/10$
Lydgate	$2/10$
Garth	$1/10$

(3)   At 1 April 1993, goodwill was valued at £30,000. No account for goodwill is to be maintained in the books of the partnership, but adjusting entries in respect of goodwill are to be made in the capital accounts of the partners.

(4)   Mary Garth is to receive a salary of £6,000. Lydgate already receives a salary of £5,000 and this is to be continued.

(5)   Partners are to receive interest on their capital accounts of 10% per annum on the balance outstanding at the end of the year. No interest is to be allowed on the balances of current accounts.

(6)   The balances on the capital and current accounts at 1 April 1993 were as follows:

	Capital £	Current £
Brooke	20,000	4,500 Cr
Featherstone	14,000	3,800 Cr
Lydgate	9,000	1,800 Dr

(7)   In addition to her balance on the capital account, Brooke has loaned the partnership £8,000. She is entitled to interest on this loan at a rate of 8% per annum.

(8)   The partners' drawings during the year were as follows:

	£
Brooke	19,320
Featherstone	16,100
Lydgate	14,300
Garth	13,600

(9)   The net profit for the year to 31 March 1994 as calculated by the bookkeeper before taking into account partners' salaries and interest due was £56,740.

The partners have asked the bookkeeper a number of questions about the year-end accounts which he is unable to answer. They have therefore asked you to answer their questions.

Assessment tasks

Task 1

Draw up the appropriation account for the partnership of Middlemarch & Co for the year ended 31 March 1994.

Task 2

Prepare the partners' current and capital accounts for the year ended 31 March 1994, recording therein the entries necessary upon the introduction of Mary Garth into the partnership.

Task 3

Answer the following questions which the partners have asked about the year-end accounts. Justify your answers, where appropriate, by reference to accounting concepts, SSAPs and/or FRSs.

(a)   We noted that, in preparing the accounts for the year, a debtor balance of £4,600 was written off as a bad debt, thus reducing profit by that amount. We understand that the debtor concerned had gone into liquidation after the year-end and that we did not know that the debt would not be recoverable until after 31 March 1994. Why did we not wait until next year to write off the debt since that is when the debtor went into liquidation?

(b)   The partnership is currently engaged in a legal case in which we are being sued for damages amounting to £53,000 arising out of a contract. Our lawyers claim that we have a very good defence to the claim and, in their opinion, it is unlikely that any damages will have to be paid. Can we ignore this claim for the purposes of our year-end financial statements?

(c)   We understand that you wish to make an adjustment in the year-end accounts in respect of goodwill arising out of the admission of a new partner to the partnership. Why is any adjustment necessary? Would any of the existing partners be disadvantaged if no adjustment was made in the accounts for goodwill?

(d)   Is there any need for our partnership agreement to be altered in the light of the balances on the current account at the end of the year?

Index